A FALCON GUIDE®

MADE EASY SERIES

Kayaking Made Easy

A Manual for Beginners with Tips for the Experienced

Third Edition

DENNIS STUHAUG

FALCON GUIDE®

GUILFORD, CONNECTICUT
HELENA, MONTANA

AN IMPRINT OF THE GLOBE PEQUOT PRESS

A FALCON GUIDE ®

Copyright © 1995, 1998, 2006 by Dennis O. Stuhaug

Falcon and FalconGuide are registered trademarks of Morris Book Publishing, LLC.

Illustrations and photos by Dennis O. Stuhaug unless noted otherwise.
Spot photography throughout © Photos.com
Text design by Nancy Freeborn
Page layout by Lisa Nanamaker
Maps on pages 130, 131, and 138 by Dennis O. Stuhaug

Library of Congress Cataloging-in-Publication Data is available.
ISBN–13: 978-0-7627-3859-5
ISBN–10: 0-7627-3859-6

Manufactured in the United States of America
Third Edition/Second Printing

FAMILYSEARCH.

WHERE
GENERATIONS
MEET

Search for   Research   R
Ancestors   Guidance

Go to Salmon Creek & give 1 last sample.

Call DeRosier & find place to pickup topsoil.

Respond to Ida Jay On Jam Pics of eclipse & Ynks

De Rosier Trucking, Inc.
Pick-ups welcome
3229 Rosedge NW Rd., Kelso   3801 Allen St. Kelso, WA 98626
360-577-1936

5605 Rosedge NW 34th St. Ridgefield Cell 360-867-3333
5195 NW 11th
Buick 2189-220740700

With grateful appreciation to Suzanne,
with whom each day begins as a joyful adventure.

Contents

Foreword

Why do I kayak? I like the rhythm of paddling and the feeling of being out on the open water, responsible for and in control of my actions. The sensation of freedom under the big sky, separated from solid ground, and the three-dimensional movement accentuated by waves and swells. When one is completely immersed in the elements, experience is heightened as increased awareness is demanded and dulled senses are rejuvenated. I cherish generating and collecting memories shared with friends, memories relived later when bridging valleys in my daily life.

In kayaking, as in few other sports, one is truly "in it" and with enough comfort to permit sustained experiences. During the daily "rat race," performance and results are pushed, and the beauty of experiencing is neglected. Out on the open water, performance and experience are again balanced.

As I look back, my education was dominated by discipline and the learning of imposed rules. At first, paddling did not come easily for me, until new concepts—obvious now—started to enter my mind. I share them with you, with a smile: *Go with the flow; it is much easier. Smile, loosen up, take it easy; you are doing it for fun. Accept what is, the way it is. Realize again and again the power of nature. Have a definite plan and be ready to change it at any time due to unforeseen conditions. How small I am in relationship to the overall.*

Kayaking Made Easy is the best-written description of the sport I have come across. I wish I had had it when I started paddling on saltwater more than three decades ago. I was immediately taken by the book's fresh, unconventional, and enthusiastic language. Romance is mentioned, and finding your own style is encouraged. The details show that Dennis has often learned the hard way, through experience.

Take this book and paddle through its contents for happy paddling on the water. The book presents a logical buildup of essential skills. It includes a great section on how to make kayaking pleasant for kids. The idea of "the box" is very good. Each member of my family (note: not only are several generations of the family prominent in the kayak industry, but they also have earned their place in national competition) has taken a personal box along for many years.

There are no age limits in kayaking. As long as you can hold a paddle, you are young or old enough to join!

—*Werner Furrer Sr.*
Kayak designer, builder, and paddling instructor

Preface

The last of the orange was bleeding out of the eastern sky, coloring the notches between the forest-dark mountains, when we launched from the head of the small bay to catch the tail of the ebb tide. There wasn't enough sun yet to burn away the low sea fog that rises along the North Pacific on a summer morning, and we glided down a compass course on our way to the edge of the sea.

We would clear the headland at the mouth of this fjord at slack tide, then turn and climb with the flood tide a dozen miles up the next deep fjord to where we'd meet with friends midway into a two-week paddling vacation. It was the wrong time of the year to watch the great gray whales migrate, but there were pods of orca in the neighborhood, and we could paddle close enough along the barnacle-crusted rocks to see the soft, brown eyes of seals hauled out and basking. An eagle crossed over us as we launched, and it came back to circle us twice before powering northward.

The tidal flow eased to nothing as we neared the low rocks of the headland. A parachute-shaped jellyfish, large enough to fill a five-gallon bucket, pulsated just under the surface as we glided along the rocks, and we delightedly pointed out the great orange disk of a twenty-rayed sun star at the limits of our vision into the depths. A boulder, a dozen meters high, jutted into the sea as the last corner between us and the fjord we came to explore, and as we rounded its sharp prow, an otter vaulted from it and splashed into the quiet water between our boats. Twenty seconds later it popped back to the surface, rising almost like a marmot in the water to see what it had startled.

This is the world of kayak touring: mist, or unexpected sun. A whale rolling up to watch you, a moose standing in the shallows with green strands of grass dripping from its mouth. A day when the loudest sound comes from waves sloshing upon a gravel beach. Seagulls croaking and rasping as they hunt along the fringes of the tide. A good kind of "tired," when even the weariness rejuvenates you.

Your touring kayak is a bridge into this world. The physical skills are within easy reach of most of us, with a little discipline and a little effort, and the foundation of kayaking knowledge may be grasped readily—and may be expanded day by day for the rest of your life.

Comfortably seated in your silent, swift kayak, you become a participant in a natural world unfortunately abandoned by all too many of us. You set your own pace, your own goals: You may enjoy an hour-long cruise along the beach, or you may embark on a monthlong voyage through these North Pacific islands—or along the Maine coast, through the Florida Keys, or from island to island along the north coast of Lake Superior.

Most marine guidebooks and charts are prepared for use with vessels limited to fairly deep water. But you and your kayak can also explore the fascinating edge where the sea and shore meet.

You may use your boat for exercise, or as a platform for fishing or bird-watching. It may become your vantage point for photography or painting. All those "mays" are at your paddle tips. The truth is that all your voyages will lead back inside yourself, and along the way you'll meet yourself again.

You won't become an expert sea kayaker by reading the following pages. You will start to become a proficient kayaker by going paddling, and you will find your way eased by what I'm passing on to you, knowledge I learned from my friends and from experience.

If we meet and paddle together, say down Kyuquot Sound, the otter may once again leap over our kayaks.

Are you ready?

Acknowledgments

No one ever paddles alone. We are accompanied by generations of silent, invisible companions; we share the water and the knowledge we have gleaned from everyone whose wake we cross. I have been particularly blessed with the privilege of paddling with three extraordinary kayak designers and builders: Lee Moyer, who by example set a standard for stewardship of our waters; Peter Kaupat, who insisted that perfection is attainable; and Werner Furrer Sr., who constantly reminded me that the ultimate reason for paddling is enjoyment. I deeply appreciate the hard work, dedication, and professionalism of Globe Pequot's editors, including Shelley Wolf and copy editor Mark Via. They make editing a high art and in doing so, unscrambled my syntax. And I take full credit for any remaining mistakes or confusions.

Wind will pick up spray and chop, and throw the wet back at you. Your spray deck will keep your boat dry; your paddling jacket will keep you warm and dry. PHOTO COURTESY BRIAN HENRY/OCEAN RIVER SPORTS

CHAPTER ONE

You Can Learn to Kayak

Have you ever sat at the water's edge and watched a sea kayak glide by? You kind of scoot around on the gravel beach, worming a little depression to sit in and digging a pair of heel holes as you gaze at the sleek boat in front of you. It doesn't look all that hard, judging from the smile on the paddler's face. She has an ear-to-ear grin, and the smooth pattern of her strokes looks like something you could do.

But there must be a trick to it, or it must take a long time to learn, you think. She was probably born with a paddle in her hands, and her folks were paying big money for sports lessons when she was just a toddler.

I'm sorry to break into your daydreams, but I have to tell you that you're no more than half right. The smile on the paddler out there is real, the grace she exhibits as she rounds the point off to your left is genuine—but the whole concept of this being so difficult that mere mortals could never learn to do it is wrong in a big way. This is an activity for today's world: low impact on you and a light touch on the world through which you pass. Low cost, low technology, and a low learning curve for the person who wants to explore all the delightful vagaries along the break where the water meets the shore.

Fact is, I'm willing to bet you can learn to paddle a boat like that in ten minutes, albeit perhaps without the grace and elegance that experienced paddler so competently exhibited. And if you and I spent an entire morning on the beach, you would be able to climb into your boat, push off from shore, and head in a reasonably straight line to a destination of your choice. In a day or so, you'd have all the skills you need to be a welcome addition to just about any group of paddlers. I don't mean a master mariner, with kelp in your hair and a compass clutched in

When filling out a birder's list, you can wait for the bird to come to your backyard, or you can slip unobtrusively into the bird's backyard aboard your kayak. PHOTO COURTESY WILDERNESS SYSTEMS

your teeth. That would be lying, and to grasp the essential simplicity of a sea kayak we have to build a bond of trust. Want to try?

First of all, let's change the name of this vessel. We'll call it a cruising kayak. That's only a small difference, but it opens up a whole world of lakes, big rivers, and small ponds. Your cruising kayak is designed to navigate quiet waters, waters in which the wind and tide are the primary forces rather than water tugged by gravity in an explosion of spray down a mountainside.

It's my experience that the cruising kayaker has an entirely different mind-set from that of the whitewater boater. The whitewater boater sits in a tool that is part of the sport. The cruising kayaker, on the other hand, shares a partnership with a subtle and responsive craft in the exploration of an activity. Sure, some people race these long and skinny boats. Others voyage for great distances with all their possessions stored below deck. Some plop their boats in the water for an afternoon's outing and a picnic. Still others churn the water over a limited course in search of exercise. Whatever works. But I notice that a fairly high percentage of cruising kayakers name their boats, while most whitewater boaters plan on replacing theirs every few years.

There's also a difference in execution, even though many of the strokes and skills can be readily transported from one kind of kayak to the other. About three-quarters of a whitewater boater's moves are reactionary, while three-quarters of a cruising kayaker's actions are based on contemplation and preparation.

Neither is more challenging, nor requires a higher level of skill or ability. Neither is a stepping-stone to the other. They are simply two separate ways of having fun on the water with a paddle in your hand.

A MINI-HISTORY

A century ago, cruising kayaks were a rarity. Sure, there were guides with canoes who would take curious travelers into the woods, but the wilderness was mainly the haunt of outfitters, "swells," and a handful of folks who made their living in the small byways of the water world. Then, in the 1880s, George Sears glided into the American consciousness with his stories of exploring the Adirondacks alone with a lightweight canoe and minimal camping gear. Sears became one of the most popular American outdoor writers, convincing his readers that anyone could follow comfortably in his wake without the expense and formality of a professional guide.

Across the pond, in England, John MacGregor modified an Inuit kayak design and developed a decked sailing canoe, which he named *Rob Roy*. MacGregor launched the clinker-planked boat in 1865, and, driven by both the wind and his trusty double-bladed paddle, he explored and wrote about the waterways of Europe. His writings, penned as often as not from within a tent stretched over the cockpit, introduced a generation of outdoor enthusiasts in England and North America to kayak cruising. (He called the *Rob Roy* a canoe, a usage that would be understood in Great Britain today, but in North America the trim craft would be called a cruising kayak.)

Maybe it was the times. Economies were vibrating from boom to bust. Americans believed in homesteading, they pinned their hopes on a dozen Western gold rushes, and they strongly valued independence and self-sufficiency. Not a bad combination. "Canoes" became the affordable yacht, whether open in the traditional manner or decked and driven by a double-bladed paddle.

Small boating was a way of life in social clubs and sporting organizations. Name a river or a body of water and odds are there was a paddler chugging along it. By the 1930s paddlers had crossed the Atlantic and had navigated most of the rivers of Europe and North America. Paddling enthusiasts had divided into two subgroups: those dedicated to whitewater thrills and those who sought the pleasures of distance.

And that's the history. The present world of the cruising kayak has its origins in the resins of the first fiberglass-hulled kayaks, constructed in the 1950s. Sure,

Touring kayaks come in all sizes. A long kayak will paddle in a straight line more easily and faster than a shorter kayak, and will do so while carrying more gear. A shorter kayak is easier to transport, easier to store, can be easier for one person to muscle around on dry land, and can prove a bit more maneuverable.

there had been plenty of wood kayaks and wood-frame and fabric-hull boats up until that time, but fiberglass created a whole market of affordable boats and a generation of designers and builders aiming for stronger, lighter, and more efficient craft. They succeeded beyond their wildest dreams. New fabrics were added to the mix, allowing designers to seek the outer limits of engineering. More than a few kayak designers and builders spilled out of the cyclical economy of the aerospace industry.

Delightfully enough, the new pastime was not particularly gender-specific. Women could match their male friends stroke for stroke in the sleek cruising kayaks, whether in circumnavigations of Hawaii or in beach-hopping explorations of remote Alaskan coasts. Kayak cruising is not an exaltation of brute strength, but a bending of skills to fit within the environment.

With the introduction of polyethylene plastic hulls in the closing years of the 1980s, mass production of kayaks became commonplace. The real-dollar price of fine cruising boats continued to fall while the quality of construction and design soared. Today, you can get a good cruising kayak for about the same price as a moderate- to good-quality bicycle. You'll spend a minimum of $1,000 with the basic accessories added in, though the total price may climb to several times that (with more technologically sophisticated materials and more specialized designs).

So, what's the allure of this sport? The beauty you'll see . . . the quizzical look on a seal's face, the dip of a gull's wing over a wave, the large eye of a whale. The feeling of being responsible for yourself, the joy in making a boat glide where you want. The exploration of a new skill and the satisfaction of tired muscles at the end of a crossing. What's the appeal? Instead of talking about it, let's go paddling and you'll discover for yourself.

CHAPTER TWO

What Is a Kayak?

I used to believe that each and every thing had its own form, and its own function. I knew exactly what a kayak was—a long, tippy boat in which you sat and which you propelled with a double-bladed paddle. Now that I am older, the distinctions that were once so clear to me have blurred, and reality seems much more important than archetypes. I have a short, fat canoe, a bare 13 feet long and a plump 38 inches across, and when I paddle down the bay from my home, as often as not I lean against my backrest and listen to the pattern of droplets flinging free from my double-bladed paddle.

A German friend of mine immigrated across the Atlantic more than half his lifetime ago to build airplanes but was sidetracked by the fragile economy of the aircraft industry into kayak building. Like me, he has lost the fine distinctions of boat types. He sits within a long, narrow sea kayak and strokes along with the power from a bent-shaft marathon canoe paddle.

Some kayaks are open on top; some canoes are decked over except for a tiny cockpit, which in turn is sealed with a fabric deck stretched between the waist of the paddler and the rim of the cockpit.

It seems as if the significant difference is that you sit in a kayak and kneel in a canoe.

Perhaps, then, kayak is function as well as form, a way of thinking about the act of traveling as much as it is the vehicle in which one travels. Starting at the bottom, a kayak displaces water. In order to float, the hull must displace a greater volume of water than the combined weight of the boat, the associated gear and equipment, and the paddler. If the hull displaces a volume of water less than this combined weight, it sinks.

Water is not overly particular about the shape of solids floating upon it. As long as we adhere to the basic flotation rule, and we are sitting motionless, we could be

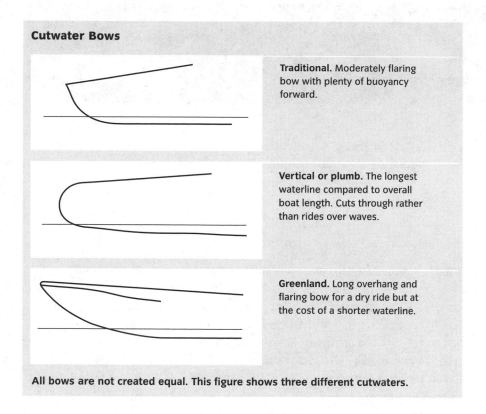

Cutwater Bows

Traditional. Moderately flaring bow with plenty of buoyancy forward.

Vertical or plumb. The longest waterline compared to overall boat length. Cuts through rather than rides over waves.

Greenland. Long overhang and flaring bow for a dry ride but at the cost of a shorter waterline.

All bows are not created equal. This figure shows three different cutwaters.

in a sphere, a cube, or a giant pencil. Once we start moving, though, all sorts of other things start happening. We become prisoners of friction and playthings of water movement.

For the fun of it, fill your sink with tepid water. Bring your fingers together so that you make a solid blade of your fingers and palm, put your hand in the water, and push it from one side of the sink to the other, palm first. You'll make a whopping great wave, the water swirling and boiling in behind your hand as it fills the hole you attempt to create. Now, turn your hand so that your little finger is the leading edge, and sweep back across the sink. You've now created less turbulence—a ripple rather than a wave—and you used much less effort in moving your hand through the water.

You've just demonstrated why a narrow kayak moves more easily through the water than a great wide one. It has to push less water aside as it cleaves ahead, and the water flowing in behind to fill the hole doesn't have to move as far or as fast. You didn't change the size of your hand, you just changed the angle of attack.

Basic Kayak Shapes

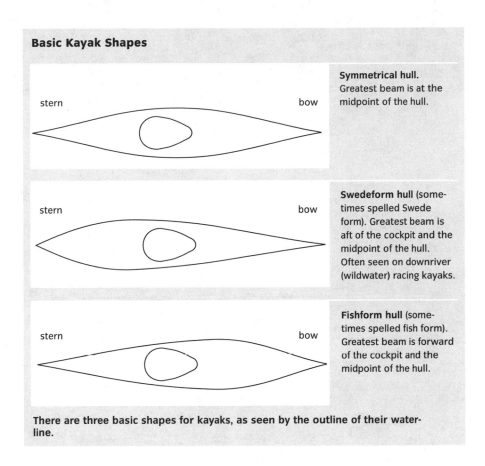

Symmetrical hull. Greatest beam is at the midpoint of the hull.

stern · bow

Swedeform hull (sometimes spelled Swede form). Greatest beam is aft of the cockpit and the midpoint of the hull. Often seen on downriver (wildwater) racing kayaks.

stern · bow

Fishform hull (sometimes spelled fish form). Greatest beam is forward of the cockpit and the midpoint of the hull.

stern · bow

There are three basic shapes for kayaks, as seen by the outline of their waterline.

If that were the only variable in the equation, the rest of this would be simple: Narrow kayaks are better. But it isn't, and they're not. To see this for yourself, stand a 2 x 10 plank on edge and attempt to balance yourself atop it. It's difficult, if not impossible. Now flop it over so a 10-inch side rests on the ground, and you can stand on this board until you get bored.

And now you've demonstrated another principle of kayaking: For boats of equal displacement—you may hear the term "volume" in many kayak shops—broader boats are more stable than narrower boats. To be technical, this principle refers to *beam,* or the measurement from side to side across the widest part of the kayak.

What you're really looking for is that old Golden Mean, the ideal compromise. Of course, there are many factors that go into kayak design, but you start with sufficient displacement to keep you afloat, the narrowest hull that will allow you to move ahead efficiently, and sufficient beam to keep you reasonably stable.

Bow and Keel Profiles

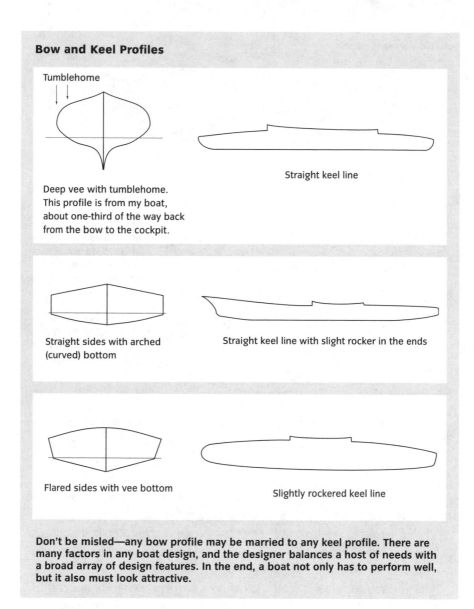

Tumblehome

Deep vee with tumblehome. This profile is from my boat, about one-third of the way back from the bow to the cockpit.

Straight keel line

Straight sides with arched (curved) bottom

Straight keel line with slight rocker in the ends

Flared sides with vee bottom

Slightly rockered keel line

Don't be misled—any bow profile may be married to any keel profile. There are many factors in any boat design, and the designer balances a host of needs with a broad array of design features. In the end, a boat not only has to perform well, but it also must look attractive.

What kind of numbers can you attach to this happy middle-of-the-road kayak? Put the measuring tape on a couple dozen popular touring kayaks, and you'll average out a boat with a beam of 24 inches and a length of just about 17 feet. A narrower boat may have less frontal resistance, but you will invest plenty of practice time in order to feel comfortable paddling. One rule of thumb is that you'll spend two full days—five to eight hours at a crack—practicing paddling for every inch whittled away from the beam. Miss a few days of practice on these toothpicks, and you'll be wobbling your cautious way one tentative stroke at a time.

Ah, but does that mean the 18-inch-beam boats are bad? Nope. When in their proper environment, they are a delight and a blast to paddle. If that's the cardiovascular, high-efficiency, and technically proficient environment you want to inhabit, then the sprint boats are the way to go for you.

THE CRUISING KAYAK FAMILY

If kayaking today represents a family of boats, then there are little clans of closely related cousins floating about. What follows is not a scientific description of genus and species, but a completely arbitrary set of introductions that will put you on at least a nodding acquaintance with the various branches of the family.

Traditional Hardshells

When you think of cruising kayaks, traditional hardshells are likely what you picture. Long and sleek hulls topped by a smooth deck pierced by a snug cockpit, sharp ends—the picture of efficiency in a marine environment. Their rigid hulls and decks may be fabricated from any of a wide variety of materials: fiberglass or other fabrics in a resin or epoxy matrix; polyethylene plastics; or wood by itself or in company with fiberglass and resin in a composite sandwich. Boats have been made of paper and of concrete—and no doubt someone right now is attempting to build a silk craft out of a sow's ear. Fiberglass boats or similar ones laid up with some of the space-age composites tend to be the most technologically advanced designs. Plastic boats moor right at the docks of modern mass production, and a builder with a well-designed boat and adequate retail outlets can bring unit costs right through what a more labor-intensive operation would call the floor. We're starting to see elegant kayaks built with a plastic sandwich material, shaped in the pressures of a hot mold. These thermoplastics are marrying the advantages of the crisp lines and shape of space-age 'glass with the cost benefits of mechanized production. It's my opinion that a novice paddler who tries equally priced fiberglass and plastic hulls will see little difference in paddling performance. Up at the performance end of the scale, though, the smooth fiberglass and resin hulls with their finer ends (bow and stern) and more rigid hulls still seem superior. At the current rate of technological change, however, I'll probably have to eat my opinions.

Frame and Fabric

These are the direct descendants of the original Arctic travelers, updated with modern components. Imagine a light framework supporting a taut waterproof fabric hull, and you'll have the concept in mind. Some frames are skillfully shaped wood, while others are aluminum. Plastics are beginning to work their way into the mix, progressing beyond mere fasteners to structural frame members. Most (but not all) disassemble with a few clips and nuts, and within minutes can be transformed into a bag of struts and braces alongside a rolled-up skin.

Cotton is the traditional fabric for decks and has been proven everywhere from whitewater rapids to trans-Atlantic crossings. Cotton doesn't need a water-proof coating, but it is heavier than synthetics and takes longer to dry. Some man-ufacturers now use polyester cloth sealed with waterproofing.

Most hulls are made of fabric coated with Hypalon, a synthetic rubberlike coating that can last thirty years. Polyester is the fabric of choice, since cotton tends to rot in the dampness. A few hulls are coated with vinyl, which is lighter and cheaper than Hypalon. A smattering of hulls are made of nylon fabric with urethane coating. Many nonfolding frame kayaks are covered with cotton canvas, which in turn is sealed with marine paints. A few specialized builders are combin-ing lightweight and flexible wood frames within a heat-shrunk and drum-tight syn-thetic fabric skin. Some are truly works of art, with designs painted on the inside of the translucent skin.

Frame-and-fabric designs are not as light as their fiberglass counterparts (again, this is true as of the time I'm writing this, but the next boat out of the shop could prove me drastically wrong). Performance tends to lag a bit behind the hardshells, with a more flexible hull that drinks up some of your paddling energy and, no matter how tightly you stretch it, still forms little concavities that slow you down. Their invaluable practicality comes rocketing to the front when you unsnap those clips and unscrew the nuts, and instead of having a great long dart to lug around, you have at most a backpack and a suitcase. If you must transport a boat, the frame-and-fabric designs become your only real choice. Yes, some of the hardshells can be unbolted into three sections, but they still don't match the tight packaging of the true folding kayaks.

Don't consider these inferior. Folding kayaks have crossed the Atlantic, poked their prows around Cape Horn and the Cape of Good Hope, circumnavigated most of Australia, and bumped into Arctic and Antarctic ice. These boats are tough. Make that TOUGH. Hannes Lindemann's Klepper model, in which he crossed the Atlantic, was bought mail order, and the Klepper folks didn't even know what it was going to be used for until after the voyage.

Incidentally, the very nature of the fabric-hulled boats gives them a neat little advantage. Many fabric boats have air sponsons along the outside edges of the hull, providing flotation but also keeping the fabric tight. Most hardshell boats contain their flotation in the tight ends of the bow and stern. As a result, many hardshells tend to rotate freely once swamped, with the bow and stern flotation keeping them buoyant. Folding boats, with their flotation in sponsons on the sides of the hull, are much more stable when swamped—and far easier to reboard.

You will pay a premium for folding boats, and as often as not a very healthy premium over hardshells. But if you want to park your boat in a closet, or fly it as luggage, it's a premium well worth the cost.

Sit-on-Tops and Wash-Decks

There are a lot of names for this broad spectrum of boats, encompassing just about every facet of kayaking. Hot rods stretch out to 20 feet and more, necked down to a bare 17 inches wide and used to race across vast distances of open ocean. I think a 30-mile-wide channel between islands rates as a vast distance, and these surf skis race such lengths between the Hawaiian Islands. At the other end of the scale, stubby wave skis shaped more like platters frolic in the crash and froth of breaking surf. Between the two extremes, midsize boats are great for lolling about from put-in to picnic, and at the same time are an ideal platform for serious cardiovascular exercise. Right now, several boats have carrying capacity for camping equipment and food, and rumor has it that at least one manufacturer is about to launch a cruising version with a wraparound fabric spray deck, a tent-like attachment that stretches from your waist to the kayak and keeps out spray, wind, and rain. At first blush, sit-on-tops appear to be creatures of the warm seas. However, with modern protective clothing designed for paddlers, including wet-suits and dry suits, these are truly year-round craft.

Opponents castigated early sit-on-tops, claiming they were not true kayaks because they could not be Eskimo-rolled in the event of an upset. Paddlers, nestled in a slight depression on the deck, simply fall off. Proponents countered by arguing that there was no reason to Eskimo-roll a sit-on-top since it was so easy to scramble back aboard following a capsize. And the advantages are many, they claimed: no claustrophobia, no being hemmed in by a narrow hull and confining cockpit. Confounding both points of view are the new sit-on-tops, with braces that allow you to use your legs to hold yourself on the boat during some radical maneuvers, which include self-rescue rolls.

A powerful argument for the sit-on-tops is their short history. There is no long tradition of the "proper" way to paddle them, the "correct" clothing to wear in them, or even the "acceptable" paddling hat. These are boats floating in the "now"; they simply invite you to splash out and have fun.

Inflatables

Not long ago, inflatables didn't seem to be a serious option for the cruising kayaker. But this was a misconception. Such companies as Sevylor were producing good inflatable boats—both for sport in the rapids and for extended trips on

A kayak, especially an inflatable one like a Sea Tiger by AIRE, is a comfortable boat for a voyage on its own but shines equally as a support boat for a larger yacht. PHOTO COURTESY MARK W. LISK/AIRE

both fresh and salt "flat" water. We're talking about circumnavigating many of Hawaii's islands and making nearly 1,000-mile voyages along the rugged and sparsely inhabited Alaskan coast with a Sevylor Tahiti, an inflatable priced within almost any paddler's budget. Now, with new materials, emerging technologies, and careful engineering, inflatable kayaks are coming into their own as safe and comfortable boats for every level of paddler. If you don't believe this, go for a spin in one of AIRE's Sea Tigers. These long and narrow arrows are a delight to paddle. While today's inflatable kayak can't match a top-of-the-design-world traditional hardshell boat for paddling efficiency, it can be paddled a fair distance while packing its fair share of the load. With their high-buoyancy hulls these boats are incredibly stable, and basic paddling techniques can be quickly acquired in them. How quickly? Whitewater rafting outfitters often trail a few inflatable river kayaks behind their big rafts on multiday trips. In a matter of minutes, with only a modicum of instruction, many vacationers can pick up the skills needed to bob down the river.

Rumor has it that a couple of other inflatable manufacturers will come out with high-efficiency puff-'em-ups. Sevylor, through its parent company Zodiac, has the rights to some pretty impressive boats in the shop, and it is only a matter of time and marketing before you'll see some of these on the water.

SOLO OR TANDEM?

You may carry an archetypal kayak in your mind, comparing the object before you with the reality that you can only see with your eyes closed. For most of us the kayak is a swift, silent, and solo boat—whether slipping along a coastline or cavorting in the froth of a rapid. The sleek Greenland-designed kayaks, with their flaring bows, certainly adhere to this standard, but the baidarkas surging out of the Aleutian Islands in the Far West were cut to a different design. Perhaps in response to a localized need, or possibly born of Russian explorations along the western North American coast, the several-cockpit baidarkas proved themselves superb sea boats as they shuttled from the fringes of Arctic Alaska to northern California. For a half century folding double kayaks have plied the waters of every continent.

Which leads to the crux of the matter: Which is better?

Sorry. There's no answer. Each has a hatful of advantages, and the art of choosing lies in matching your needs to the conditions in which you'll be paddling.

Most of the time when I paddle with my companions, we look like an undisciplined horde pouring down the surface of the bay. But appearances can be deceiving, because we've paddled together long enough to marry up the group safety practices that support each of us. We sure don't look it, though. One friend is a physical fitness fanatic, and in his long and narrow boat he darts ahead and lags far behind, much like a coursing dog during the first miles of a backpack trip into the mountains. Another is a fisherman, and his boat is merely the platform that carries him to the fishing grounds. A third paddles a high-volume, beamy kayak stuffed with cameras and the paraphernalia of his art. Still another "gunkholes" along, gunkholing being the habit of poking into every nook and cranny along the way.

With these as friends, it's pretty obvious that we don't paddle the same kinds of boats and that we don't cruise along like a line of trunk-to-tail elephants. With our unique personalities and our different needs, it's also obvious that we're all in solo boats. Any attempt to put a sprinter in with a fisherman inevitably leads to bruised egos and disagreement. So the solo cruising kayak gives us the solitude and control of our immediate destiny that is all so rare in today's hurly-burly world.

Double kayaks, on the other hand, are greater than the sum of their parts.

There are many good reasons for choosing a double kayak. Two paddlers of

If you yearn for that perfect photographic image, then a kayak is the magic carpet that can bring you across the natural world quickly, silently, and almost invisibly. It carries your gear and provides a stable platform for your camera. PHOTO COURTESY WILDERNESS SYSTEMS

equal strength and skill will go faster and farther or will arrive at their destination less tired if paddling one double kayak rather than a pair of solos. A double is more stable than a single of equal design. A double allows paddlers of differing strengths and skills to paddle as one with the least emotional friction. A double enables a strong-paddling parent to carry a child in the bow cockpit—and, with the station wagon–size boats with a center cargo hatch, can allow a family to paddle together with the floating equivalent of a playpen amidships. In a group, the double can carry a tired or injured paddler.

And now for the real reason to paddle a double. It's fun. You can share, you can chat, you can be a second pair of eyes with a ready "look at that" in response to the roll of an orca or the breath-like shadow of a loon across a lake.

My wife and I dreamt of owning a double kayak and saved for years for a Klepper Aerius. This big, folding kayak had been for half a century the boat of choice of explorers and wanderers, and we saw it as the perfect vessel for cruising close to home as well as for packing compactly on air flights to odd corners of the continent. Coins were stashed in a secret jar; the occasional bill was tucked away; the check from an odd job was earmarked. I finally ordered our dream boat, and it arrived on the eve of Valentine's Day while my wife was halfway across the country playing in a tennis tournament. I lugged it up to our second-floor family room, put it together, and spent the next couple of hours carefully gift wrapping the boat—all 17 feet—with a big red bow around the middle. My wife flew in at 10:00 P.M., walked into the family room at 11:00, and shrieked at 11:01. We carefully hoisted the (by now) unwrapped boat out an upstairs window, across the garage, and atop our van. Twenty minutes later, in the drizzle, we were floating on a lake with the lights from the shore glittering in the night.

"Oh," my wife exclaimed. "We forgot to christen her. We forgot the champagne."

There are moments when you just can't say anything. I handed her a goblet and popped the cork.

You can't do that in a solo boat.

Doubles, especially the bigger ones with the center hole, certainly can carry more gear than can a single kayak. You can load aboard the multi-burner stove, the big water jugs, even the kitchen sink. This carrying capacity is a definite plus, but don't be misled into thinking a double can carry twice as much as a single. Two solo boats can easily and efficiently carry more weight than one double kayak. Your double may be 50 percent bigger (I just made up that number, but it's in that range) than one solo boat, but it is not as big as two solo boats. Think about it. Put two solo boats side by side, with the bow of one just about at the cockpit of the other. Then with a chain saw cut the bow off one boat and the stern

off the other. Scoot the mutilated hulls together sideways and glue them into a whole. The pieces you have left over show the volume you lose.

So you're teetering on the edge of laying out a bunch of bucks for a touring double, and you still need a few reasons to make the final plunge. After all, it always helps to have someone pushing at you from behind and insisting that your idea was pretty good in the first place.

The baidarkas of western Alaska two centuries ago were built with three cockpits—for bow and stern paddlers and a passenger in the center. Today's version, like this Osprey triple from Pygmy Boat, is a versatile alternative to a fleet of kayaks: Two people can paddle with or without a center passenger, or a single person can paddle solo from the center cockpit while keeping the boat in good trim. PHOTO COURTESY JOHN LOCKWOOD/PYGMY BOAT

Here are four reasons to buy a tandem kayak:

1. You have a family. Once your child is of a size to be trusted in a cockpit alone, a double becomes a necessity. Drop a strong and skillful paddler into the stern hole, and a child into the bow cockpit, and you can kayak-camp and kayak-cruise at your leisure. One adult can handle most of the touring doubles, giving up a little speed and distance for the real pleasure of watching a child come face-to-face with a beautiful world. If your family includes a child and a pair of adults, add a single to your fleet. The child and one adult can paddle the big boat while the other adult paddles solo. Soon enough the adults will be back in the double while the child paddles off on his or her own. Lifting a double down from atop a car and lugging it to the water's edge is a challenge for one person, but it can be done.

2. Doubles are romantic. Trust me.

3. You'll always be paddling with a partner, if not a whole group. Despite the best of intentions, accidents happen. You might sprain a wrist, develop a blister on one hand, come down with tendonitis, be weakened by the flu. If you're paddling in a double, your companion can obviously help you out. And with a double in a boating party, an ill, injured, or tired paddler can switch over to the big boat and continue to camp or to safety. Your option in a party of solo boats is to rig a towline, which, while doable, is seldom satisfactory to the towee or to the tower.

4. Life's about sharing. Sunrises, the ripple rings spreading out from a drop of rain, an otter diving over the midsection of your boat as you glide around a rock on a rugged coast. Ghosting along a line of houseboats while a dulcimer and a recorder play Christmas carols with the stars diamond bright and a lantern on a pole bobbing at your stern.

A caveat: Some people should never be bridge partners nor ride a tandem bicycle together. Paddling should be fun, and if your and your companion's paddling styles clash, you may well be happier in a pair of solo boats.

Whatever you decide, your basic kayak is going to be the kayak you like. You may prefer to paddle in a single kayak or team up in a double; you may embark on a monthlong voyage or an afternoon picnic; you may leisurely glide along or strain to hold top speed. The pleasure of paddling lies in finding your own style.

CHAPTER THREE

What Is It Made Of?

We have a regrettable tendency to believe that our toys are the most sophisticated and technologically advanced that could ever be imagined. There's a story, perhaps apocryphal, that in the waning days of the nineteenth century there was a movement in Congress to abolish the U.S. Patent Office on the grounds that everything that was worth inventing already had been. The truth of the matter is that ten millennia or so back an Inupiat in the high latitudes of North America figured out that he could build a skeleton of wood and bone strikingly similar to his own rib cage and over that stretch a treated hide to make a floatable object—the first kayak.

The kayak, incidentally, was the hunter's boat, while the larger, open version became the umiak, or boat that was used to transport large numbers of people or household goods. That's why today, although there's no linguistic evidence to back it up, the umiak is known as the woman's boat and the kayak as the hunter's or man's boat.

Every boatbuilder believes that he or she alone has the secret to the best boat design, and that's why each builder changes the design inherited from some other boatbuilder—if only in some tiny detail. Perhaps that's a North American trait, this constant effort to improve on the past rather than follow in the wake of tradition. Whether or not the proto-Inupiat knew of the ancient Irish coracle (oddly enough, also a hide skin stretched over a frame), builders rapidly developed a long, sleek craft in which the paddler faced forward and drove the boat toward the future, unlike the European tradition of having the paddlers facing aft and seeing their past diminish as they drove on toward an unknowable goal.

What all this means is that people of immense technological skill and incredible engineering sophistication devised a boat that in concept was mature well before Xanthippe's nagging drove Socrates out into the courtyards to walk about and teach. Fact is, the ten-millennia-old Inupiat hunter would probably feel pretty much at home in today's Feathercraft or Klepper, and could drop right into a Dagger plastic cruising kayak with only a few grunts of amazement at the rigidity of the skin.

THE FOUR BASIC DESIGNS

For a few seconds let's throw all talk of materials overboard. There are four kinds of cruising kayak hulls. The direct lineal descendant of the Inupiat kayak is today's rigid frame and flexible fabric skin boat—Klepper, Nautiraid, Pouch, Feathercraft, Folbot, and Kayak Labs, to name the most accessible builders. There are at least a dozen other builders, somewhat smaller, and the best of their boats are equal to the best cruising boats that have ever been built. In these boats you can cross the Atlantic; you can paddle your way around the ends of the continents; you can circumnavigate Great Britain, Australia, or North America. John Dowd, one of humankind's great small-boat paddlers, writes of being blown into Auckland on the hundred-knot breath of a hurricane—which he acknowledges is a far greater tribute to the quality of the frame-and-skin kayak he was paddling (or in this case, leaning well out of and hanging on a fierce brace) than it is to his own forethought. Dowd and his boat survived the wild ride into the New Zealand harbor with no ill effects other than exhaustion.

The second hull is the child of evolutionary technology—the step-by-step improvement in materials engineering—that gave us the monocoque design. Dictionary words aside, the monocoque hull is one in which the skin is the structural component rather than there being a rigid skeleton supporting a flexible and yet watertight skin. Crane your head inside the cockpit of a cruising kayak formed of plastic or glass laminate, and although you may see thickened areas providing additional strength or abrasion protection or bulkheads that seal the ends of the boat into watertight compartments, basically you're looking into a craft in which the material of the hull and deck supports itself. You might see a beautiful kayak formed of thin strips of wood edge-glued into a graceful hull and wrapped with a layer of fiberglass. These, too, are monocoque hulls.

The third family of cruising kayaks is the puff-'em-up variety of high-tech and well-engineered inflatables. Not too many years ago, inflatables were simply big doughnuts that caromed down rivers like demented billiard balls. Today, inflatables have carved out a well-respected niche in the performance market, from sporty solo boats capable of playing in significant whitewater to massive rapid transit vehicles with a middlin'-to-fair-size crowd on board. Some inflatables, such as the venerable and still outstanding Tahiti, have ventured into incredible waters with a spirit untopped by their hardshell cousins. Don't step back from these well-engineered and versatile boats until you've spent some time in their cockpits—and don't spend time in their cockpits unless you want an eye-opening and positive paddling experience. In my view, inflatable cruising kayaks lack the ultimate cruising efficiency of their hardshell brethren, but their advantages of portability, storability, and paddling ease may well erase a small loss in on-the-water efficiency.

A fourth form, more commonly launched from home workshops but in truth not very common at all now, is the rigid frame covered with a rigid material. Some boats were made of frames cut from plywood and covered with plywood sheathing; some were made of bolted-together frames planked with solid wood (one 17-foot kayak designed around the midpoint of the last century was planked with 1-inch-thick solid wood and must have weighed the proverbial ton); and a few were assembled much like traditional canoes—planked up over forms and with steam-softened ribs shaped to the inside of the hull before the boat was popped from the forms. The hull was made in one piece, the deck in another, and the two were mated like clamshells.

That's *how* boats are put together—not necessarily with what. Kayaks have been and probably will continue to be built out of any imaginable material. Hide has fallen into disfavor, but more than a few boats have been laid up with paper. Aluminum is more common among canoes, but at least a few enterprising craftspeople have hacked and welded an approximation of a kayak from the white metal. Civil engineering colleges routinely race paddlecraft formed of concrete.

VIRTUES OF THE COMMON MATERIALS

The overwhelming majority of today's modern kayaks are fabricated from one of four materials: fiberglass and its cousins, polyethylene (plastic), fabric, or wood. Peeking over the horizon is a new family of plastic sandwiches, which are shaped in a hot mold. Design-wise, they shape a boat as sophisticated as any of their fiberglass cousins, with the advantages of machine-accurate production. What's best? To answer that, you have to paddle into the builder's mind. The choice of hull material teeters atop a pyramid of strength, weight, and cost, measured against the builder's vision of how the boat must perform. Unless you have some idiosyncrasies in the recesses of your mind, remember that you're buying a boat and not a material.

Fiberglass

Let's start with fiberglass. In principle, it's simple. Visualize a few layers of fabric soaked in a resin (usually polyester, vinylester, or epoxy) and draped tightly within a female mold. The fabric may be traditional fiberglass, or one of the high-strength materials such as Kevlar, or any of a number of proprietary cloths. Don't be surprised if the boat you find is a sandwich of a number of materials, combining the virtues of each.

The resin sets and becomes rigid, and a sleek and stiff hull is created. That's in principle. In the real world, builders have concocted an incredible variety of resin formulas poured over an equally staggering number of fabrics in their search for the strongest, toughest, and lightest hull. A hull's strength is indicated in its ability to retain its shape under stress, without cracking or splitting. Its toughness depends on its ability to withstand the sandpaper-like abrasion of landings as well as the dings and nicks of day-to-day existence. Everyone is concerned about weight, but few people stop to think that the bare hull of a boat only accounts for about one-fourth of its total weight. The other three-quarters comes from the seats, coamings, hatches, hardware, bulkheads, and the gizmos that you hang on or around your craft. Even at that, you yourself will outweigh your boat by two to three times. Nevertheless, you don't need to pack around a lot of excess weight, so if you can pare away a few unneeded pounds from your kayak and equipment, you will be better off.

Most fiberglass sea kayaks have a layer of pigmented resin on the outside of the hull and deck. It's called the gel coat. This layer, in addition to carrying the bright colors of the boat, provides a wearing surface against the abrasion of beach landings as well as shielding the resins and fabrics from the piercing rays of the sun.

Where does cost come into this? If you add strength, if you add toughness, or if you reduce weight without diminishing the first two, you're going to add money into the pot.

A fiberglass hull should be rigid. It shouldn't creak and flex underneath you, and it shouldn't develop patterns of hairline cracks at stress points nor have its tape pull away from its seams. When you shift your weight from the shore to the cockpit rim, you shouldn't feel the deck slump in, and when you slide your weight onto the seat, you shouldn't feel the cockpit rim compress toward your hips.

Run your fingers along the seams, or under the edge of the cockpit. A smooth finish is a good sign. Not an ironclad guarantee of a fine boat, but certainly a good sign. Stick your head deep into the cockpit and look out through the side of the hull. If the gel coat is of uniform thickness, the light coming through the hull will be uniform. If you have splotches of light and chunks of shadow glimmering through the gel coat, you should suspect an uneven gel coat or a hull of unex-pectedly varying thicknesses.

Unless you're an Olympic racer, don't be enticed by claims of lightness. First of all, in the real world of boat production, reinforcement means both strength and weight. You can build a light boat of superlative strength, but you will pay for it. Pay for it originally, and pay for higher repair and upkeep from the everyday knocks of paddling. If you desperately need to spend money, pop for a really good

The kayak is the ultimate fishing machine. Your paddle strokes easily propel you to your favorite fishing grounds, on salt or fresh water, you can carry a huge assortment of gear and tackle, and it is stable and quiet. Best of all, at the end of the day you merely lift it to the rack on your car and head for home; you're not constrained by a need for ramps or expensive moorage fees. PHOTO BY STEVEN COOK/WILDERNESS SYSTEMS

paddle and let the boat rest in the hands of the water.

Look for bubbles, scabs, or what looks almost like colorless rust—these are all symptoms of flaws in the manufacturing process. They may just be cosmetic, or they may be cosmic.

Last, take a look down the hull or the deck. Don't expect a mirror-smooth finish, but are you looking at a major wavy surface? That's worth being a bit concerned about.

A few manufacturers can supply "take-apart" fiberglass kayaks. These are rigid-hulled boats that have been cut into three or four pieces. The sections can be bolted into a single, strong, and waterproof hull—and since the sections can nest somewhat, the take-apart hull is a bit easier to store or transport.

Plastic

Back in the Dark Ages of chemistry, ethylene was one of the oddities of petrochemical production. It was a kind of waxy-feeling substance, apparently without a lot of practical use. But one day someone discovered that you could string huge numbers of ethylene molecules together as polyethylene. A whole new plastics industry was born. While today fiberglass is still the most popular building material for cruising kayaks, polyethylene plastic is nipping right at its heels.

If you string ethylene molecules together into long chains, you have linear polyethylene. Hook the molecules so that the chains also extend sideways, and you have cross-linked polyethylene. Cross-linked is a more rigid material, more resistant to damage and requiring less interior bracing. Linear polyethylene is a tad less rigid and strong, but it is far easier to repair by an amateur if it is damaged. The other major difference is that with current technology, linear polyethylene is very easy to recycle while cross-linked is out on the fringes of the possible. That *could* change with one twist of a test tube, of course.

Concerned about recycling? Figure that just about any blackish part of a plastic kayak probably saw the light of day first as some other part. Virtually every boat manufacturer uses recycled plastic in seats, coamings, deck plates, and other non-hull components. Remember when you puddled every one of your watercolors together? The resulting mess was sort of a deep muddy gray— certainly not one of the more appealing shades on your palette. The same thing happens with recycled linear plastic. As of yet, there is little color separation of the plastic going back into the hopper to be remelted, and with the blues and the reds and the greens and the yellows going in, a mucky gray oozes out. While manufacturers could add a very substantial amount of pigment to the new plastic (and beef that up with more plastic to make the mix as strong as it was the first time around), it's more efficient and practical just to add a little black to bring the mix to a marketable color.

Even with this information about the recycled portion of the boat, you might as well admit it: You have a nagging feeling that somehow plastic just isn't socially correct. Yes, plastic is made from petrochemicals. But isn't it better to create a renewable resource from the crude bubbling out of the ground than to burn it up in making electricity or creating auto exhaust? You can cut down forests to make wood boats, dam rivers to produce electricity to refine aluminum, or . . . well, the point is that just about anything we use carries an environmental cost. A piece of polyethylene plastic lying on the ground is inert and won't be leaching toxic substances into the earth. Collect that piece, chop it up, and it can be remelted into new forms. That includes the sad moment when your boat is thoroughly thrashed. It can be recycled into the raw material for a new craft.

In most linear plastic boats, you're likely to find interior supports such as bulkheads, walls, ribs, and even stringers. These aren't a sign of a "weak" boat that has been beefed up but are a mark of sound engineering taking full advantage of the structural characteristics of plastic.

In addition to two kinds of polyethylene, there are two ways of forming polyethylene boats. Both methods produce fine hulls. Each starts by melting polyethylene pellets within a mold. Rotomolded hulls are formed by rotating and tilting the mold to spread the polyethylene and to allow thicker buildups in such wear areas as the keel, stem, and stern. The other method, blow-molding, uses air pressure to force the molten plastic into every nook and cranny of the mold.

If you were to weigh plastic and fiberglass hulls of equal quality, odds are that the fiberglass hull would be a touch lighter. You might also notice that the corners and edges of the fiberglass hull are a little sharper than those of its plastic counterpart. Most of us, though, wouldn't perceive these minor differences once the hulls are in the water. What we would notice, however, is the weight of our wallets after buying the boat of our choice. Given boats of equal quality and design, mass-produced plastic hulls tend to be more economical than labor-intensive fiberglass hulls.

Frame and Fabric

Frame-and-fabric boats date back to the origin of the kayak, and for at least the last fifty years have supported hulls of consistently fine quality capable of undertaking incredible voyages. Virtually every boat of this type comes with a hull made of a fabric treated with waterproofing coatings and a deck of a lighter and quite water-repellent fabric, stretched over a frame. Some manufacturers prefer a wood frame; others build an aluminum one.

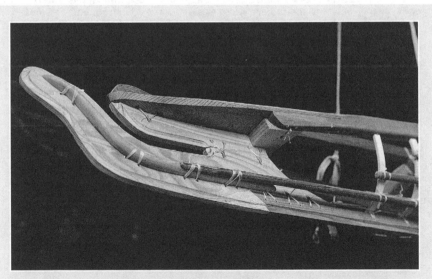

Builders of traditional frame-and-skin kayaks lash the components of the frame together just as the original builders did millennia ago. The result is a flexible hull that glides over the waves rather than forcing its way through. That's why the earliest kayakers referred to "riding" their kayak rather than "paddling" it. This kayak is a Spirit Line boat.

Wood has a special attraction, a beauty and grace that fits so well into the quiet world of the cruising kayak. We sometimes step back, though, afraid of what we imagine to be the cost of craftsmanship or the difficulty of building one ourselves. Don't! Keith Ligman was just nine years old when he started mowing lawns and then shoveling snow to raise money for his own kayak. Two years later, he bought a kit boat, a GoldenEye 13-foot single kayak, from Pygmy Boat. It was daunting when he unpacked the parts, but with guidance from his father over the winter of 1995 and into the spring of 1996, he built his own trim and beautiful craft. By the middle of the project, Keith made the transition from being told each step to grasping the flow of work on his own. It's the kind of education and reward many of us wish we could have experienced. PHOTOS COURTESY PYGMY BOAT

One paddler prefers aluminum, saying it requires less maintenance, while the paddler in a boat with a wood frame counters (while varnishing) with the claim that aluminum must be equally cleaned and protected from saltwater corrosion. The wood-frame advocate says that wood is easier to repair in the wilderness, while the aluminum-frame paddler simply points to the tube repair kit that comes with most aluminum boats. As with hull color, the choice really boils down to the taste of the paddler.

A more significant choice may involve cockpit layout. Some frame-and-fabric tandem boats have individual cockpits for each paddler, while others have a large cockpit holding both paddlers with a two-hole spray skirt or spray deck covering the cockpit.

A second major option involves methods of keeping the fabric skin taut on the frame. Some boats have a snug-fitting skin snapped to the frame, with the final skin tension coming as the paddler inflates air bladders within the skin structure. The military version of the Klepper, for instance, has four such bladders that provide a near-rigid skin along with amazing stability and flotation. Other manufacturers go with a skin that must be pulled tight and hooked to the frame—a slower, more difficult, but less expensive alternative. Assembly time can range from five minutes to half an hour, depending on model and manufacturer.

Wood

Wood-hulled cruising kayaks have been around a century or more. Historically, hulls were laid up with lightweight lapstrake or smooth planking over steam-bent ribs, much like traditional canoes. A few were and still are built with sawn frames and solid planking.

Today there are two common techniques in building wooden kayaks. Strip-built boats are constructed out of narrow strips of thin wood fitted over a mold (or frames), with each strip of wood edge-glued to its neighbors. Hulls and decks are formed separately and removed from their molds before being coupled together. Most are covered with a layer or two of fiberglass and resin. Stitch-and-glue boats are shaped out of accurately cut "planks" of thin plywood that are wrapped around molds and then "stitched" together along each edge with wire "thread." They are also covered with one or more layers of 'glass and resin. You're also still liable to see the odd kayak built with interior frames and covered with a plywood skin.

Wood boats tend to be very strong, very light, and very expensive. Part of the cost is in the nature of the raw material. Straight-grain, knot-free wood usually comes from old trees and is pricey. At the same time, craftspeople who work with wood are willing to put in the extra touches that transform an eminently practical hull into a work of art. You're likely to find inlays, painted decorations, and a host of special flourishes. Since it takes somewhere between 100 and 150 hours to hand-build a wood kayak, it's easy to see how costs can quickly mount. Yes, some builders can launch a boat out of their shop in less time (some will take even longer), but the creation of a wood kayak is as much an act of love as the manufacture of any quality product, and the buyer will in one way or another pay for that time.

Inflatables

An inflatable kayak is a series of airtight tubes engineered into a long and relatively narrow form, with a floor joining the tubes. Backrests, seats, and foot braces may be added; spray decks, however, are an uncommon option. Some inflatables have the floor supported above the water level, and valves or slots in the floor allow water to drain away.

Multiple air chambers offer more security. If one chamber oozes air, the others will continue to support the kayak and passenger. The additional walls and seams, however, do add weight to the craft.

An inexpensive kayak may be built of unreinforced or unsupported polyvinyl chloride (PVC) plastic or rubber. The low initial cost is counterbalanced by a more fragile hull and normally a less efficient design.

Most enthusiast-caliber inflatables are made with a base fabric topped with an airtight and abrasion-resistant coating. Nylon has been the most common base material, with polyester catching up in popularity. Some manufacturers are now fitting inflatables with fabrics such as Kevlar—used in bulletproof vests—into high-wear areas for light weight and durability.

The most common coatings are neoprene, Hypalon, PVC, urethane, and ethyl propylene diene monomer. Not all fabrics or coatings are created equal, even those with the same name. As a rule of thumb, the higher the percentage of coating compound found in the coating material, the better the quality. For instance, a compound with 65 percent neoprene would probably be of better quality than a compound with 40 percent neoprene.

Puff 'em up and paddle away. Today's technology has created excellent inflatable kayaks, such as these Sea Tigers from AIRE. PHOTO COURTESY MARK W. LISK/AIRE

The fabric's fineness is measured by *denier,* which is the weight in grams of 9,000 meters of yarn. The greater the denier, the heavier the yarn. Don't grab this number too quickly, assuming that heavier yarn indicates strength. The weight of the yarn does not indicate the tightness of the weave, nor the bursting or tear strength of the fabric.

A balanced weave is a fabric with its warp and weft—that is, the lengthwise and crosswise threads—made of the same denier yarn. An unbalanced weave has the warp and weft made of different denier yarn.

It's important to remember, and to repeat, that you're buying a kayak and not a material. You should start with a dealer you trust and with whom you can communicate, a design that fits your desires and needs, and a reputable manufacturer. You want a boat that fits you, that will carry you safely and efficiently on the voyages you dream of, and that you can learn to love. The function you seek determines the incidental material of the hull.

CHAPTER FOUR

Outfitting Your Basic Kayak

Forget the brochures, forget the fancy ads, forget the advice and the sales talk: A cruising kayak is simply basic transportation. There are a whole crop of gadgets guaranteed to make your paddling experience a more glorious one that really just don't cut it in the small and self-contained world of the kayaker. You don't need 95 percent of all the gizmos on the market, and if the truth were told, you're probably better off if you can even avoid exposure to half or more of them.

Let's take a look at the goodies you might consider when you fit out your bare hull. The truth is that you're not going to have a lot of choice on some of these items unless you simply adopt a blank face and ceaselessly repeat to the salesperson the list of things you do and do not want on your basic boat. First you'll be told that you have to have whatever is on the showroom floor. Then you'll be told that you absolutely need to invest in whatever is bolted to the demo boat. Don't ignore that advice. From the folks who run kayak shops, you might learn that most of those goodies are really important, vital, or at least convenient. But you still can ask for, demand, and ultimately receive just exactly the boat you want. You must balance what you think you know with the caliber of advice that is offered. Ultimately, you'll be the one paddling the boat.

SEATS

Start with a seat. Every kayak needs at least one. Some manufacturers realize that all paddlers' bodies are not alike and equip their boats with adjustable back supports. My personal choice is a back-band type of support that is adjusted by a line fed through a jam cleat on the side of the seat itself. Some adjustable seats have a

We dream of paddling to distant shores, but more often we grab a few hours out of a hectic day and cruise in the shadow of skyscrapers. PHOTO COURTESY WILDERNESS SYSTEMS

curved back panel hinged in some fashion on the bottom, with an adjusting mechanism that allows you to dial in the angle of the most comfortable back support. I'm told these work, although I have never paddled with one.

I have, however, paddled a boat with a solid back support rigidly molded into the seat itself. I suppose that if only one person were to paddle such a boat, he or she could pad out the rigid support so that it fits properly and comfortably. Consider this a challenge of adaptability.

Last, and perhaps least, are the kayaks that are shipped without any form of back support. You can't paddle them effectively until you cobble together a back support system. We're not talking comfort here. You need to be locked into your kayak (you'll learn how in chapter 12) in order to send it gliding across the water. The backless seats are designed to have a dry bag behind the seat, so one solution is to use the bag as part of the seat assembly. The drawback is that you can't go for an evening's paddle down the bay unless you are packed for a long sea journey.

You're going to spend quite a lot of time in that seat, so you should look at a couple of other things. First, the seat should be rigid within the boat. Mine has a thin foam pad between the bottom of the seat and the hull, and shaped pieces between the outside of the seat and the hull/gunwale. The seat doesn't sway on its hangers dangling from the coaming. Beware, however, of seats that are suspended well above the hull. Low is beautiful, because low means you have a lower center of gravity and thus more stability.

In terms of fit, you should check the front of the seat for an upraised lip, and you should be aware of your own position within the seat. If the front edge of the seat presses against the back of your thighs when you're in a normal paddling position, you'll soon be in extreme discomfort. After a few minutes of paddling, the pressure of that seat lip can send your feet into tingling sleep, and in a few more, numb them totally. Answer? Pad the bottom of the seat with thin layers of tapered closed-cell foam (closed-cell won't hold water like a bath sponge) until you're comfortable.

THE COCKPIT

The seat, in many ways, determines the size of the cockpit. The pros and cons of size can be boiled down as follows. Small cockpits mean small spray decks, and a small spray deck may be set more tightly and is less likely to be blown off than a larger one. You are also less likely to lose a smaller, tighter spray deck when rolling your boat. Larger cockpits mean boarding and exiting are easier, and larger items may be stowed in the cockpit itself. Folks who customarily launch off exposed beaches and paddle in turbulent seas seem to prefer smaller cockpits. I'm not a smaller person, and I like lots of open room around me.

SPRAY DECKS

Some people would have you believe a spray deck, or spray skirt, is an accessory. No way. It is as much a part of your kayak as the more rigid part of your deck. It should fit quite snugly around the cockpit coaming, snugly enough so that it won't pop off if a bit of wave falls on you, and yet be stretchy enough so that you can pop it off in an emergency. Some spray skirts have a fabric handle that is sewn across the narrow point at the front of the skirt. I make my own spray decks using neoprene, and I tie a practice golf ball onto the elastic cord that holds the spray deck to the coaming. The ball bounces around right at the front of my cockpit, and it is easy to find and pull if I need to strip the skirt off.

Some paddlers like coated nylon spray decks because they dry easily, although they do require an elastic cord or (in most cases *and*) suspenders in order to keep them up around the torso. Others (I'm one) prefer neoprene spray decks, which, since they are stretchy, fit closely about the torso and still allow a

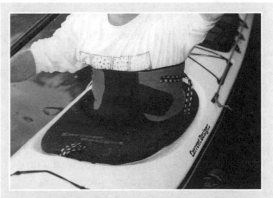

Water can splash over the lip of your cockpit, drip from your paddle, and mist over your kayak as rain or fog—and that's why we don a spray deck fitting closely around our waist and snapping over the rim of the cockpit. PHOTO COURTESY BRIAN HENRY/OCEAN RIVER SPORTS

full range of motion. On the downside, they seem always to be damp.

Unless for some reason you want a wet lap, get in the habit of always wearing your spray deck. Most paddles come with drip rings, and most drip rings let a steady trickle of water down the paddle shaft that is destined to fall onto your lap. You may be quick, but I doubt you can pop your spray deck into position in the few seconds between the time you hear a wakemaking powerboat and when the wake rolls up on your boat.

For paddling in protected waters and when you want quick access to your belowdecks, half-deck spray decks are available. Think of an awning stretched over a frame, spanning the distance from the front of your cockpit to just before your torso. They'll shed water drops from your paddle as well as not-serious splashes and spray sneaking over your bow.

FOOT PEGS

To paddle, you must have your feet solidly placed on a structural support. No question, that's part and parcel of how we kayak today. You have a variety of options. Some foot-peg assemblies are formed right into the hull itself. Other foot pegs are part of adjustable systems, in which the distance from the back support to the foot peg may be mechanically varied. The third alternative is the foot peg as the control pedal for the rudder system. Without getting into the pros and cons of equipping your kayak with a rudder system (okay, I will—I think a full rudder system is invaluable), bear in mind that most control pedal systems may be adjusted for proper fit. If you are fortunate enough to be exactly the same size as the model used in setting up a nonadjustable system, then I suppose you could live with one. But most of us couldn't.

If your feet rest against a solid bulkhead, you can glue foam blocks to the bulkhead as footrests. It will take a while to get the fit right, and you'll spend most of that time upside down in the hull gluing or shaping foam. Adjustable foot pegs are a LOT easier, especially if more than one person may paddle the boat.

BULKHEADS AND HATCHES

When it comes to interior design, you and your kayak have two choices. You can opt for an open interior from bow to stern, or you can divide your kayak into a series of rooms with waterproof (so they say) walls called bulkheads. Today, "bulkhead" is the trendy word in kayak fashion, and you'll find satisfactory reasons to flow with the crowd. Front and rear watertight bulkheads create air chambers at each end of your kayak, which in turn provide you with substantial buoyancy (remember all those awful submarine war movies in which the crew clangs massive doors shut as they wait out a depth-charging?).

With a gentle paddle stroke and a little patience, you can voyage into those places where the water is stretched into a thin film and you feel as though you're gliding across a heavy dew. PHOTO COURTESY SPLASHDANCE

But wouldn't such a design radically limit the amount of stuff you can pack with you? What about camping? Not to worry. If you erect waterproof walls within your hull, you can still gain entrance to the two holds via hatches. There are two common types of hatches. One is circular and, much like a short, fat bolt, can be screwed into or out of a deck fitting. The other type may be of any shape—usually rectangular or trapezoidal—and is held in place by clips or by lines passing over it. These commonly have a gasket between the hatch and the deck fitting to keep them watertight.

There is no perfect hatch. While quiet-water kayaking, take it as an act of faith that all hatch systems will, at the least convenient moment, choose to leak. This is not too bad. Remember to pack anything you want to keep dry within a waterproof or "dry" bag. That's the old "belt *and* suspenders" theory. Even if a hatch does leak, it will take a long time for enough water to trickle in and affect your buoyancy.

It might seem that bulkheads and hatches are the wave of the future. But like the song says, "It ain't necessarily so." You are limited by the physical size of the hatch as to the gear you can carry. Obviously, if you can't get it in the hatch, you can't stow it inside. Also, bulkheads add weight.

On one of our boats we have a rear bulkhead and hatch, but just a void under the forward deck. Some folks would suggest that in this arrangement I should have a small screw hatch up near the bow, which would allow me to reach in and push or pull on the small gear bags I tend to shove forward. I don't do this. Instead, I have a long cord lashed to the first bag that goes in the bow. It is not elegant, but when I tug on that cord and pull the first bag out, all the bags I loaded after that one come with it. My mountain dulcimer, which I could never fit through a hatch, goes up under the bow.

FLOTATION

If you don't have bulkheads, or if you have only a rear bulkhead, you'll need inflatable "flotation" bags secured in the ends of your boat. Don't just push them in through the cockpit—make sure they are secured in place. It would be embarrassing to watch your kayak sink while your flotation bag drifted merrily away. Flotation bags may hold more than air. Several makers build bags that may be opened and filled with your gear, resealed, and then inflated.

Consider safety. If you have the ends of your boat sealed off—by bulkheads or flotation bags—with one just behind your seat and the other just ahead of your foot pegs, you have limited the amount of water that can enter your kayak in the event of a miscalculation. "What's a little water?" you say. A big, high-volume cruising kayak with no interior walls or flotation bags can swallow up a ton or more of that liquid. That's a lot of weight to move, and a lot of water to pump out!

Don't be smug if you have a folding kayak with air sponsons built into the hull. That is not enough. Sure, those sponsons will keep your boat afloat if swamped (with decks awash), but you'll still be left with a lot of gallonage sloshing about. Secure flotation bags in bow and stern, and you'll displace some of that water.

I've been told in all seriousness by some sit-on-top or wash-deck paddlers that they do not need flotation bags because their hull is a huge flotation chamber. They shouldn't be so smug. A friend paddling 5 miles off the Puerto Rican coast realized his sit-on-top was sluggish and popped the inspection hatch open to take a look. Significant water lurked inside, to his surprise and dismay. Fortunately, another paddler in his group had a portable pump, and the crack in the hull that had let in the water was small enough so that only one drop at a time could ooze in.

When you consider a hatch for your own needs, you must realize I've made an assumption. I thought you might like to load your boat up with gear and paddle off on a multiweek expedition. But if you look at your kayak as an exercise machine, with the potential of serving as a ferry to an occasional picnic, don't even bother with a hatch. Or if your idea of camping is a short paddle from inn to inn, you don't have to worry about stowing tents, sleeping bags, and stoves. The simpler your needs become, the more elegant your boat becomes.

RUDDERS AND SKEGS

Down the road a piece, after you've paddled a bit, you'll discover that rudders are not designed to turn a kayak. Your weight and your paddle turn your kayak; your rudder helps you go straight. Given that, most kayaks either come with a rudder system or can have one added at the shop.

Rudders come in three forms, two of which are practical. We'll dispose of the third with a merciful shot to the head. On rare occasions you'll come across a kayak with a rudder that is fixed permanently in the "down" position. The last one I saw had a cotter pin holding the rudder blade fully immersed. Even if you believe that you will *never* run into shallow water, *never* attempt to land on a beach, and *never* have to adjust your rudder depth to counter a crosswind, this design is still a pretty stupid idea. Kayaks are nosy, prowling-shallow-water-and-tiny-bay boats, and you don't need that barn door permanently hanging down back there when you do venture into all those nooks and crannies you thought you'd never explore.

The other two kinds of rudders retract, and each style has advantages. One design lets you retract the rudder out of the water into a flush well on the deck. With the rudder thus locked, your foot pegs are rock solid and the rudder blade is protected—even while you transport your kayak. On the negative side, you need two lines (one to raise, one to lower), you must remember to center your rudder before retracting, you have a more complicated mechanism, and you have to be prepared for the *thump* as it whacks into your deck.

The second design merely lifts the rudder blade out of the water and dangles it like a rooster's tail in the air. These are mechanically simpler—one line both lifts and drops them—and most can be removed and stowed inside during transport. In any weather condition that would affect a raised rudder, you'd probably want the rudder down anyway. The disadvantage to this design is that you have no way of locking your foot pegs in position when the rudder is out of the water. As you apply paddling or leaning pressure to each pedal, the rudder waves in the air.

Your principal concern shouldn't be the rudder-retracting design, but the link-age between the rudder and the foot pedals. First, is it smooth? Second, is it likely to foul on anything? Third, when it breaks, can you jury-rig a repair?

Not all rudder systems are foot operated. Easy Rider has a one-line control system quite suitable for physically challenged paddlers who cannot use a foot system. Basically, there is a line from one side of the rudder, while the other side of the rudder is connected to an elastic cord under pressure. Loosen the line and the kayak turns one way; apply a moderate pressure on the line and the kayak goes straight; pull even harder and the kayak turns in the opposite direction. You don't always hold the line, but secure it with a jam cleat.

Your last choice is a skeg. This is a fixed-direction rudderlike blade mounted on the stern that you can dip deeper into or remove from the water. Don't dismiss it out of hand. It provides precise and mechanically simple directional control in wind and sea. It does not, however, offer the quick and easy fine-tuning a rudder provides.

All the talk here of rudder options assumes (I did it again) that you are paddling a single kayak. If you're in a double, there is no debate. I have yet to see a double kayak that doesn't require rudder control.

CARRYING TOGGLES

A canoe is easy to carry. Toss it up on your shoulders and you can take it along for a comfortable walk over a pretty good distance. Your kayak won't cooperate like that. For a short distance you can hoist it up on one shoulder and crab along—this difficulty is not a function of weight but of bulk—and odds are you'll be tired well before you get to your destination. What's the solution? Cooperation. You and I can carry your boat together, one at each end. I suppose we could each cradle an end of the kayak, but it is easier to use one hand and a toggle. The most common deck fittings you'll find are either loops or toggles (3- to 4-inch cylinders 1 to 1½ inches in diameter) at each end of the kayak. Some are molded into the deck (a bad design, because they are difficult to replace) and some are threaded through a small hole in the very ends of the boat (a simple and effective solution to the challenge of replacing frayed loops). The hole is sealed off with fill, which keeps it waterproof.

I find that a fabric loop, even on a light boat, is uncomfortable after a few steps and, when you toss in a few bags of gear, cuts deep into your hand. The toggle is a lot easier to hold onto while carrying. Part of my preference might come from my river background. It is a common practice for decked boats to have a grab loop of some kind—to grasp while retrieving a swamped boat. Many paddlers believe that if you perchance stuck your fingers through a fabric loop on a swamped boat in a current and the boat began to spin about—why, you would be locked into that loop until rescued. I don't know if that has ever happened, but I believed it. That's why I carefully modified my fabric loops into toggles.

If you stick a short, stout stick through a loop, or through the loop that attaches to a toggle, two people can share the weight of one end of a boat almost as if they were packing a litter.

A bow line is also smart to have. That's a line extending from the bow loop back at least to the cockpit. Use it to tie your kayak securely after landing, or at a dock. I've seen folks beach a kayak and walk away from it . . . only to find it snatched back to the waiting arms of the water by the tide, a wave, or even the

Deck Fittings

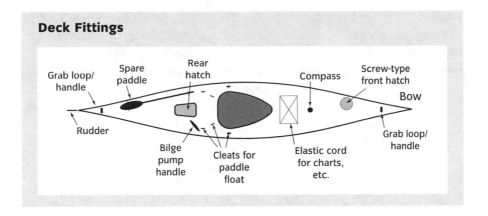

wind. That may never happen to you, but like the belt-and-suspenders theory, it is far better to be safe than sorry.

Most cruising kayakers like to run lines fore and aft from their bow to their stern along both sides. A kayak, especially when wet, is as slippery as a greased pig. If for any reason a person in the water or another boater has to grab on, those lines will allow it. You can also tie little eyes in those lines, for securing odd bits of gear.

I have four pad eyes arranged on a largish square just ahead of my cockpit. Elastic cord is strung through each of the eyes, for the perimeter, and then twice across the middle in the shape of an X. This is my chart table, as well as the spare pair of hands I use to temporarily hold a floatable object. If it doesn't float, I tie it to one of the eyes on the fore and aft lines I mentioned earlier.

PADDLE FLOATS

Just behind my cockpit I have two pad eyes and two cleats, the lashing system I use in setting up a stabilizing system in the unlikely (I hope) event that I capsize. A paddle float, made with a spare paddle and a float, is a temporary outrigger used to stabilize a swamped kayak, allowing me to reboard. (Look at the section on rescues in chapter 13 and you'll see the arrangement.)

Some kayaks are molded with a groove in the deck to help hold the paddle at right angles to the kayak. Handy, but not vital.

Easy Rider's Peter Kaupat has engineered a permanently mounted float rescue system. He developed a swiveling mount that is attached behind the cockpit, with a pole with a float on its free end. One tug on a line and the pole swings out perpendicular to your kayak.

Whatever system you use, it has to be hell-for-leather stout. You'll put a lot of strain on the mountings, and as with parachutes and life jackets, you can't afford a failure. Make sure the fasteners holding the cleats to the deck will not pull out and that the deck itself is stout enough to resist tearing. I've seen cleats mounted with screws and with pop rivets—neither of which would prevent the cleat from ripping free. I have a reinforced deck and hold the cleats in position with bolts mounted through a steel backing plate under the deck.

Because I know these cleats are securely mounted, I'll use one as a towing bitt in the unlikely event of having to tow another kayak. Incidentally, the expression "to the bitter end" doesn't refer to a taste at the end of an experience. The "bitter end" of a line or rode ("rode" is just nautical talk for the rope holding an anchor) is the last part of it that is secured to the bitt. When you're at the bitter end, the whole rest of the line is stretched out and you're at the last of it.

SEA ANCHOR

A sea anchor looks much like a small fabric parachute, and when opened underwater, it pretty much holds you in one place despite the forces of the wind. You need only a few deck fittings to stow or deploy one. The bitter end of the sea anchor rode is usually a loop or bridle that fits around your cockpit rim. This rode leads forward and through the bow loop. That keeps your bow pointed at the sea anchor when it is deployed, and into the wind and usually the waves. When voyaging, the sea anchor is kept folded under the elastic cords on your deck, all set to use with the rode simply kept through the bow loop.

There's another use for a small sea anchor, requiring one additional deck fitting. I do like to fish, and I do like to take pictures—and a kayak can be blown all over a bay with just a light breeze. I'll fly a small sea anchor off the midpoint of my kayak, right next to the cockpit. I have a fairlead and jam cleat right to hand, to secure it. With the sea anchor out 10 or 15 feet, I can sit rock solid over the precise place that will deliver dinner as soon as a fish lurking there bites. My kayak turns sideways to any wind, and I can fish or make images from my chosen position. Doug Simpson, the founder of Feathercraft, taught me this trick.

PADDLE PARKS

As the name implies, a paddle park is a place to (temporarily) park your paddle. I've seen paddlers mounting something that looks like a broom clip on their deck, snapping their paddle into the jaws. I use one of the cleats on my foredeck. I put my paddle up against one of the horns of the cleat, and then slip a loop of elastic cord over the paddle and under the opposing horn. Quick and simple, and it keeps the paddle from drifting away.

You don't need to tie everything but the kitchen sink atop your boat. At best, you'll set up little dams that will kick waves upward into your face or down your neck. At worst, something will slip or untie, and you'll see a billfold's worth of goodies sink into the depths. If nothing else, you'll cramp the paddling efficiency of your kayak.

COMPASSES

I believe in compasses. Every kayak should have one, whether a permanently mounted deck compass or a hand-held unit. See chapter 14 for the types you could have on your boat.

BILGE PUMPS

Water stays on the outside of the hull and you sit inside the hull—separate and distinct existences. Right? Well, not really. Every kayak I know has at one time or another been filled with water. If you and a friend are in a shallow, warm pool, you can invert a water-filled kayak and rock it from end to end in order to dump the last of the water. But outside of that pool, it's a different story. Let's say, because it is an easy bad habit to slip into, that you were paddling without your spray skirt snapped around the coaming. Since your mind was a thousand miles away and you weren't paying any attention, you didn't notice that you drifted out of the channel and were gliding right along the edge of the dredged drop-off. And you didn't notice the yacht plowing up the channel. Really—all these things can and do happen. The wake from the yacht hit the shallows, mounted into a curl, and right in the middle of your daydream dumped all over you. You prevented an upset with some quick paddle moves, but you're hip deep in channel water.

Your first instinct is to rant and rave at the inconsiderate jerk who drenched you. Your second instinct . . . well, I hope you planned first, because your second instinct is going to need a bit of preparation. You want to get the water out of your kayak. A bailing can is awkward at best in the narrow confines of your cockpit and probably won't do more than irritate your already frazzled nerves. If you had thought ahead, you would have had a bilge pump mounted on your kayak. You could start working the handle, and a steady flush of water would immediately sluice overboard.

If you didn't have access to a permanently mounted bilge pump, you could have purchased a portable pump and stowed it safely under some of the elastic straps on deck—with a lanyard tying it to your boat in case of a mishap. Shove the bottom down into the bilge, and start working the handle up and down. Remember to direct the stream of water overboard.

You should also have a big sponge tucked alongside your seat. You can mop up the last few dribbles of water with it.

It's bright out on the water. You'll want a hat or a good pair of sunglasses.

SAFETY EQUIPMENT

A simple weather radio, tuned to the National Oceanic and Atmospheric Administration's (NOAA) permanent broadcast channels, should be an essential component of your boat. Check it the night before you launch, the morning you launch, and the morning and night of each day you're on a paddling trip. If you head north of the border, the Canadians offer a similar 24-hour radio weather forecasting network. You're only talking about a few bucks, tops, and knowing when not to paddle is perhaps as valuable as knowing where to paddle. If you're expeditioning, you might consider an EPIRB, government slang for an emergency radio locator beacon. Pull the tab and this little transmitter begins to shriek out a distress message. You have to register and license each EPIRB, but if you are paddling into unknown seas, the paperwork may be worth it. Paddling closer to home, you might consider a cell phone or VHF marine radio. Neither are cheap, and there's always the risk that any electronic gizmo will fail at the worst possible moment. So you need some other safety measures at your disposal.

As the operator of a real boat, you have the obligation to carry signaling devices in case of emergency. The law says that's an emergency flashlight (blinks an SOS), a strobe, or flares. The first two are down near the "not-good-enough" mark for those who paddle close to the sea, as we kayakers do. I keep a two-faced (clear and red) signaling mirror and a piercingly loud whistle taped to my PFD (personal flotation device; see chapter 5). A bright flashlight is also needed for any night paddling, just to tell other craft where you are. Some paddling friends keep extremely bright strobe rescue lights pinned to their PFDs, to help locate them in case of an accident at night. Some paddlers I know use "light sticks," chemicals in a tube that when activated glow with a green or blue light. Start one, and it is good for most of an evening and allows you to keep track of other boats in your party. Radar reflectors fall into this category. But if you know how and when to use a radar reflector, you know more about paddling than I do. A basic reflector is several interlocked pieces of aluminum held as high as possible off your deck. It makes you visible (highly visible, one hopes) on radar screens and will possibly prevent a major collision. I've never used one, but those who cross shipping lanes believe in them.

A sea anchor looks like a small fabric parachute, and when opened underwater, it water works just like jamming your paddle down into the sea floor. It will hold you in position relative to the water and prevent the wind from blowing you about. If there is a current, you're going to go with the current. Also, if you're tired, you want to eat, or you need to mend a boat or a person, the sea anchor will keep your bow into the wind.

You're not going to need a sea anchor for casual paddling around a pond, but it can be a valuable tool when voyaging. Practice with the sea anchor under good conditions so you know how to use it when it is needed.

The bitter end of the sea anchor line or rode, as discussed earlier, is usually a loop that fits under your cockpit rim. Choose a line such as nylon that has some stretch to it, to take the shock out of being pulled and dropped by waves while held at the end of the line. Make that a little stretch—if you used a long piece of shock cord, I could imagine you pulling back from the sea anchor with the wind and waves and then suddenly shooting forward like the pocket of a slingshot.

This line leads through the bow loop of your kayak and to a ring or fitting to which the shrouds of the sea anchor are also attached. The line should be perhaps three to five boat lengths long—say, 30 to no more than 50 feet long.

A paddle leash such as this one from Mark Pack Works has a Velcro wrap for the paddle shaft and a clip to hook to a secure deck mount. With a leash, you'll never drop your paddle and watch it drift away—or, just as bad, not see it as it bobs out of sight.

You'll need another light line, a bit longer than the total length of the sea anchor line plus the sea anchor. This retrieval or "tripping" line fastens to the apex of the sea anchor and leads back to your cockpit (and a nearby cleat). With the main anchor line you could pull yourself up to the sea anchor, but you'd still be left with the anchor deployed and holding you in position. Pull on the tripping line, though, and you'll collapse the chute and make it relatively easy to retrieve. You'll have to pull in both the anchor line and the tripping line, but that's not hard.

Some folks simply stow their sea anchor under the elastic cords on their foredeck. That works, but the fabric can flap around and catch both the wind and any stray waves. Others keep their anchors in a fabric tube, kind of like an umbrella cover. This makes a neater package and still allows easy deployment.

A paddle float is a sort of do-it-yourself outrigger that can be mounted in an emergency to let you clamber back aboard your kayak. You lash your spare paddle to your rear deck and attach a float to the outboard paddle blade. A bleach bottle provides 8 pounds of buoyancy, enough to support you as you slither into the cockpit, and a commercially made float that slips over your paddle blade can provide as much as 30 pounds or more of buoyancy. Never use your personal flotation device as the float on the end of your paddle.

I'm not certain if a paddle leash or tether is properly a piece of boat gear or paddling equipment—I suspect that depends on whether this chunk of line attaches the paddle to you or to your boat. I've heard proponents of each, and both views have some righteous points on their side. The bottom line is that all three of you—kayak, paddle, and you—should remain together. From river paddling days, the cardinal rule was that you should always keep a grip on your paddle because you could use it as a swimming aid even away from your boat. Equally, you should never allow yourself to be attached to any object, because it could snag on the river bottom. I carry those arguments around in my thoughts and am inclined to tether the paddle to the kayak even though wind could sweep both out of my reach in the event of a mishap. If I grasp the paddle, and the paddle is attached to the kayak, then I have the kayak.

There's one last piece of safety equipment you should have with you, and it can be priceless—your own good sense. You'll probably never need emergency or rescue equipment if you paddle within your own capabilities. Accidents can happen, but it is up to you to reduce the possibility of one.

CHAPTER FIVE

You and Your PFD

WHAT YOU MUST HAVE

There are two sets of laws regulating PFDs (personal flotation devices). One comes from the U.S. Coast Guard, and it flatly states that you must have at least one Type I, Type II, Type III, or Type V PFD—the more accurate term for life jacket—aboard your kayak for each person aboard. If you want the numbers, that's U.S. Coast Guard Regulation Title 33, Chapter 1, Part 175, Subpart B. The regulation stipulates further that they all have to be wearable PFDs (that's what the various types mean, among other things) and that those old faithful and ineffective square seat cushions no longer make the grade.

Those are the *minimum* federal requirements. States may and do set stricter standards. Some states demand that PFDs be worn at all times, usually as a move to protect children, but the laws are changing across the country. Get a copy of your state's boating laws and regulations from your state boating law administrator, normally in the department of Natural Resources or Parks but at times in Game or Fisheries, and in a couple of cases in the state police. If you can't find the office, call the nonemergency number for a local metropolitan police force and ask for the marine patrol division.

The second set of laws is a little more stringent. This covers the natural laws of common sense. If you're stupid enough to venture out on *any* body of water without a PFD, you're rolling the dice with death and the odds are stacked against you.

But you don't have to worry, so you say. Because you aren't planning to paddle far out to sea where most drownings occur. Well, nine out of ten people who drown are in inland waters, and most of them are within a few feet of safety. According to the Coasties, who are charged with collecting such information, most of the victims own PFDs but die without them.

Okay, so I'm on my soapbox. If I paddled an aircraft carrier, I might feel differently, but in the small world of the kayak, the sea is awfully close and awfully personal. I wear a PFD not out of fear but to show my respect.

WHAT THE NUMBERS MEAN

When you start shopping for a PFD, you'll find two sets of buoyancy numbers. One is the minimum buoyancy supplied by that class of PFD. For Type I, that's 22 pounds. For Types II and III, it's 15½ pounds. Type Vs range from 15½ to 22 pounds. Before you start adding up how many PFDs it will take to keep you afloat, remember that the PFD is keeping you afloat *in the water*—and most adults require only an extra 7 to 12 pounds of buoyancy to keep their faces dry. The amount will depend on your body fat, your lung capacity, the water state, and whether or not you have 5 pounds of fishing weights in your pockets. Also, keep in mind that you're looking at minimum buoyancy. My Type III PFD actually provides about 21 pounds of buoyancy at sea level.

The second buoyancy number identifies the weight of the person that PFD was designed to support, and again that's going to hinge a bit on who you are and where you are.

The Coast Guard divides the world of PFDs into five kinds, of which four meet the requirements for kayaks (and canoes) of any length. Type IV—the square seat cushion or the life ring—is meant not to be worn but rather to be thrown to a person in the water. Paddlers need to wear their PFDs. For most purposes, three of the remaining kinds aren't all that practical. Type I is the big, bulky "offshore life jacket" with a minimum of 22 pounds of flotation, designed to float most unconscious people faceup. It is also the most bulky type of approved PFD and probably the most uncomfortable to wear while paddling a kayak. Type II, the "near-shore buoyant vest," is the traditional horse-collar life jacket with a minimum of 15½ pounds of buoyancy. It can float an unconscious person faceup, but not as efficiently as a Type I. The Type II is not designed for comfort while paddling. Type V comes in two categories: special-purpose devices that are only approved in specific situations and hybrid devices that combine at least 7½ pounds of foam flotation with inflatable cells that when inflated bring the total flotation to 22 pounds. Special-purpose PFDs are limited to special uses or conditions. One pullover PFD is considered to be a Type III when worn, but take it off and it no longer meets the requirements.

That brings us to Type III PFDs, which are the "flotation-aid" vest-type PFDs worn by most paddlers. They have a minimum of 15½ pounds of buoyancy. They are comfortable, but won't necessarily roll you faceup in the water.

After all that I can hear you: "But what's the best one for me?" Well, let's look into this together.

DESIGN

Head over to your local canoe and kayak shop and look at the PFDs on display. You'll find most are either waist length (called "shorties") or have a definite break in the flotation above and below the waist tie. That "cuff" or "skirt" below the waist tie can be folded out so that it does not interfere with a spray skirt.

Some of these PFDs look like they are made of a series of vertical tubes, while others seem to be made of panels. Either design will work for you, and I don't know of a safety difference between the two. Early on, some paddlers felt that the vertical-tube PFDs moved with their body while the panel designs didn't, which was uncomfortable.

You might run across a "float coat," which is a full jacket that offers the buoyancy of other Type III PFDs. These have a place in the boating world, but I wouldn't want to wear one in a cruising kayak. They're warm to hot jackets to begin with, and as you build up plenty of body heat while paddling, you may be tempted to strip off that hot coat.

FIT

Now that you've selected a design you like, you need to get the right size. We're not talking sweatshirts here, and an extra large doesn't fit everybody. You want yours (the *personal* in personal flotation device means just what it says) to be snug without constricting. That's why PFDs are made in different sizes.

See here on the sides? Those are adjusting straps. By snugging down on them, you can start with an approximate fit and customize it to your body. Let me help you for a moment. If you go into the shop wearing a T-shirt and adjust your PFD to fit over it, you may find yourself feeling like a sausage with a T, a vest, a sweater, and a paddling jacket all stuffed into that PFD. Wear your paddling clothes when you try on a PFD, and if you can't take it on a real paddle, at least sit on the floor and see if you can stretch through your paddling motions.

When you try on a PFD for size, check especially the armholes and the fit around your waist. Your PFD should have ample arm openings so you won't fight the armhole with each stroke. My PFD has narrow straps over my shoulders, which give me a full range of arm motion. Your PFD should also be snug around your waist. Type III PFDs are designed not to ride up when in the water. If your stomach is larger than your chest, however, some riding up might occur. At worst, and with a bad fit, you might literally slide down inside your PFD until your arms hang up on the armholes. I suspect this is more likely if you open up your side adjusting straps all the way or, without thinking, totally release the side cords in a lace-up adjustment design. I learned to paddle on rivers, and I like a whitewater PFD. Despite my appreciation for good cooking, the girth of my stomach hasn't caught up to the circumference of my chest; to hold the bottom in place, my PFD has a pair of crotch straps that go from the back of the PFD between my legs and snap to the front. I don't wear these while cruising, but I have them as an option.

A caveat for women paddlers: If you have a boyish figure, PFD manufacturers assume you can cram into a "unisex"—read that as "for men"—PFD. If you're a little more curvy, the better paddling-oriented PFD manufacturers now offer both traditional front-zipper and side-entry PFDs that acknowledge the gender difference. Kokotat, Lotus Designs, Perception, and Extrasport are four well worth examining.

A good rule is to wear your PFD as the outermost layer of your clothing. Some folks will wear their poncho or slicker over their PFD, with the supposition that otherwise you can trap a large quantity of water under your poncho and erode the lift of your PFD. As far as I know, however, this is just a theory. If it helps, I don't wear anything atop my PFD. I'll squirm into my spray skirt with the tunnel pulled up toward my armpits and then wrap my PFD around myself. This way, if I get clobbered by spray or a wave, the water will drip down (eventually) to the kayak and then to the sea. Sort of the way rain slides down the shingles on a roof. If I pulled the spray skirt *over* my PFD, water could trickle down my front—and let me assure you that during most of our coolish year I don't need a damp trickle there.

Okay, snuggle into your normal paddling clothes and your new PFD and clamber into your kayak. Most of you will be pretty comfortable. A few folks, though, will find the PFD shoulder straps up around their ears and their nose rubbing on the zipper. DON'T attack your PFD with a pair of scissors in an attempt to get a better fit. It isn't the PFD's fault. Odds are the foot pegs/rests inside your kayak are adjusted too far forward and you have to stretch to reach them. As a result, you're slumping in your seat, almost like a chaise lounge, and that's why the PFD is all scrunched up. If you sit up, like your mother said, you'll paddle better, breathe easier, and your PFD will fit much more comfortably.

COLOR

The fashion mavens have discovered PFDs, and you can find them in any color you want. I figure that international orange or lime green can be seen in most conditions. Considering a camouflage pattern? Why would you want any bit of survival gear in colors hard to see and thus hard to find? As for me, I choose even my packs and dry bags in the brightest colors I can find—or, more properly, in the brightest colors that I find hardest to lose.

CARE

PFDs don't last forever, although with sensible care they will hold up for a number of paddling seasons. To test your PFD once you've had it for some time, plop yourself in the water with it on and see if it can support you with your chin out of water while you have your arms and hands motionless under water. If the water line is up to your eyes, it's time to retire this piece of equipment.

Most Type IIIs fasten with a zipper. I think a big-toothed plastic zipper works better than a small-toothed metal one, but neither will work if it is filthy with sand and dried salt. Keep the zipper clean! Many PFDs also fasten with snaps and buckles. Do the same drill, and keep them clean. Once they start to visibly corrode, or rust, it's time to replace the snap or the PFD—unless you want to hang your life on a corroding and weakening piece of gear.

It's not hard to kill your PFD. People have been known to use their PFD to cushion their boat and protect their car finish while driving to the launch, to cook a damp PFD dry by draping it on a hot radiator or over a fire, to cut off the bottom of their PFD if it seems a little long, or to use their PFD for a kneeling pad or a boat fender. Dumb, right?

PFDs FOR CHILDREN

Children are not adults. That seems obvious, and yet some supposedly adult folks attempt to dangle their kids in PFDs far too big for them. The kid will be uncomfortable and in an emergency could well slide out! I've seen kids literally slip down in their PFDs until only the shoulder straps can be seen above the surface and their arms hang up in the bottom of the armholes. So use PFDs that fit your children. Today, you'll find PFDs for infant, child, and youth—with chest sizes on the labels.

Speaking of that, a couple of years ago in Maryland a father was drafted into helping with an elementary-school water education class. His job was to help the second-graders put on their Type II PFDs, which all fastened in front with cloth ribbon ties. Down the dock marched a line of kids, all proudly wearing their PFDs, and all with the ties on the underneath side of the PFDs. For a moment, I wondered *why* the parent in question tied the bows on the inside . . . and then I wondered how he did it. I don't know to this day. But you should understand *how* to don and adjust your and your child's PFD before you need it.

CHAPTER SIX

Power to the Paddle

A paddle is the final link in that power train that begins when your feet press against the pegs and ends with you moving briskly through the water. Let's spend a few minutes here on the beach considering why paddles are the way they are. First of all, kayak paddles have one thing in common: a blade at each end of the shaft. Now, you don't actually need a kayak paddle to paddle a kayak—historically, people have gotten around in long, skinny boats quite well driving a single-bladed paddle. But we're not going to talk about them. Let's focus, for now, on the basics of double-bladed kayak cruising.

From drawings and descriptions it appears that for a couple of thousand years, dwellers of the Far North used a fairly short kayak paddle with unfeathered and narrow blades. "Unfeathered" means that the two blades are in the same plane—if you put an unfeathered paddle on the ground, both blades will rest flat. (Feathered paddles have the two blades set at an angle to each other.)

Those canny early paddlers, perhaps hampered by a shortage of raw material, knew that long narrow blades worked quite well if one had to maintain a steady paddling cadence over hours and hours. The narrow blades were and are a masterful design given the two parameters of physical strength and available materials.

If the sport had grown only in a linear fashion, the narrow unfeathered blades would be the only paddle we have today. About a hundred years ago, however, outdoor enthusiasts who adopted the kayak as a sport discovered that while narrow blades were great for high-gear cruising, the narrow faces would cavitate, or lose their grip on the water, during powerful bursts of acceleration—such as when sharply turning or leaping ahead out of a standing start. Big blades didn't have such trouble. By the late 1960s you could find paddle blades wide enough to hold a large pizza. The wide blades offered a massive grip, but on the down side they were nearly impossible to paddle for any great distance.

Around this time sprint racers figured out that a big, broad blade waving around in the air during a race was an aerodynamic no-no. Those racers discovered that if you canted the two blades of the paddle at about right angles to each other, then while one blade was planted in the water the other would slice cleanly edge-first through the air. And thus was born the feathered blade.

If you're cranking out a hundred paddle strokes a minute, this design makes a difference. But if you're gunkholing and exploring with me, you'll probably stroke at a more leisurely pace and never feel any air resistance, regardless of the paddle design.

An asymmetrical paddle blade like this Werner Paddles Camano looks unbalanced in the air, but remember that it enters the water at an angle. When properly inserted into the water, there are equal areas on each side of the paddle shaft, and there is little tendency to twist.

Some big-water paddlers, who venture into the wilds of the ocean or the tumult of wind and storm, claim that if you're paddling with the wind on your beam—anywhere on your side—a feathered paddle can be wrenched right out of your hands by a gust. The theory is that while the blade presents a knife edge toward a forward motion or wind, at the same time it presents a big sail to the side and may be grabbed and slewed over your head. This has never happened to me, nor to my paddling companions, but on the other hand, we're more likely to sprawl out on the shore when the wind rises. "You have to learn to drop your shaft when the wind hits," is the conventional wisdom.

If both blades of a paddle face the same direction, as in the top paddle, the paddle is "unfeathered." If the blades are set at an angle to each other, as in the bottom paddle, the paddle is "feathered." Although once the blades of most touring paddles were set at right angles, today most blades are set at 70 to 80 degrees—which seems to prevent sore wrists.

About 80 percent of all better-quality paddles are feathered at an angle of 80 degrees. Some folks believe that a 90-degree feather leads to wrist inflammation and tendon damage and that a less severe rotation prevents this trauma. There doesn't seem to be any advantage to having the blades angled at less than 45 degrees to each other.

The "big sail" theory doesn't seem to detract from the feathered paddle's popularity. About three out of every four solid-shaft paddles have feathered blades. Okay, so what else is important in a paddle?

LENGTH

Let's start with length. There's no easy rule to selecting a paddle length. Paddles are sold in centimeter lengths. Shorter people or people who paddle shorter boats can use a shorter paddle, perhaps as short as 210 centimeters but usually up around the 220-centimeter mark. A 230-centimeter cruising paddle is close to average and just about anyone can use one. If you're well over six feet tall and paddling a 33-inch-beam double, you might need a 250-centimeter paddle.

If you like to paddle at a slow cadence, or relatively few strokes per minute, you will be happier with a relatively longer paddle. If you like to paddle at a brisk clip, consider a shorter paddle. If you're not sure, do some experimenting. Find a boat shop on the water, and on a day with a 10- to 15-knot wind, try a variety of lengths and the same blade shape. You'll know when one fits.

Power Face

Back

The blade of a touring paddle may be flat, as in the bottom paddle, in which case either side of the blade may be used as the power face. Other blades, as in the upper paddle, are shaped much like the bowl of a spoon with a concave face and a convex back. The spoon blade grasps the water much better than a flat blade, and the vastly increased efficiency more than makes up for the minor inconvenience of dissimilar fronts and backs. Both feathered and unfeathered paddles may have either spooned or flat blades.

BLADE SHAPE

You *could* get by with a square of plywood nailed on the end of a pole. In fact, that might make your paddling easier, because you could use either the front or the back of the paddle for any stroke. Some time ago, however, paddle makers found that if the blade was shaped ever so slightly like a spoon, it would grip the water more easily and provide less cavitation in the water. Later, they discovered that the top and bottom half of the blade could be shaped differently to provide the most mechanically advantageous energy transfer. Generally speaking, cruising paddle blades will be quite a bit longer than they are wide.

SHAFT

The shaft does more than just hold the blades. It allows the paddler to apply power and to control the angle of the blades. A less well-engineered shaft will be round. Most paddlers prefer an oval shaft. The oval shape fits more comfortably within the hand, and the muscles in the hands and forearms soon learn the relative position of grip and paddle blade angle.

Some paddle shafts are solid, and the blades are held in a fixed position. That's super. My wife paddles with such a blade, and I just ordered a new touring paddle for myself with a fixed shaft. Other shafts come apart in the middle, with a variety of locking mechanisms, which allows you to switch between a feathered and an unfeathered paddle. A take-apart allows you to find your favorite configuration.

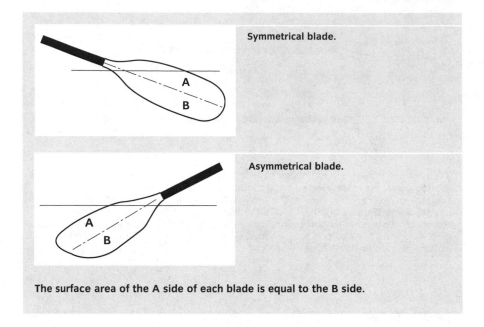

Symmetrical blade.

Asymmetrical blade.

The surface area of the A side of each blade is equal to the B side.

Not only that, a take-apart is a lot easier to stow as a spare. I would be pressed to find a 220-centimeter space for a full-length paddle on my rear deck.

You can improve your grip with a couple of simple tricks. First, put drip rings on your shaft near the blades. These prevent water from running down the shaft. Second, use the same tape tennis players wrap around their racquets to improve the gripping surface.

When it comes to that, all tennis players don't use the same size grips. You can, if you shop about, find paddle shafts of different diameter. If you have small hands—and this may be important to women paddlers—find a small shaft.

MATERIALS

Materials? Wood is pretty. A fine-crafted wood paddle is a thing of beauty and could cost you as much as $400. At the other end of the scale, a moderately good paddle can be found with an aluminum shaft and plastic blades for about $80. I have one, from Lee's Value Rite, and it serves as a working paddle and a great spare. Generally speaking, you'll find middle-of-the-road paddles with fiberglass shafts and fiberglass blades. These do good duty and will take the abuse of pushing off from a beach and driving all day. As you work into the composites with graphite and a host of space-age products, you'll see the price ratchet up steadily. You might like to paddle the top-of-the-line lightweights (I do), but you might be nervous bashing one about (I am).

WEIGHT

Look for a paddle that weighs about 2 pounds, 4 ounces. If a paddle weighs over 3 pounds, it will pile-drive you right into the ground at the end of five hours. If it weighs less than 2 pounds, it lightened your wallet a whole bunch and/or it is a little on the fragile side for thumping on rocks, beaches, and the rest of the paddling world.

Secondly, look where that weight lies. Heavy blades will weigh on you. Light blades and a heavier shaft are easier to paddle—after all, you're going to be swinging that weight thousands of times in a short trip.

WINGING IT

I can't talk about wing paddles from a great deal of personal experience—although they are certainly race-proven. I've gleaned my opinions from friends who swear by them. A wing blade looks like a spoon with an attitude. The power face is cupped in almost 2 inches, the back is convex, the top edge is curved over, the shape is asymmetric, and the blade itself might be twisted. It's also hung off the shaft at an angle of up to 10 degrees. Why do all this? Because a wing *could* give you a longer, slower stroke rate with more power and more speed, and because its paddle path turns every stroke into a mini-brace, which helps stabilize or balance your kayak.

The paddle forces you to use your lower back and stomach muscles. You insert the paddle blade up near your feet, as with a conventional forward stroke, but instead of coming right alongside the hull with the stroke, you let the blade float out at an angle. The power zone extends a foot or two beyond your hips.

Will it work? I'm going to find out. The touring paddle I just ordered is a fiberglass wing.

CHAPTER SEVEN

Let's Go Paddling

Kayaks—and most especially cruising kayaks—are tippy. This is a well-known fact, attested to by hundreds of summer camps and perhaps thousands of pages of carefully reasoned analysis by writers who wear outdoor clothing. Right? Well, you can find out for yourself.

Give me a hand and we'll carry your kayak down to the water. Fact is, I'll walk out into thigh-deep water with the bow of your boat and carry on this conversation from the water. As we talk, keep an eye on your boat. No, it won't drift away, because I could nudge it back shorewards. Let's see how long it takes for this tippy boat to turn turtle. Five minutes? An hour? Three hours?

What do you mean this little demo isn't fair? You agreed that kayaks are tippy, and all we're doing is testing out this bit of common knowledge. I'll push the boat back to shore, help you aboard, and bring you out here into water 2 or 3 feet deep, and we can chat all day—or until I get cold. You will not flip over like a chicken on a rotisserie and do a face plant in the brine. Absolutely not.

First of all, virtually every cruising kayak manufactured today is inherently stable. It takes a substantial outside force to overcome your kayak's tendency to remain deck-side-up. Yes, you can get hammered by a breaking wave in the surf or you can hang your own weight so far over the side that gravity overwhelms buoyancy, but during the vast majority of paddling hours, you'll be riding in one of the most stable boats that ever put to sea.

A moving kayak is more stable than a sitting one. Later in this book you're going to be introduced to braces, in which you use your paddle to increase the stability of your kayak. With a typical paddle and a typical range of upper body motion, you'll be able to reach out 4½ feet on either side of your boat. Remember: Your paddle is part of the *gestalt* of your boat. As you learn to become one with the kayak, you'll realize that your boat is not just 24 inches wide—the apparent measurement from gunwale to gunwale—but is really 9 feet wide from the tip of the paddle extension on one side to the tip of the paddle extension on the other. Nine feet makes for a beamy boat, and with that dynamic width at your fingertips, you'll be rock solid on the water.

WHY KAYAKS FEEL TIPPY

"But the boat feels tippy."

Yes, that's right. Well-designed kayaks wiggle easily in the water. You'll lean your kayak in order to turn it. You'll also soon find that it's easy to tilt your boat a few degrees, harder to make it lean a bit further, and then it's downright difficult to add even a little more angle. This phenomenon is called secondary stability. It means your boat is easy to lean, but hard to turn over.

Secondary stability is not a force of nature, but is part and parcel of the designer's trade. Flat-water sprint boats, found in Olympic racing, have little inherent stability. Everything but straight-ahead speed has been sacrificed at the drawing board.

No matter how convincing I may be on paper about the ultimate stability of cruising kayaks, the minute you feel the boat wiggle under you, your inner ear will tell your brain in absolute terms that I am a liar. "Hey, this thing is wobbly, we're going to slip, and then we're going to *fall!*" Maybe it's the lizard part of your mind, just a centimeter or so off the brain stem, that's so worried, but whatever part of your thinking system it is, believe me, it will be persuasive. Wrong, but persuasive. You'll simply need to *show* this precursor of rationality the error of its ways.

Anyone who has never been in a kayak thinks they know how tippy they are. In truth a kayak is so stable you can stand up and cast in comfort while fishing. PHOTO BY STEVEN COOK/WILDERNESS SYSTEMS

Degrees of Stability

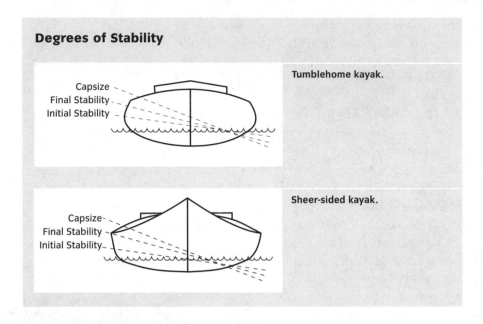

Tumblehome kayak.

Capsize
Final Stability
Initial Stability

Sheer-sided kayak.

Capsize
Final Stability
Initial Stability

BOARDING YOUR KAYAK

There is no right or wrong way of clambering into your kayak, but there are methods that are easier, more graceful, and probably less likely to transform you from a paddler into a swimmer. Let's carry your kayak out into your backyard or onto some other secluded spot. Bring your spray deck, your PFD, and your paddle, and I'll carry one end of your boat while you carry the other. If you want, stow your gear in the cockpit as we walk.

With your kayak on the soft grass, your first step is to slip into your spray deck. Some people step into the center hole and pull the skirt up, while others try to hold the skirt over their heads and wiggle up through the hole. I've never had much luck with the skirt-over-head technique; whenever I've tried, I've merely ended up stuck in the hole. When you're getting in, pull the top edge right up to your armpits. When you're in the kayak, you can slip the skirt down a bit, but as long as it is as high as possible, you are less likely to jam it between yourself and the cockpit rim.

Now, put on your PFD. Yes, you're in your backyard and this is just practice. But put it on anyway. It's a good habit to get into, it shows the proper respect for the sea, it's the right example for the children—and besides, boarding your kayak is a lot different with than without a PFD.

Next, sit down beside your kayak, right next to the cockpit and seat, with your feet extended toward the bow. If you feel like it, let your hip touch the gunwale—

Boarding Your Kayak

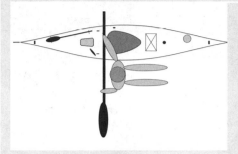

1. Place your paddle across the rear deck of your kayak, with one blade flat on the ground and the other just beyond the opposite edge of your deck. Sit or squat next to your kayak, about at the cockpit. Put one hand on the paddle shaft near the blade and the other hand at the cockpit with your palm on the shaft and your fingers curling around the cockpit rim. Push up on your arms so that most of your weight is supported on the paddle.

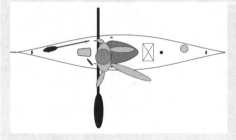

2. Shift your weight over the kayak, above the rear rim of the cockpit, and at the same time put your leg (the one next to the kayak) into the cockpit opening.

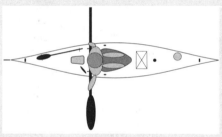

3. Still using your paddle to support your weight, put your other leg in the cockpit for stability. You'll probably be more comfortable if you keep a little more weight on the side of the paddle still touching the ground.

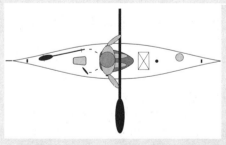

4. Push your weight forward a little so you're right over the cockpit, and lower yourself onto the kayak seat. Bring the paddle in front of you.

Boarding works equally well from a beach, a low bank, or a dock. Practice the first time on dry land, and you'll see—if not the first time, at least in the first few times—how easy it is to board your kayak.

Getting out? Just reverse steps one through four. Until you're comfortable getting in and out, keep a fair percentage of your weight supported on the paddle blade resting on the ground. You will be surprised how quickly you outgrow the need for that extra balance and simply scoot in and out of your boat.

The first time you feel your boat come alive in the water can be intimidating. You try to remember a score of lessons and dozens of instructions, and all the while your boat is wiggling underneath you. That's when a guiding hand from your instructor really feels good! Whether in a club or in a class, a good instructor will share paddling skills and steer you away from bad paddling habits. PHOTO COURTESY OCEAN KAYAK

if not, keep within a few inches of the hull. Put your paddle behind your back so that it crosses your boat just behind the cockpit. If you're using a feathered paddle, slide the paddle across your boat until the blade is on the far side of the boat and stands vertical. The other blade should rest flat on the ground. If you have an unfeathered paddle, slide it across until one blade is flat on the ground and the other is just beyond the deck.

With your hand that is next to the kayak, reach over and hold the paddle shaft with your palm while wrapping your fingers around the cockpit coaming. Place your other hand on the paddle shaft right about the small of your back. Push up, so that your weight is supported by your feet and your hands. You might hear your kayak creak a bit, because it's not accustomed to supporting your weight while aground, but it will do so without overly complaining.

Now lift your leg next to the boat and put it in the cockpit. Shift your weight from the grounded blade of your paddle until you are poised over the cockpit. Bring your other leg aboard. If you paddle a typical Pacific Northwest kayak, with a big cockpit, you'll be able to lower yourself into the seat and then extend your feet forward under the deck. If your boat has a small cockpit, you'll have to slip your legs forward as you slide into the seat. Don't worry, this move is almost automatic. (It is a truism that you can't assume anything when going to sea. But for our on-the-lawn boarding practice, we'll assume that the kayak shop helped you adjust the backrest of your seat and set the rudder pegs at the right length.)

With your feet on the rudder pedals (or foot braces), lean forward just a bit and bring your paddle across the spray deck in front of you. Hook the elastic at the back edge of the spray skirt around the cockpit coaming behind you, and once it is hooked, grab the front edge in both hands and snug it over the front edge of the cockpit. The sides sometimes will just roll into place and sometimes may need a bit of a boost. Most spray skirts have a loop or handle at the front. Reach out and grab that loop or handle. Make sure you know where it is.

Reverse the sequence to get out. Unhook the front of your spray skirt, release the back edge, put your paddle behind you with one blade flat on the ground and the other just beyond your deck, and lift yourself out of the cockpit. Shift sideways and move your legs to the ground.

You got it! Try it a couple more times, and you'll be surprised how easy it gets.

YOUR FIRST LAUNCH

Now let's go to the beach. I'm going to walk alongside you on your first launch.

The bay we've chosen stacks all the cards in your favor. The water is shallow and warm, and the sand beach angles easily into the clear water. There are no other boats on the bay, and therefore no wakes to slap up alongside your kayak. And we're in luck. There isn't another person on the beach. We rest your kayak so that the front of the cockpit is just past the water's edge and then turn the boat so that the angle between the beach line and the keel line is about 45 degrees. That's not a critical measurement, so don't worry if you don't have a protractor.

Put your paddle across your deck just behind the cockpit, just as you did when you practiced boarding from the lawn. One blade should be

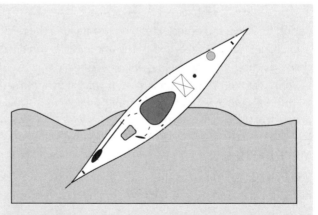

When possible, you'll find it easier to launch when your kayak is at an angle of about 45 degrees to the shoreline.

Your first launch off the beach into a wave can be frightening, but it doesn't have to be. To help you gain your sea legs on your first solo paddle, let a skilled friend tug you off the sand and through the first wave. Your next launch will be a piece of cake. PHOTO COURTESY OCEAN KAYAK

flat on the sand, the other extending just beyond the deck. Now, either squat, crouch, or sit down right next to the cockpit, like you did on the lawn. I suggest doing this from the shore side, unless you really want to sit in the water. Now get in your boat. You already know how. If you sat in damp sand, you'll probably have a little wet sand in your kayak, but that's no big deal. Now snap your spray skirt into place, like you learned on the lawn.

WET EXITS

You may get the idea that this is a progressive series of lessons, and something's about to be added. You're right. We're going to learn another way of exiting your kayak.

There was a good reason why we angled your kayak across the shoreline. The bow of your boat is floating. Scootch a bit forward, with a bump of your hips, and give a light push with your paddle on the shore, and you're afloat. If you were exactly perpendicular to the shore, you'd have to drag your stern 8 or 9 feet down the beach before it was in the water, and since the beach angles down while the water under your bow is flat, you'd be in a boat supported at the ends and high in the middle—guaranteed to dig a major gouge with the stern. And there you'd be, supported on the sharply angled bow and stern of your kayak while you and the broader midsection are wobbling well up in the air. You thought a boat in the water felt "tippy"? If you come straight off the beach (or, conversely, land by slamming straight into the beach), you're going to learn a whole new definition of "tippy." If you were absolutely parallel to the beach, you'd have to slide the whole length of your boat sideways before you sloshed into deep water, and kayaks are designed to move ahead rather than sideways.

With your PFD fastened and your paddle in hand, I'm going to walk you out into stomach-deep water. At first, that's measured on me. We'll cheat this first time and let you grasp the golf ball (or the loop) on your spray skirt. As soon as you're ready, shift all your weight to one side. As you do that, I'm going to help a bit, and you're going to be part and parcel of your first capsize.

I'm not particularly worried. After all, you're the one who is upside down and held into a suddenly very confining cockpit. The main reason I'm not concerned is that you're going to tug the loop and so strip the spray skirt away. Put one hand on each side of the cockpit and shove—just straighten your arms and don't worry if you are shoving up or down. You're really just shoving out. As you straighten your arms, your rump will lift out of the seat and your legs will slide right out of the boat. You might actually, though unintentionally, push the boat ahead a bit while straightening and that will just speed your exit. And an exit it is. Or, more precisely, a wet exit.

Why did we go through all that?

Most of us, when first inching our way into a kayak cockpit, think just how tight and constrained a small boat it is. That little bump on the top of your spine may start wailing, "We'll soon be trapped, we'll turn over, we're not going to be able to get out. . . ." What your primitive brain is saying is loud and very, very convincing. But as we've seen, your brain can be wrong.

Since your boat was set up with a rear bulkhead, all we have to do is keep the boat upside down as we lift the bow—and the water rushes out. If it didn't have bulkheads, we would have to alternately lift the bow and stern until all the water poured out the cockpit.

Now let's return to the beach and get back into the boat. After a few times, boarding your boat gets easy. If you're feeling sporty, pull your boat up alongside a low dock and use the same technique to get from the dock to your boat. It works exactly the same way.

HOLDING YOUR PADDLE

Hold your paddle with both hands so that the middle of the paddle shaft is centered between your thumbs. You don't need a death grip on the paddle shaft; just wrap your fingers loosely over the top of the horizontal shaft and cradle the weight of the paddle on the balls of your thumbs and the web between your thumb and index finger. If you grip tightly, you'll wear yourself out.

In fact, if you really want to grip, go to a lumberyard and buy a 3-foot chunk of 1½-inch dowel. When you're watching television, just grip that dowel as hard as you can for as long as you can. After about fifteen minutes or so, you'll get that urge out of your system and be willing to paddle with relaxed hands.

To put more of your muscle power into a paddle stroke, move your hands out toward the blades. How far? Determine your maximum efficient hand spread by holding your paddle horizontally over your head, upper arms horizontal. Slide your hands out until your forearms are vertical. That's your forearms, not your puffy sleeves in a breeze.

Hold the paddle over your head with your upper arms horizontal and your forearms vertical. You probably will have to inch both hands in and out a bit until both your elbows make a right angle. This is the maximum power position for paddling. No, no, no—not the position in which you have to work the hardest or make the maximum effort. This is the hand position that gives you the maximum mechanical advantage and the maximum leverage when manipulating your paddle. It's not a bad spot from which to start.

Are you afraid you might forget just how far apart to spread your hands? Don't worry too much—you're not in international competition. It really doesn't matter if you're a whit or so off. You can just flip your paddle over your head, lock your elbows into a right angle, and there you are. If you want, keep your hands in posi-

Grasp your paddle so that the knuckles of your control hand—the hand that rotates a feathered paddle—line up parallel with the paddle blade on the same side as that hand. The first few times you go paddling, you'll find yourself looking to see which direction your paddle blade is pointing. By always aligning your knuckles and blade, you'll instinctively know the position of the blade. If you choose to use an unfeathered paddle, you still align your knuckles and blade, even though you won't be rotating the paddle.

tion and lower your paddle in front of you. Have a friend loop a thin strip of duct tape around the paddle shaft just beyond your little fingers on each side. By the time the tape wears off, your muscles will remember where to reach.

YOUR FIRST STROKES

Go ahead and flail at the water a bit. There you go in a wobbling fashion, straight as a snake's tail, but *you're paddling!* Your first paddle is an exciting moment. You're a captain, you're in total command of your craft. The boat does what you tell it to do. Not necessarily what you want it to do, but certainly what you tell it to do.

Now that you've burned off a little excitement, let's see if we can increase your fun quotient by making your paddling a little easier. You were pulling with your upper arms as you splashed about, and even after ten minutes or so — if you're honest—you'll admit that your upper arms are a bit tired.

Let's run a small test. Stand on the beach with your paddle held vertically in front of you. Turn it so that the power face of the blade on the ground is facing you. (Some instructors call the power face the "front," but we all mean the face of the paddle that "pushes" against the water.) Look up at the blade in the air. You'll have to look up, because most touring paddles are 220 to 230 centimeters long and few of us are 7 feet tall. If the power face of the upper blade is aimed at your right, you have a right-hand-control paddle. If the power face faces your left, you have a left-hand-control paddle. If the power face faces you, you have an unfeathered paddle. And what if the power face faces away from you? You've either let the paddle twist as you gawk at the upper blade, or you have a paddle with a serious identity problem. If you have a break-apart paddle, you might have simply slipped the two halves together incorrectly. If by some strange chance the two halves match up backward, release the lock (often a button) and twist the paddle blade around to where it should be.

With feathered paddles your control hand (right for a right-hand-control paddler and left for a left-hand one) will lightly grip the paddle shaft and will allow you to rotate the paddle with your wrist to put each blade precisely into the water vertically. You won't change this grip as you paddle. Your other hand forms a ring within which the paddle shaft rotates as you immerse first one blade and then the other.

Hold your paddle out in front of you, horizontally. Look at the knuckles on your control hand. The upper edge of your paddle blade next to your control hand should line up with your knuckles at the base of your fingers. Are you the kind of person, like many of us, who is likely to relax your control hand and forget the most efficient position? Not to worry. Many paddles will give your muscles and your fingers a quick clue if your positioning changes. Paddle shafts are oval, not round, and they will feel different if they shift within your hand. If that isn't enough, try taping a matchstick to the paddle shaft right next to your top knuckle line. You can feel the matchstick, and this will let you position your control hand easily.

If you choose an unfeathered paddle, both hands work as control hands. You'll line up the upper edges of your blades with the row of knuckles across the base of your fingers.

Let's start off paddling an unfeathered paddle (some of the instructions for using a feathered paddle will come from these directions, so read on). We'll begin with a stroke on the right side. Extend your right arm so that your elbow is straight and your hand is about at the same level as the peak of your deck. At the same time, bring your left hand back almost as if you were going to put a shot, that is, right to the front of your left shoulder. I keep the midpoint of the paddle above the lower edge of my sternum. Many paddlers prefer a slightly lower position—you'll discover what works best for you in time—but I believe that a slightly higher paddle position, with the midpoint of the paddle shift near your solar plexus, gives you a more efficient paddle stroke. The submerged blade is closer to the centerline of your kayak, it is closer to vertical, and more of your energy is translated into go-ahead force. A lower paddle position, with the midpoint around your navel, means the apparent path of the blade as you put the power to it will be a "C." The first part of the stroke will push your bow away from the paddle blade, the mid-part of the stroke will move you forward, and the last part of the stroke will pull your stern toward the blade. This ongoing wiggle won't be very noticeable, but it will be real and it will erode part of the energy you brought to your kayak this day.

Insert the paddle blade in the water as far forward as you can comfortably reach without slouching forward. You're getting that blade forward with a combination of upper body rotation and arm extension. You'll be reaching right around your foot, but you don't have to check this distance exactly. It's just what happens. Don't bang at the water; don't pretend you're a beaver and the paddle blade is your tail. Just slip the paddle in.

How deep should it be placed? If you don't put the blade in the water, you can't develop any power. If you plunge it deeper than the throat of the blade, you're just using up leverage without gaining any paddle face. Without being too particular, try to just submerge the blade.

Forward Stroke

Kayak movement

Apparent path of paddle blade

Once the blade is in the water, let your right arm begin to draw the paddle back. Simultaneously, push forward with your left hand, palm forward and fingers relaxed, as if you were aiming that hand right at the bow. Create an imaginary line right down the center of your deck, and don't let your pushing hand cross over that line. You won't lose marks for doing so, but you will over-rotate your torso, tire sooner, and lose power. Don't lift your left hand too high, either. I've watched people lift their left hand in this paddle stroke much higher than their eyes; there is no benefit gained from doing so. If you keep your left hand at shoulder or perhaps chin height, you're less likely to drip water on yourself, and the power from the blade in the water will actually serve to stabilize your boat. Keep the blade as close to vertical as you comfortably can, because that position gives you the maximum power face. Also, keep the paddle blade as close as you can to perpendicular to the keel line of your kayak. If you angle the blade forward or backward, it will want either to climb out of the water or to dive deeper—and the energy you use to correct this is better spent in moving the kayak. If you let the blade angle into or away from the perpendicular position, it will want to drift away from the side of your kayak or sheer into it—again, correcting this will be a waste of energy.

The energy portion of your stroke should kick in as the paddle passes from your knees to your hips. Once the blade is past your hips, all you're doing is prying up on the water, simply because of the angle of your hands. It's better that you lift the blade from the water and, as you do so, continue until your right hand is up by your right shoulder and your left arm is fully extended. You're now in a mirror-image position of the first stage of the stroke you just completed. Insert the blade and keep paddling!

To paddle with a feathered blade, start by holding your paddle in front of you, both arms extended and your elbows held almost straight. This isn't one of those military-movie exercises where you have to hold your paddle in front of you until you drop. All we're going to do is see how your control hand works.

If the knuckles on your control hand are properly lined up with the top edge of the blade on that side, the other blade should be more or less horizontal. Rotate your control hand back toward you and, at the same time, raise your forearm just a tad by cocking up your elbow. Keep a firm grip with your control hand and let the paddle shaft rotate within the circle of your thumb and index finger of your other (noncontrol) hand. You'll find it easy to rotate the control-hand blade so that the bottom edge goes forward and the top edge back until the blade is about horizontal. At that point the other blade will be perpendicular to the water with the power face pointing toward the stern of your boat.

Try this a couple of times, and pretty soon your hands will know which blade is vertical and which horizontal. Some people will try and cheat by letting the paddle shaft rotate within the grip of their control hand. I suppose you can do this if you want, but if you do, you will never become a confident paddler.

Which hand should you use to control the paddle? As a guru from the 1960s would advise, just do what feels right. Arbitrarily, we'll say you're right-handed and you paddle a right-hand-control paddle. That's probably the norm. It is not an iron-bound law, however. My wife is left-handed, and she prefers a right-hand-control paddle. I don't know if that's a triumph of education over nature or if it does indeed reflect an innate preference for right-hand paddles.

Most people who use a feathered paddle start stroking on their control-hand side. The first half of the stroke with a feathered paddle is exactly the same as for

The beach is an excellent classroom. You can learn how to adjust your boat's footrests and seat for comfortable and efficient paddling, how to hold your paddle, and how to rotate your torso and plant your paddle blade in the water for a smooth and powerful stroke. You'll do it without concerns about being tossed about by waves, blown by a breeze, or even toppling (accidentally) out of your boat. PHOTO COURTESY OCEAN KAYAK

an unfeathered paddle. The same reach, the same paddle placement as far forward as you can reach without leaning forward, the same pull backward, and the same punch forward with the upper hand. The first difference comes as you begin to lift the control-side blade from the water as it passes your hip. As the blade clears the water, rotate your wrist back and slightly cock your forearm at the elbow. This will bring the noncontrol blade perpendicular to the water just as you insert the blade in the water near your foot.

At the end of the power phase of your stroke, just as the blade passes your hip, lift the blade from the water. As you lift the paddle and blade with your non-control hand, rotate your control wrist forward and straighten your arm. This will turn the control-hand blade until it is vertical and ready to insert into the water.

If you don't think about this cycle, it comes pretty naturally. But if you try to think through each stage, it may seem awkward, uncomfortable, and downright silly. So don't think about it, just do it.

Whether you're paddling an unfeathered or a feathered paddle, don't go wind-milling down the bay with the tips of your paddle carving perfect circles in the air. A circle would lift one blade too high and plunge the other too deep. The proper shape your blade tip should make is an oval or an egg shape.

Now I'm going to be just a bit negative for a minute and assume you're making a few mistakes common to novice paddlers. In your first few strokes, you're probably not keeping the paddle blade as vertical as possible and you're probably not keeping the blade at a right angle to the keel line. Both of these positioning flaws reduce the apparent size of the power face and decrease the efficiency of your stroke. You may not be putting the entire blade in the water, or you may be plunging the blade far beneath the surface. Check to see if you're swinging your top hand across the center line of your deck. To gain a little extra thrust, you're letting the blade trail well past your hips. In the effort to reach as far forward as possible, you're probably leaning forward rather than keeping your back vertical. You probably have a death grip on the paddle shaft, and despite this you've let the shaft rotate in your control hand.

How do I know you're doing all this? Because I've made each and every one of these moves, and although I swore I wasn't guilty, a jury of my peers has hooted and pointed at my quirks.

LEARNING BOTH STROKES

We've spent a fair amount of time together, a lot of it with me in the water beside you, but all we've accomplished is to start to describe the motion of a basic forward stroke. While you can paddle with what you've learned thus far, you'll feel like a weakling when your arms get tired after a few minutes. What you've learned is how to use the guiding muscles in your arms. What you'll learn now is how to use those guiding muscles to direct the big muscles in your back, shoulders, and abdomen—and from these muscles you'll find it's possible to paddle easily for hours at a stretch. "But," you ask, "with all the time we've spent on just one stroke, how many more strokes do I need to learn?"

If you read all the paddling books and magazines, hang out with paddling gurus, and attend all the paddling symposiums, you'll hear of dozens of absolutely required paddling strokes. The people who use them probably like them. Before we start planning a long curriculum of basic strokes, though, take a look at your paddle. It has two faces—the power face and the back. That's it. Likewise, you have two paddling options. You can use the power face to create resistance in the water, or you can use the back side of the blade to create resistance. Two types of strokes. (Okay, you also have a top and bottom edge to each blade and you could slice the blade through the water edge like a hot knife through butter. And when you miscalculate your blade angle, you're liable to do just that. If the mistake is totally unexpected and you're driving with full force, you could find yourself transmogrified into a swimmer. I hope you'll have time to take a good breath before the experience. I didn't.) You can apply those two strokes in different ways,

With a few almost effortless strokes, you can set your kayak to gliding over the clear water.

at different angles, and at different times in order to make your boat respond in the manner you hope it will, but those are all the tools you have.

WHAT MAKES A STROKE WORK

Before we go on, let's give some basic thought to just what a paddle stroke is. Well, you already know, right? You put the paddle blade in the water and you pull the blade back toward yourself. Wrong! If you were sitting on a large rock, with ropes securing your body to the stone, that's what would happen. But a boat is not a rock, and you're not tied down. You reach forward and anchor your blade in a fairly inflexible medium. Think of reaching forward with an ice ax and driving a point into a smooth sheet of ice. When you pull on the shaft, the point isn't going to move. You move, sliding forward and toward the point. When you put your blade in the water and pull, the blade doesn't move. You pull yourself toward the blade. You have your feet, placed on the rudder pegs, stretched out in front of you, and as you pull yourself forward, you push your kayak ahead with your feet. If you didn't push the boat ahead, you'd pull yourself into a little ball up in the bow.

PUSH AND PULL

Back to the forward stroke. When we first began paddling, you were moving your kayak by simply pulling with one arm and guiding the paddle with the other. What we're going to do now is change your pulling hand from the sole source of power into a moveable fulcrum. You'll keep your power developed by pulling on the paddle, but we're going to add more thrust. Let's imagine that you merely insert the blade into the water and hold the paddle in position with your hand next to the immersed blade. Now, with your upper, guiding, hand, you press forward on the other end of the paddle shaft. As you press forward, you turn your paddle into a lever pivoting around the fulcrum of your lower hand. See how the blade moves? That propels you ahead!

Now combine the two moves. As you pull with your lower hand, push with your top hand. You won't double your power, but you will increase the total paddle power by about a quarter to a third by pushing with your top hand. If you throttle back so that the total power at the blade remains the same, your pulling hand will only have to work two-thirds to three-quarters as hard to produce the same result. Overall, you're working just as hard, but your arms are sharing the work rather than putting all the effort into one bicep.

To make this work, keep the relative speed of both arms/hands about the same. It's easy to get too pumped up and shove with all your might—completing the forward push before your pulling hand has even started back. Keep the cadence down as you learn how your muscles should feel, and keep all your motions light and gentle. You don't have to knock out the heavyweight champion of the world, so there is no reason to drive hard into that top-hand push. Yes, I noticed that you're almost throwing a punch with your pushing hand, and that's absolutely the right way. But keep it easy and smooth.

For some reason, many paddlers start out with their pushing hand right at shoulder level—where it should be—but then they push first up to higher than eye level and then in a downward plunge at the end of the stroke. If you do this, you start flailing all over the place and you lose much of the effectiveness of the push. I did, and I had to learn first how not to send my hand in a great arc before I could learn to keep my pushing hand level. Paddling suddenly got a lot more fun for me. I was working less and getting better.

ADDING IN THE POWER MUSCLES

You've made good progress controlling your arm muscles. Now let's throw in the big guys and see what happens. Step one is to check that you're seated firmly in your boat. Your feet are on the pegs and your back is comfortably pressed against the seat back. Your legs are up against the underside of the deck, but you're not so constricted that you can't relax your legs and lower your thighs. Your hips fit snugly in the seat—you've padded the seat for a perfect fit. You're one with the boat from the waist down, while your torso can rotate freely. Remember, you're not in a chaise lounge. You want to be sitting erect. Fuss with this until you're comfortable, because you're not going to paddle with the least effort and best result until the boat is an extension of yourself.

Now you're going to learn to work with the maximum effort of your muscles. When you have to pick something up, you squat because that brings your major thigh muscles into lifting, rather than your out-of-position back muscles. When you lift something heavy from a tabletop, you use your biceps rather than your little finger. And when you paddle, you'll use the big muscles of your torso and back rather than the smaller muscles of your arms to scoot yourself along.

The next step is to start your stroke, just like you've been doing, extending one hand ahead to plant your blade. Take a mental snapshot of what you're doing right now. Your shoulders point directly out to the sides of your boat, perpendicular to the keel line. If your boat is perfectly aligned north and south, you have one shoulder pointing due west and the other east. All your drive is coming from your arms. Now, reach farther. Don't lean forward. Rotate your torso. Don't try to twist yourself up like a towel you're trying to squeeze the last dribble of water from, but just swing a comfortable distance. You will likely rotate your paddle-side shoulder forward about 45 degrees, or one-eighth of a circle.

It is all too easy to think you are rotating when in fact you're just pumping your elbows in and out. Look down at your PFD zipper. If the zipper continuously points at the bow, you're riding on your biceps. If the zipper moves back and forth, through an arc of 4 inches or more, you're rotating your torso.

So, what have you done?

First, by rotating your torso while keeping your back vertical, you've increased your reach forward. This is good, because you've increased the length of your effective, vertical stroke. Even more important, you've wound yourself up like a spring and you're all set to uncoil with the big muscles of your back and belly. As you start the pulling portion of your stroke, not only will your arm come back but your shoulder will rotate back and add power to your stroke. Your shoulders will rotate from about 45 degrees ahead of amidships to 45 degrees aft of amidships, or through an arc of a quarter circle. This is not a precise measurement. One person will rotate easily, and another will be tight. One of the better bicycle match sprint racers of recent years was massively muscled, and every time he attempted to turn his head to look behind, he forced the bike into a sharp little jag. He literally couldn't turn his head and torso against the tightness of his massive torso muscles. And yet he was an Olympian.

As your pulling shoulder comes back, your pushing shoulder goes forward, accelerating the pushing motion of your top hand. Both sides of the paddle stroke gain power.

You may find this hard to measure, but in the primary power zone from your knees to your hips, most of the power will come from the uncoiling muscles in your back. The smallest amount of energy will come from your upper pushing hand, with your lower pulling hand providing the middle ground of energy. Think of what you're doing as moving a spring smoothly back and forth, sort of like a Slinky marching across the surface of the water. Your arms will not be straight as an arrow, but will be bent just a tad at the elbow to keep the paddle shaft away from your chest.

Now you'll see why it's important that your feet be firmly on the pegs and your hips be snugged into the seat. When you're driving ahead with your right paddle blade, you'll feel your right foot push on the right peg. When you drive ahead with your left paddle blade, you'll push on the left peg. If your kayak seat were too wide and you hadn't filled it in with hip pads, you'd slide from side to side with each stroke. Each slippage represents energy that could have moved your boat ahead.

How powerful are your back and abdominal muscles? Let's find out. Turn your elbows off, with no pulling or pushing with your arms. Start with your kayak dead in the water, and concentrate on using just your torso twist to drive your paddle. Sure, this is counterproductive, but we're isolating your power and not practicing paddling for a few strokes. You'll feel the big muscle down the front of your stomach tense and stand out, and the top of your thighs will grow warm from shoving your feet.

Right away I know what you're thinking: "If I really twist, I'll go really fast!" Sorry—it doesn't work that way. Kayaking is a way of becoming one with the water and the environment, not a way of overcoming it. Be gentle, move with calm deliberation, and concentrate on the grace of what you are doing. What we're looking for is an elegance of movement.

The worst thing you can do is to think of each movement as a separate act. Cock a wrist. Extend an arm. Twist. All your moves should flow together in a current of motion, indivisible. There are no absolute rules in the art of paddling. By way of example, consider the proper motions of a tennis stroke and then watch films of Bjorn Borg on the court. In a classic tennis sense, he fell far from perfection. The only thing he did right was to put his own motions into a fluid grace that worked for him—and in doing so he won a lot of tennis matches.

CHANGING SPEED BY CHANGING GEARS

So far we've been running in low gear. That's another way of saying we've been using a lot of arm and torso motion in order to move our paddle a relatively short distance. Remember, upper arms horizontal, forearms vertical, and elbows at a right angle. That's your power position. Now let's shift into a cruising gear.

High gear—more paddle strokes per minute but less of your muscles used on each one—comes as you slide your hands toward the middle of the shaft. Bring them in no farther than the width of your shoulders.

Hold your paddle in both hands, with your hands a comfortable and equal distance from the middle of the paddle. Keep your elbows at your sides, and bring your hands up so that your index finger knuckles are right next to the little bones that protrude at the top outside rear of your shoulders. The midpoint of your paddle should be around the little vee where your collarbone connects to your sternum. You're now holding your paddle in the high-gear slot, where you will get the maximum paddle blade movement with the minimum of hand and arm movement. It will take more muscle to move the paddle, but you'll be able to keep up a higher paddle cadence more comfortably, and for a longer distance and a longer time. You might want to put a circle of tape around your paddle shaft just inside of each thumb position to remind you where high gear rests. You can put your hands anywhere between the tapes marking your "high" and "low" gears, depending on the amount of power you want to apply to the paddle.

STOPPING

Up to this point, we've put all our efforts into going ahead, more specifically into going straight ahead. But what happens if you paddle up a long, straight slot between a pair of immovable objects and you find that the two shores—be they rock, log, or the towering side of a barge—are coming together? Well, before you panic, let's learn how to stop.

First of all, even if you were really pushing along, you're probably only making a speed of about 5 knots. You can just stop paddling, and you'll glide to a halt. But if it looks like you'll glide for 75 feet and you're but 60 feet from the end of the water, you have a significant challenge. You're going to be the test subject in a deceleration test. A loaded kayak at cruising speed packs an immense momentum. Before you say that 5 knots, or 5 miles per hour, isn't all that much speed, just remember that insurance companies run their crash tests for bumper protection at 5 miles per hour, and some vehicles can sustain thousands of dollars of damage when colliding square on with an immovable object.

The moment you stop paddling, you're going to learn another surprising thing about your boat. It won't slow in a straight line. Try rolling a hoop down the road, and as it slows it wobbles off center and eventually flops into a constricting spiral. Your boat will behave similarly, though perhaps not to that extent.

No problem. All you have to do is stop. Let's see. Your right foot is on the right rudder peg and your left on the left—where's the brake peg?

In your hand. Hold your paddle low across your body, about midway between your belly button and your solar plexus if you have a low-decked boat, or midway between the deck and your solar plexus if you have a steeply peaked deck. You're going to be putting some weight on the paddle—or force, if you prefer. You want the effort from your paddle focused down low where you can transmit it to the back band of your seat rather than keeping it high where your stomach muscles will have to strain to keep your back from arching. Tuck your elbows in toward your sides, with your arms slightly bent and flexible. Your paddle should be in its normal position, with the back of the blade toward the front of the boat. Dip the blade into the water for a second or two, letting your torso rotate back to take some of the energy from the blade. You'll find it easier if you cant the top edge of the paddle just slightly toward the front of the kayak. With the blade angled just slightly, the force of the water against the nonpower face will attempt to push the blade up and out of the water. If you had the blade canted the other way, with the top edge of the blade back and the bottom edge slightly forward, the paddle would be inclined to dive deeper into the water. In a worst-case situation, you'd lose control of the paddle and could even lose the paddle entirely. Push forward with your hand slightly to counteract the pressure on the back of your blade.

What you've done is to jam your blade into a relatively immobile substance as your kayak slides by. The water will grip your paddle blade. The energy is transferred from the paddle to your arms and torso, down to your lower back and rump, and from there is applied to the backrest of your seat and the rest of the kayak.

But now we've caused another problem. We've stopped one side of your kayak. I know, if you stop one side, the other side is bound to stop, but we've applied the brakes by the paddle blade some distance out from the side of your boat. If you just dip the blade in on your left side, the bow of your kayak is going to swing to the left. That's simply a force of nature. Fortunately, there is a simple solution. Dip the paddle on one side, burn off the energy you can by rotating your torso and flexing your arms, and then retract the blade on the first side and dip the blade on the other. You need only two or three seconds on each side before you switch sides.

You've managed to stop your boat, and to stop it about where you wanted. That's great—you could have stopped by ramming at full speed into the barge moored right alongside, or you could have stopped by thudding bow-first into the chunk of granite that's effectively blocking the end of the channel. But you still have a problem. You're bow-on to the granite, and you're between the barge and a log boom. If the world had been kinder, the granite boulder would have been a beach and you could have landed, picked up your boat, turned it around so that the bow was back down-channel, and then paddled in a straight line to where you started.

Oh, and one more thing: The distance from the side of the barge to the log boom is just a little narrower than the length of your boat. Even if we had been practicing turns (which will come in a few pages), you couldn't have turned around anyhow.

BACKING

Fortunately, kayaks can go backward. Remember when we started paddling forward, and you found that your kayak moved ahead because you pulled with your paddle and pushed your kayak along with your feet? We're going to build on that, but turn it all around. Keep your feet on the pegs, exerting enough pressure to keep your knees up against the bottom of your deck and your rump securely braced against the back of your seat. You remember the position. But now you're going to push yourself along by pushing your back against your kayak. Did you and a friend ever ride in a little red wagon, with one of you steering and the other facing backward over the end pushing with his or her feet? We're going to do that in your kayak, with you sitting in the back of the little red wagon.

You just stopped your kayak, remember? And so you're sitting, wondering what to do next, in the middle of the narrow channel. If you thought about it, you probably shifted your hands out to the outer tape mark, to the low-gear slot, when you put on the brakes. You needed power to resist the forces shimmering up your paddle blade. Leave your hands in this position, because you're going to need a little power to get going, but just as with backing up a car, you're not going to need speed to get you out of this situation.

You might lean back toward the stern just slightly, or you might try to keep your back straight and vertical. Both positions work; do whichever is more comfortable. But if you lean forward, you'll lose the ability to rotate your torso. Keep your paddle in its standard paddling position, with the power face aimed aft toward the stern and the upper edge of the control-hand side aligned with the row of knuckles at the base of your control-hand fingers. Some people will try to flop their paddle and put the power side toward the bow. If you do this, you'll lose the control of blade angle you've been trying so hard to master, and you won't gain any power. Really, you already have more power and speed than you'll need here. Just like in the stopping maneuver, only the back side of your paddle blade will be used.

Either side will work for your first backward stroke, but as with the forward stroke, it seems natural to start on your control side. If you have a right-hand control, rotate your torso clockwise until your shoulders point about 45 degrees from straight out abeam, or just about as far around as you learned to coil in the forward stroke—remembering, of course, that in the forward stroke you rotated your shoulder blades forward and now you're rotating your shoulders back. Both arms should be comfortably bent, with your elbows fairly close to your body. Insert the paddle blade as close to vertical as is comfortable, with the blade perpendicular to the keel line and the point of insertion about 2 feet behind your hips. Obviously, you're going to be lowering your hand next to the blade, and in doing so you'll raise your opposing hand. There's no reason to lift that hand above shoulder or chin level, and there's equally no reason to push that hand well forward. You may find that you're dropping your shoulder on the paddling side and raising your shoulder on the other side, and as long as you're not skewing yourself into some odd corkscrew shape, that's perfectly normal. Don't be concerned. You'll know if you're doing it right because you'll be comfortable. If it doesn't feel right, it probably isn't.

Uncoil, rotating your paddle-side shoulder forward, and as you rotate, you'll apply pressure to the paddle blade stuck in the water. Since the blade is relatively immobile, what you're doing is pushing yourself in the opposite direction—and if you shove yourself toward the stern of your boat, your back and rump will shove your kayak in the same direction. As you push against the paddle, you'll find yourself leaning just a tad toward the stern of your boat. That's natural, and just a matter of the physics of muscle movement and leverage. All the power won't come from your unwinding torso. Apply pressure with your relaxed palm as you extend your arm toward the bow, and use this pressure to guide your paddle. As your hips move back past your paddle (the first time you do this you'll swear the paddle is moving forward, but what you're really seeing is something analogous to sitting on a rear-facing seat on a train and watching the telephone poles appear at your shoulder and rapidly recede in the distance), turn up your throttle and apply maximum thrust until your knees reach your paddle blade. Retract the blade just after your knees pass.

The closer to vertical, and the closer to perpendicular to the keel line, you keep the back of your paddle blade, the more surface you will have to grip the water and the more power you'll be able to generate. For a moment, let's flop out of the kayak and float in the water stomach down with your shoulder touching the bow and your eyes just below the surface. We'll let someone else get in the cockpit. Put on some goggles so you can see better. For easy measurements (these numbers bear no relationship to the real shape of a blade, but I can't do complicated sums in my head) we'll assume that the paddle blade you're looking at is 12 inches long and 12 inches wide. So you have 1 square foot of blade surface. If the blade is absolutely vertical and at a perfect right angle to the keel line, every bit of that surface presses against the water.

Now, the paddler is getting a little lazy. His or her top hand has moved far forward of the hand next to the blade in the water, so that the paddle shaft and thus the blade is at a 45-degree angle to the water. From where you're watching, up at the bow, the apparent height of the blade is now only 6 inches. Sure, the real length is 12 inches, but the column of water pressing against it is only half that. Now, the paddler's arm is still lazy, and the blade cants off 45 degrees from perpendicular to the keel line. From your viewpoint, the blade that had appeared to be 12 inches wide is now only 6 inches wide. The apparent surface has just been reduced by half again, so we're down to one-quarter of a square foot of blade surface. Just by not taking full advantage of the paddle stroke, our paddler has lost three-quarters of the paddle surface.

Let's let our substitute paddler go off and practice somewhere, while you get back in the boat and avoid the mistakes you just observed. For maximum power, keep the paddle close to the side of the boat, with a little power used to keep the blade down and most of your power spent in keeping a straight line parallel to the keel line.

As you lift the paddle blade from the water, your shoulders will be rotated and your hands will be moving in the proper position to begin the next stroke on the opposite side.

Nothing, though, is simple. What you have is a powerful stroke, one that will move your kayak backward—but your boat was designed to track in a straight line going forward. Backing up can be a challenge, with the stern of your boat darting unexpectedly sideways. Think of your kayak as a wind vane—it wants to point into the wind. If you twirl the back end of a wind vane around, or attempt to fling an arrow feathered-end first, the resulting action will be at best erratic.

Try inserting the lower outside corner of your paddle blade into the water first, a foot or more off that imaginary point a couple of feet back from your hips. The apparent movement of the blade toward the bow will be in an arc, something like one side of an arch, until you retract the blade as it passes your knees. This is an unbalanced stroke, but it will work! You'll start by going straight astern, but the last part of the stroke will really pull the bow toward the paddle side. The alternating stroke on the other side will pull your bow to that side, and you'll glide backward in a wiggling line.

You're right. This is not the most efficient way to move astern, compared to a straight line. What this does do, though, is present you with a whole series of potentially correcting strokes. If your kayak begins to turn to the right, put a little more muscle on your next stroke on the right side. You could also reach out a bit farther to the right and exaggerate the arc of the stroke a little more. We're not talking about major corrections here, just little nudges that keep you going in one direction. Backing up (or in nautical terms, "backing down") is a compromise between the two extremes of this stroke.

The faster you paddle, the more likely you are to shift your weight and the more likely you are to let your boat swing widely out of alignment. Keep it slow, keep it easy. If you back up slowly, you'll need smaller corrections and you'll actually go faster than if you paddled very quickly and burned off all your energy and speed with abrupt course corrections.

You'll also find that peering back over your shoulder is inconvenient and uncomfortable at best, and one of the reasons that you'll veer off course. Line up the point of your bow with an object on the shore, and keep those two marks in line for three or four strokes before you crane your neck around.

That's all there is to backing. You can plant your paddle blade in the water and pull yourself up to it, or you can plant your paddle blade in the water and push yourself away from it. Every variation of these two strokes involves either a change of direction in the force exerted or a combination of the two forces. I think most paddlers know this, at least in their muscles, even though many will articulate the names of all sorts of variations. My friend Steve pointed the two-stroke truth out to me while teaching a basic canoeing class, and it's made my time on the water easier.

TURNS

We've managed to board our kayak, paddle in a straight line, stop, and back up. That would be enough, if all waterways were 9 feet wide and a zillion miles long. But because no body of water fits this description, our skills aren't enough. We need to learn how to turn our kayak, at the speed and angle we wish, in order to explore the world passing alongside.

Sweeps

Think about what's happened to the kayak as we paddled. When we inserted the blade close to the gunwale with the blade close to vertical in the water and pulled ourselves right past it, we went straight. If we held our paddle closer to the deck while we inserted the blade in the water next to our knees, it was much harder to keep the apparent path of the paddle exactly parallel with the keel line. We had planned on moving straight ahead, but the apparent path of the paddle looked like a "C" with the open mouth of the letter wrapping around the cockpit. We were actually inserting the paddle ahead of the center balance point of the kayak and shoving the bow of the boat sideways during the first part of the stroke—until the paddle stuck straight out sideways from the cockpit—and then pulling the stern of the boat over to the blade in the last half of the stroke.

And good that we did! Why? The straight-ahead, right-down-the-keel-line stroke applies power and thus speed to the boat. But when we "sweep" the paddle around in an arc, we've enacted the "sweep" stroke, one of the basic steering strokes.

Let's back up a step. No one can make an absolutely vertical, straight-ahead stroke. To do so, you'd have to insert your paddle through the bottom of your boat and pull yourself right up and over the shaft. Anytime you put the blade in the water, even as close as you can to the gunwale, the center of your paddling effort is going to be off the center of the boat and there will be a tendency for the power

Sweep Stroke

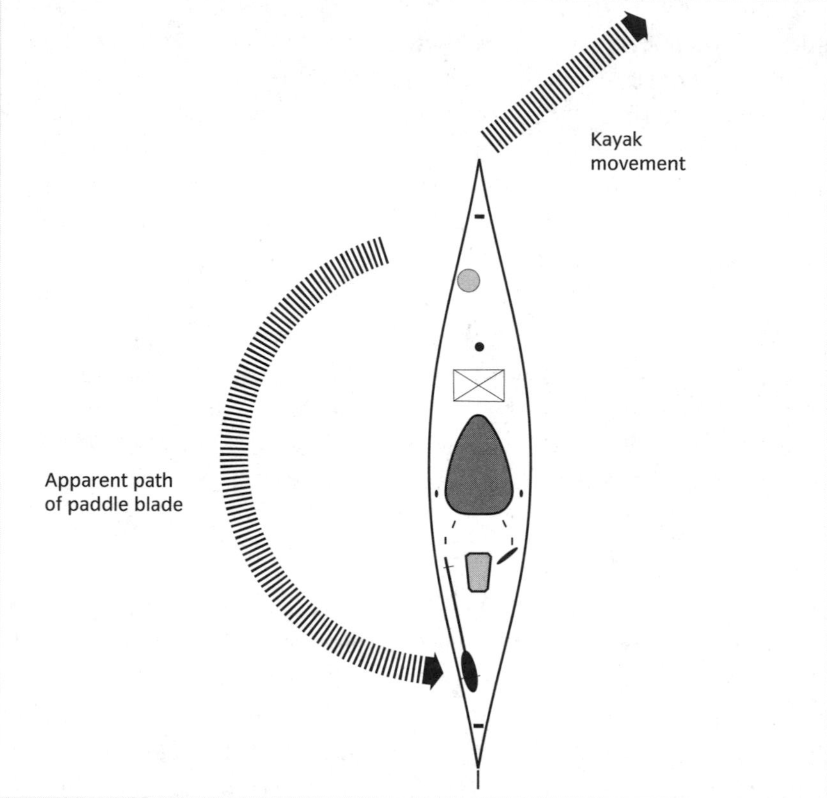

Kayak movement

Apparent path of paddle blade

The motion for the full sweep stroke is in three separate parts. The first third of the stroke (in this case, with the paddle on the left, or port, side) moves the bow to the right, while the middle third of the stroke moves the kayak ahead. The last third pulls the stern to the left and pivots the bow to the right. The net result is a strong turn to the right.

to turn your kayak. At the same time, you're instinctively going to resist splashing your paddle in up around your bow and twirling the blade in an enormous half circle from bow to stern. It violates all the things you've learned about pushing, pulling, and direction. You may or may not articulate this, but you know it.

Back in the boat, and now we're cruising down the bay. Something catches your attention over to starboard, and you'd like to swing over that way to investigate. What do you do?

You could try putting more force on each stroke on the left side of your boat. Remember, every forward stroke is unbalanced just a bit off center, and a few hard strokes might push your bow around. For that matter, if you're really forcing one side, you might just as well ease up on the other to make the paddling even more unbalanced and the turn easier. The next logical step would be to paddle on the left side only, with no strokes on the right. You can't get more unbalanced than that.

This may not turn you in time, however. Big, lazy arcs will eventually get you around, but we have a few other tricks in our bag. When you plant that paddle blade on the left side of your boat, push away from it as you pull yourself forward, and you'll push the bow of your boat to the right, through the first half of the stroke. As the paddle passes perpendicular to the keel line, or straight out from you, start pulling the stern toward the blade, which increases your right turn. It's natural to attempt to rotate the blade in the water, with the lower edge ahead of the paddle shaft. If you do that, however, it will seem as if you're lifting the entire ocean (even though you're really lifting only a few gallons). In addition to making your stroke less effective, you're wasting a lot of energy.

To make this stroke as comfortable and natural as possible, keep your paddle shaft fairly low and as close to horizontal as you can while keeping your hands off the deck and the blade fully in the water. You don't even have to be moving ahead in order to make it work. You can, and you should know how to, pivot your boat in a circle just by a series of sweep strokes.

You can exaggerate this stroke by shifting your hands so that the hand near the immersed blade is at the midpoint or so of your paddle and the other hand is at the throat of the upper blade. This gives you a much longer reach and increases the sweeping motion. But this move is risky—you can lose the muscle memory in your hands of the orientation of the blades and, in the worst case, could send a flat blade hydroplaning along the

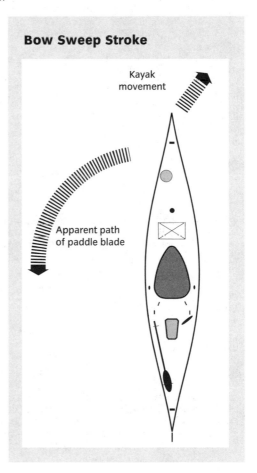

Bow Sweep Stroke

Kayak movement

Apparent path of paddle blade

surface. Better, just extend your arms while doing this stroke. You could, if you wish, lean forward a bit to plant the blade as far ahead as possible, which in effect increases the effective length of your paddle and also increases the power of the sweep.

The first third or so of a typical sweep stroke both gives you forward power and starts your turn. The middle third moves you ahead, while the ending third really cranks your boat around. Okay, you saw this for yourself about the third time you tried a sweep, but it's the kind of thing you want to keep in mind when you start to plot a change in direction. You don't really have to sweep from bow to stern. Just use what you need.

So far, we've been concentrating mainly on the strength of your arms (with some assistance from your torso), and while that works, it also means you're working too hard. You have other muscles that you can bring into play! The total amount of work being done will be the same, but you've already seen the advantages of letting more muscles share the effort.

Shifting Your Weight

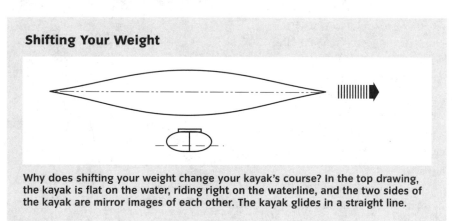

Why does shifting your weight change your kayak's course? In the top drawing, the kayak is flat on the water, riding right on the waterline, and the two sides of the kayak are mirror images of each other. The kayak glides in a straight line.

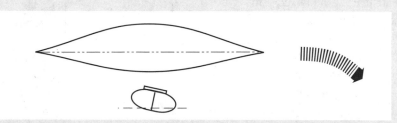

In the lower kayak, the paddler's weight is shifted to one side and the kayak is cocked up at an angle. There is more hull on one side of the centerline than on the other, and the angle at which the hull cleaves the water is now distinctly different from the centerline. The kayak's outline appears shorter, because as the kayak is rotated to the side, the rockered ends are lifted above the surface.

Press ahead with your foot on the stroke side, as if you were attempting to scoot the kayak along just with the power in your leg. At the same time, press upward with your stroke-side knee. When you do this, you will almost naturally shift your weight toward that lifted knee.

Think about what's happening to your boat as you shift your weight. Even though you're more comfortable in your kayak now, having paddled a bit, it still wobbles from side to side underneath you. Your kayak has a long, straight keel line with vertical flat surfaces at the bow and stern. Every time you try to turn while sitting flat on the water, you shove these great kayak walls sideways through the water. Now, think of the "footprint" your kayak leaves when viewed from below. Each side is a smooth arc, and each side is the mirror image of the other. When you shift your weight to the stroke side, to the outside of the turn, you cause your boat to heel, and in doing so you create a new underbody—or underwater—shape. You no longer have a long, straight keel line with symmetrical sides supporting your weight. The stroke side, where you've shifted your weight, is now shaped like a much wider and shorter arc, and the side from which you've shifted your weight is a very narrow arc. By shifting your weight and leaning your kayak partway over on its side, to a certain degree you've lifted your bow and stern out of the water.

It's unlikely that you're paddling in a mirror-smooth pond. Odds are that waves are reverberating about, and they probably are big enough to move you up and down. Do you want to attempt a turn when you're in a trough and your bow and stern are deep in the waves ahead of and behind you? This doesn't make much sense to me. When you're in a trough and your ends are deep in the water, your boat is pretty well stuck in one direction. Wait until the crest of the wave is under

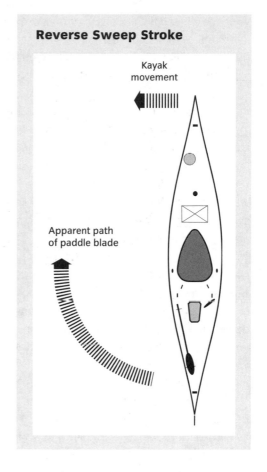

Reverse Sweep Stroke

Kayak movement

Apparent path of paddle blade

your cockpit and the ends of your boat are dripping water in the air. You'll dramatically reduce the lateral resistance on the ends of your kayak, and turning will be much easier. You probably won't have both ends of your boat out of the water, at least not in your beginning days, but any reduction in wet surface out on the ends will help.

How much muscle should you put into the sweep? A properly designed cruising kayak is going to resist your attempts to send it off in a new direction. After all, some designer spent a lot of hours and brain power in figuring out how to keep it from turning. The key is to watch your blade. If you're skidding it through the water, you may have the musculature of an ox, but you're merely plowing the water and losing the efficiency of the stroke. Ease up. You should see little eddy swirls peeling away from the edges of the blade, but you shouldn't see turbulence and aeration in the wake of the blade.

Every kayak paddle, by definition, has two blades—one on each end of the shaft. With one blade you can sweep-stroke your boat around to a new course. But you have another blade just hanging out on the other end and ready to work. Let's say you want to make an abrupt change in course and perhaps even slow down a tad. That neat thing you spied earlier is still off to starboard, but unless you really crank a corner, you'll glide right on past the only narrow little channel you can follow to it. To turn sharply and abruptly, turn your sweep stroke around and make it a reverse sweep stroke.

Keeping your back vertical, rotate your torso to the right with your right shoulder back a comfortable 45 degrees or so. Keep your right arm mostly straight and as far behind you as comfortable while your crooked left arm comes around until your left hand is right off your solar plexus. Plunge your right paddle blade into the water vertically, close to the stern of your boat, with the power face aimed aft and the back of the blade toward the front of your kayak. That's the normal paddle position.

Keep your paddle shaft low, just off your deck, and your blade completely immersed. Drive the blade, back side forward, toward the bow of your boat in a great C-shaped arc. Let your uncoiling torso drive the paddle, and use your sweep-side arm to guide it and maybe add just a bit of power.

The first third of this stroke will really snap your boat around and could startle you. And rightly that it should. This stroke is going to seem unstable. You're going to be perched right on top of the paddle when you start the move, and you'll notice that you're taller in the boat and that you won't seem as totally connected to your kayak. On the other hand, you're getting a major amount of support because of the weight and pressure you have on the paddle blade. I started serious paddling in the stern of a slalom C-2, a decked two-person canoe designed to turn and twist in whitewater, and it wasn't long before I could almost lift the stern of the boat out of the water as I snapped it around with a reverse sweep.

The second third of the stroke continues the turn, but also quashes much of your forward motion. The last third is the weakest part of the whole, in which you pull your bow over to the paddle blade, but you can dial in a few extra ergs of energy by leaning a bit forward in the last few degrees of arc. Withdraw the blade before you slam your boat into it. This isn't a joke; it can happen.

I said earlier to keep the blade as close to vertical as you can while swinging through the arc. If you tip the top edge of the blade a bit forward as you apply forward pressure, the blade will almost want to hydroplane up and out of the water. If you cant the lower edge forward, the blade will want to dive.

If you have any way on, which is a nautical way of saying you're moving, the first third of a stern sweep is a powerful steering tool.

Sweeps in a Double

So far, you've been practicing your sweep strokes in a solo boat, a K-1 if you prefer. K, of course, for kayak and 1 for the fact that you're the only person in it. What about a K-2—or what we sometimes call a tandem and sometimes a double? If you're paddling in the bow in a two-person kayak, the area of an effective sweep is the arc from ahead to perpendicular to your hip, or the front half of a sweep. Any attempt to sweep from abeam aft will just stir the water about, as you have a lot of boat sitting behind you.

If you're in the stern, however, just the reverse is true. Your sweeping arc of power is from a point perpendicular to your cockpit aft toward your stern. If you were so bold as to swing your paddle through the first half of the arc, say from just off your knees to straight out abeam, you wouldn't be sweeping your boat into a turn but would be "prying" or shoving your boat sideways.

Rudder Strokes

So far, we've thought of strokes as active motions, as movements you execute with your paddle in order to push or pull the ends of your kayak into a new direction. The rudder stroke, which under the right conditions smoothly causes your kayak to change direction, is a different sort of stroke. It is not a *dynamic* stroke— in other words, it doesn't entail your moving your paddle. Instead, it relies on the motion of the water past your paddle blade to do its work.

With the rudder stroke you create a temporary rudder near the stern of your kayak with your paddle, and by changing the angle of the blade in the water, you can change the amount of turn you want. It follows the same principle as the rudder at the stern of a sailboat or at the tail of an airplane. It only works if you are moving relative to the water. If you're drifting along at the same speed as the water—no matter what your speed relative to the land—the rudder stroke is ineffectual. As a bit of frosting on your dessert, you won't lose as much boat speed while you fine-tune your direction as you would with a reverse sweep.

Start off almost as if you were setting up for a stern sweep, rotating your torso to the right while extending your right arm aft to just off the rear deck and bringing your left hand around until it is almost over your right gunwale. You're still looking at that neat thing over to starboard. Insert your blade into the water as close to vertical as possible, with the power face aimed at your hull and the back aimed out. Keep your left hand at the gunwale and push out with your right hand, and your boat will gracefully arc toward the right. The more you push, the steeper the turn—and the more resistance you'll cause with a resulting loss of speed. The faster you travel at the start of the rudder stroke, the more pronounced the turning motion.

Now some variations. Some boating authorities suggest holding the paddle shaft out and away from the hull, which allows you to set up a sharp turn toward the paddle side and a less efficient turn away from the paddle side. This works. You can do the same thing by setting up your rudder stroke on the other side. Others suggest locking your hand next to the blade against the gunwale and moving your top hand back and forth as if you were steering with a tiller. On paper, this technique gives you better leverage. I can't praise or criticize this, however, because I can't get the hang of it.

One variation that works well for me, which I thought I discovered when surfing down the front of a wave until I found out that everyone else had made the same discovery, is the precise and delicate adjustments you can make by changing the angle of the blade in the water. No, not by pushing the whole blade in or out, but by slightly rotating the paddle shaft so that the top of the blade either angles slightly away from the hull or slightly toward it. Use this technique with a rudder stroke to boost your turn, or by itself for microcontrol.

PUT YOUR STROKES TOGETHER

Few paddlers use the rudder stroke by itself. Come to think of it, few paddlers use any stroke by itself. All strokes flow into one another as paddlers attempt to gain the greatest results with the least energy expenditure. Most stroke techniques spring from common families: The rudder, the reverse sweep, and the sweeping low brace (you'll learn about braces in chapter 9) all build from a common foundation. Discover the common elements and move from one stroke in sequence to the next, and you'll find an amazing wholeness in your paddling. You won't be restricted to stammering over one paddling word, mentally translating it, and then flailing about for a second and then a third word. You'll think in kayaking sentences with a fluent patter rolling off your blade.

Sorry, but there's no magic formula to make it all work so easily. You'll have to learn by rote, until you reach that surprising point when you're no longer thinking but merely doing.

How can we help that happen? Stretch out before you clamber into your boat. Touch your toes, windmill your arms, and do the light exercises that should be part of the tune-up of your body every day. And relax.

Don't put your fingerprints into the paddle shaft. All you really need to do is lightly push with the pads of your palms. Support your paddle in the circle of your thumb and index finger, but don't worry about imprisoning it.

Speed comes slowly. Paddle slowly, and the speed will come. If you paddle at a cadence of twenty or so strokes a minute, you'll feel how the strokes fit together. Triple the stroke rate, and you splash about and veer wildly from left to right. If you stroke with a feather-light touch, your correction strokes will also be light and smooth. Pull hard on that shaft, and you'll have to correct just as hard if you've made a major error.

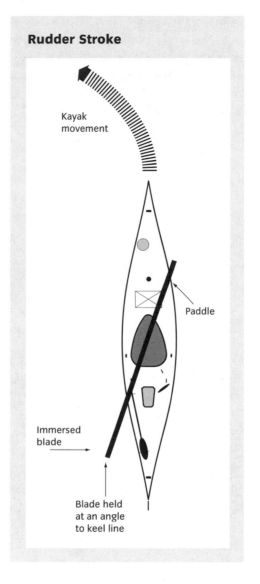

Rudder Stroke

Kayak movement

Paddle

Immersed blade

Blade held at an angle to keel line

If you have access to a good gym, test your arm strength. If you're like most people, one arm is stronger than the other. (That's positive thinking. I just heard another paddler make the same bet, saying that one arm was weaker than the other. If you think negative, you'll paddle negative.) Don't let one arm overpower the other. The easiest way to do that is to keep your strokes light and easy as you learn. For that matter, don't let your paddle shaft creep through your hands until one hand is up against the throat of a blade and the other is around the shaft's midpoint. It's very difficult to go straight with that as your driving tool.

The last tip is hard to do. Don't look at your paddle, don't look at your bow, don't focus on your compass, and don't close your eyes to concentrate. Pick out a bright mark on the far shore and paddle toward it. You'll soon paddle straight and smoothly toward your goal.

CHAPTER EIGHT

Draw Strokes

What happens when you've ended up not quite exactly where you wanted to be? Your boat is in the right alignment with the poles, you're in good balance and with the normally dry side of your boat toward the sun, yet you're a few feet away from the desired dock, rock, or beach? You could, if you so desired, start forward again and make a big, swinging circle with the fond hope of this time inching within grabbing range of your target. That could be the best solution. I was paddling against a flood tide and precisely calculated where I would have to be to snag onto the end of a finger pier. I even knew to the stroke how much power and time it would take to put me there. Or I thought I knew. I'd like to think a boat wake or a vagrant puff of wind scrambled my best-laid plans, but the truth is that I glided to a serene halt about 3 feet beyond grabbing distance—and once I was halted, the wind and tide conspired to whirl me away. The best course of action in that narrow, current-ridden passage would have been to drift back a few meters, put on enough speed to catch the eddies along the shore, and hop back up to the dock.

SLIDING SIDEWAYS

There are times when you don't have to take such a circuitous journey to gain just a few feet. A kayak, designed to travel straight ahead, is willing to scoot quite comfortably sideways if you're willing to work along with it. How? The draw stroke, the subject of this chapter.

THE POWER OF THE DRAW

When you wanted to go straight ahead, you planted your paddle in the water up around your knees and then pulled yourself up to that immobile blade. Going sideways works exactly the same way. Plant your paddle firmly in the water straight off

Draw Stroke

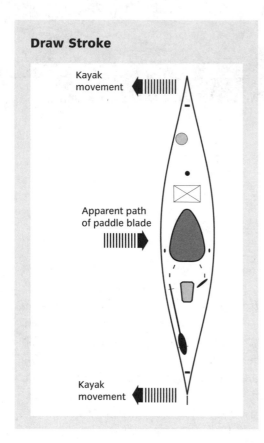

Kayak movement

Apparent path of paddle blade

Kayak movement

your cockpit with the power face of the blade aimed right at your hip, and pull yourself over to the shaft.

To do this, start off by holding your paddle in that basic position that should be familiar by now. Since this time your destination is over to your left, rotate your torso to the left until your shoulder is back about 45 degrees from being perpendicular to your boat (I suppose you're getting tired of these numbers, but they are the angles that work for most of us). Reach straight out from the side of your kayak and, while keeping the paddle as close to vertical as you can, plant your blade in the water. This is one of the few strokes in which you can raise your top hand—in this case your right hand—higher than your chin, and it might be convenient to do so as you strive for that vertical plant. It's my suspicion that most kayaking shoulder injuries are caused as paddlers force their hands up above their shoulders and apply stress at an awkward angle.

You're not going to reach out 9 feet and drive the blade throat deep into the brine. Few paddlers can, when keeping their weight centered, reach out 36 inches; two and a half feet might be a good working goal. If you're a small person in a beamy boat, don't be discouraged if you can't reach past 2 feet. With the blade in the water, your left arm will be straight and your right arm will be cocked somewhere around a right angle at the elbow. Remember that all the dimensions and angles given in this book are no more than hints. If they work for you, great. If another way proves more comfortable, that's okay. You write your own test.

So now you've stuck the blade in the water. The stroke itself is simplicity in action. Pull in with your lower left arm. You might want to push with your top hand a smidgen, but this is only going to be 5 percent of the paddle force. You'll scoot your boat right over to your paddle.

The first few times you try this, you're not going to get your paddle directly out from your kayak's center of lateral resistance. What this means is that your pull will not be perfectly balanced between the ends of your boat. Either the stern or the bow will move more than the other end. If you pull, and your bow swivels right around to your paddle, you might counter by planting the blade a little farther back next time. If the stern comes around, plant the blade a little more forward.

We haven't said anything about using your rudder or skeg, and I hope that you have it neatly tucked up in the air like the tail of a proud rooster. That broad blade is an anchor on your pivot, and will keep your stern nailed right to the water.

Now, let's say you're leaning over the left side of the boat and you're skidding the boat sideways to the left. Friction is grasping at your hull, and the combination of your weight and the drag all along the bottom as you slide across the water is going to dip your port gunwale. Bad news. No, you're not going to see your hull trip and suddenly spill over. But you are causing more drag and thus making more work for yourself than need be. Push your left knee up against the deck—remember, we're still moving left—and the torque will rotate the boat back level. I sometimes think I overdo this and actually lift up the leading gunwale so that the kayak's flat bottom attempts to slide up on the water, but I think this is more illusion than reality.

This may sound like a joke, but it isn't: Don't run over your own paddle. I've seen stretched-out tennis players sprinting for a dying drop shot get their racquet under the ball at the last second but end up standing on their racquet grip and imprisoning themselves. You can do this with a powerful draw stroke. The bang as you collide with your blade can jostle your paddle out of your hand, and you could even jerk in surprise and overturn yourself.

Before it comes to that, when your paddle is within a foot of your hull, smartly rotate your control hand and swivel your blade power face back toward the stern. You can then either cleanly slice your blade up and out of the water in the first stages of another draw stroke or you can use it as the last bit of a conventional forward stroke. Lifting is easy. Just extend your left (lower) arm until it is straight.

Some folks may think this is a less than balanced stroke, and in those fractions of a moment when the blade is in the air, they may have a point. But think of a ladder, or a person standing with his or her legs apart and plenty of weight on each foot. It's hard to rock them. You can put a great weight on your draw stroke, and that paddle will be as steady as if it were set into concrete. During the drawing motion of the stroke, you effectively extend the width of your kayak by the distance the blade is from your hull.

LEARN TO SCULL

Is there a way to keep the effectiveness of the draw stroke without that pause as you lift the blade from the water? Yes. You can start sculling when you're balanced out there in the first stage of a draw stroke. The sculling draw stroke is a logical extension of the draw itself just as the draw is an extension of the forward stroke.

Now, before we get involved in the mechanics of the sculling stroke, let's go for a car ride. I'll drive, and you play just like a kid in the passenger seat. Remember how you used to be an airplane in the car? You'd make a blade of your hand, and as long as your hand was horizontal, it would just float in the wind outside the window. If you tilted your hand up a bit, your arm would swoop up toward the sky like the wing of a plane. That's just what we're going to do, once we get back into the kayak. But first we're going to stop by the river and play with your paddle. Go ahead, step out there on the rock so you can reach to where the current is swift.

Plant your paddle firmly in the water, so that both edges are precisely aligned with the flow of the current and the water passes smoothly across the power face and the back of the blade. It would help if the paddle shaft were more or less vertical, but this is not imperative. Set your arms so that you can rotate the paddle shaft but the shaft cannot pull away from you. Now (this is the tricky spot, and if you aren't ready, you may be surprised off your rock), rotate the paddle so that the upstream blade edge turns away from you into the current. That paddle is pulling away from you! Just like your hand rising in the onrushing air past your car window. If you were holding the paddle firmly and the rock were slippery, you'd be pulled directly toward the paddle and into the water.

You've just learned all you need to know about sculling. From here on out we need only talk about refinements. What do you mean, you don't understand? Your muscles do—trust me.

Back to your kayak. Get into your cockpit and start your draw stroke. Once your paddle blade is immersed, though, I'm going to freeze the action. It's okay, I'm bracing you. Your paddle blade isn't all that smart; it acts the same whether moving water is striking its power face or the moving blade is exerting force on still water. It knows its own angle and the feel of the water deflected off the blade.

Back to real time. When you did your first draw stroke, you set your power face so that it aimed directly at your boat, at your hips. That's where we'll start now. Your lower arm is bent just a bit and is poised to put all the power into the stroke. Your upper arm is arched, and your hand is all set to be the solid fulcrum around which your paddle will twist. If you don't think I'm watching, you might attempt to move that upper hand around so that you grip the paddle shaft from underneath—perhaps you think the angle you've made is uncomfortable, awkward, and certainly not very effective. This would not be a wise move. When you

Sculling Draw Stroke

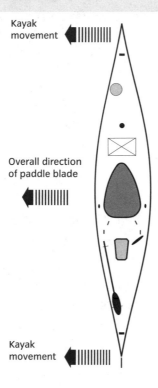

Kayak
movement

Overall direction
of paddle blade

Kayak
movement

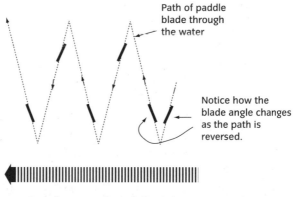

Path of paddle
blade through
the water

Notice how the
blade angle changes
as the path is
reversed.

Overall progress through the water

No, the arrows aren't wrong! You advance the paddle away from your kayak in a
short series of Z motions, and you pull your kayak toward the paddle blade. It
sounds like one of those perpetual motion machine scams, but it really works.

keep your hands in the normal paddling position, you're ready for any surprises that may be poised just out of eyesight, waiting to catch you unaware. I don't know exactly what is waiting to catch you off guard. If I did, I could warn you. But I do know that Loki (the mischief-making Norse god) or Coyote (the trickster from the desert in Native American legends) is just quivering with anticipation. One time I saw a totally distracted paddler shift his weight out of balance and at that precise minute get blindsided by a duck. He flailed about, which worked out fine because he got his arms moving just before he turned into a swimmer. You can't plan for a duck attack, but if you're alert as you paddle, you'll be better prepared to deal with one.

Rotate the paddle shaft so that the bow edge of the blade is canted out 20 or 30 degrees from the keel line of the kayak. Too small an angle and you won't get any bite on the water, too big an angle and your blade will stall instead of slice. You'll be able to feel the pressure on the power face and experiment a bit until you get the correct angle.

Now, using just the power from your lower arm, push the paddle toward the bow of your boat on a path parallel to your keel line. You may have seen all kinds of diagrams showing figure-8 patterns, lazy-S patterns, and even jagged lightning bolt or interlocked-Z patterns. These are all right, but they each focus on the aggregate motion of your boat and paddle and not on the way in which you do the stroke.

Move the blade from just behind your hips to just ahead of your knees—the normal 4-foot or so sweep of your blade. As you move the blade, you'll feel the paddle tug away from you. Don't let it go! The paddle is going to climb away from its location in the water, by a few inches, but as it attempts to move away from you, it is going to drag you along. Think of the paddle as a horse, yourself as the harness, and the kayak as the cart. The horse moves the harness, and the harness moves the cart. All together.

The scull works as a series of little motions. Somewhere around your knee, stop the blade, reverse the angle so that the stern edge of the blade is now angled out at a 20- to 30-degree angle, and bring the blade smartly and in a straight line parallel to your keel line back to just past your hips.

You think, "Hey, this can't work. I'm starting around midships and working toward the bow, so I'm going to pull my bow around but leave the stern wallowing back there." If you were doing just one stroke, sure. But you're working first one end and then the other, and the inertia of your hull will dampen out abrupt swings. You might find that either the bow or the stern does advance faster, and that's because for one reason or another you're a bit unbalanced. If your stern is lagging, either move the paddle motion farther astern or put a little more oomph in the stroke toward the stern.

You'll set up the blade angle with your control hand, be that the top or bottom hand when you're moving your boat. Change the angle with the same little twist of your wrist you used with a feathered paddle. (See, I told you all these strokes connect.)

The sculling draw is a long series of continuous motions. What you don't do is move the blade . . . stop . . . change the angle . . . stop . . . move the blade . . . stop. Instead, strive for a constant, uniform flow, without a discernible break in the motion. The first time you do this, your motion will be jerky. That's fine, but you will smooth out as you practice.

You'll find that, just as with the draw stroke, the combination of your weight on the stroke side of your kayak and the friction along the keel line will tip your stroke-side gunwale down. This means you're putting more boat in the water, and in doing so you're increasing the friction. If you ski, your feet and knees know all about sideslipping with skis flat on the snow. Edge and you'll stop. Push your stroke-side knee up against the thigh pad and deck and scoot your hip toward the paddle to keep the boat as flat as possible and to let it sideslip as easily as possible.

A draw stroke has more quick power. A scull provides constant power, plus it offers you an apparently wider base and more stability.

For the fun of it, set the blade angles backward and with each scull have the paddle push the boat. This is slow, inefficient, and could be better done with a regular scull or draw on the other side (why else does a kayak paddle have two identical ends?). But the reverse scull is a beautifully precise way of moving a boat a few inches without switching sculling sides, and it is a powerful learning tool as to how and why the stroke works. Give it a shot.

CHAPTER NINE

A Bracing Experience

From the low cockpit of a cruising kayak, the sea presents an in-your-face experience. The spray that washes over the deck is very personal, the waves that lift and drop you echo in the pit of your stomach, and the wind curls and eddies around your ears. While at sea, you will get wet and you will teeter up on edge, and unless you learn to be comfortable within the arms of the sea, you will find these experiences to be upsetting in every sense of the word. I don't mean to disturb you, nor to frighten you from all bodies of water. But you have to understand the basics of paddling skills, and you have to equally understand what to do when by mischance or misjudgment you exceed the boundaries of stability.

Remember that at all times you have two immense aids: the knowledge of your own body position and the absolute support of that which at first would appear to be the most fluid—the water upon which you float.

How does a kayak use the support of water to balance? Climb aboard, and let's take a look.

Your kayak is bilaterally symmetrical. That's a fancy way of saying that the right and left halves of your boat (divided right down the keel line) are mirror images of each other. Buoyancy, then, is the same if measured an equal distance out on each side, perpendicular to the same spot on the keel line. The net effect is that the boat is perfectly balanced at the keel line.

Your body is symmetrically balanced, too. If every muscle in your body suddenly spasmed and you were locked in a painful rigidity, your weight would be balanced on a plane that passes through your body vertically through your sternum and spine. In other words, your weight is centered within your body. If you were sitting in your cockpit and we started measuring the combined weight of you and your boat in horizontal layers from the bottom of the keel to the top of your head, as if you were made of cakelike layers or sedimentary bands, the center of your total weight would be somewhere around your navel.

Think of that point, that concentration of weight, as the focal point of all the forces pushing downward, or the center of gravity. There is another point that is the focus of all the forces that are supporting you and your boat. The forces that keep you afloat are concentrated in a point called the center of buoyancy. Your center of gravity will remain somewhere near your navel. Your center of buoyancy, however, won't. It changes with each degree of tilt or list as different parts of your kayak hull are immersed in or lifted from the water.

If your kayak is absolutely level, your center of gravity, center of buoyancy, and keel line are all in a vertical line. If you shift your weight to one side, the center of gravity will thus be to one side of the center of buoyancy, and your kayak will tilt to that side. If your center of buoyancy didn't move, you'd just continue right on over. As your boat begins to tilt, however, it puts more of the widest beam into the water. This alters the center of buoyancy and moves it in the direction of the added support— and in effect moves the center of buoyancy back under the center of gravity.

The center of buoyancy, despite our occasional hope and wish, is not indefinitely moveable. If you extend your center of gravity past the furthest adjustment to the center of buoyancy, you'll capsize. That's as true for a kayak as it is for an aircraft carrier. Kayaks, however, come with a built-in device that manipulates the center of gravity—you. That's right. You can shift your weight, you can tilt your torso, and in doing so you can preserve the balance of your boat.

To see how this works, we'll start by locking your body into a rigid whole. Now, start to topple your body to one side. All too quickly, you'll pass the point of no return where your center of gravity overturns your buoyancy and you capsize.

Now, suppose your boat is tilting to one side. Instead of keeping your body rigid and in line with the keel line, twist at your hips to keep your upper body vertical. This keeps your belly button over the keel line and you upright. What could have rocked you up on edge? Perhaps you're gliding sideways on the face or the back of a wave, and because the surface of the ocean is tilted at that point, you're also tilted. Perhaps you're thrown about in the wake of a careless powerboater. The why doesn't matter. What does matter is that you were able to twist your body to keep your weight and buoyancy in line.

THE HIP FLICK

Was this a fluke? Hardly. Come and sit in the placid bay and let's play a bit. With your paddle in the basic forward stroke position and horizontal, wiggle your boat a bit just using your hips. To do this, make your torso vertical and let your rear be the pendulum of a clock with your hips the pivot point. If the left side of your boat is low, press down with your right cheek and at the same time push up against the deck with your left knee. Your boat will rotate under you, from up on its beam end to a horizontal position. With any balance whatsoever, you can snap your kayak back to level with what will become an instinctive move. When talking to a bunch of experienced kayakers, just nod knowingly when they mention hip flicks. Those are what you've just been doing.

The hip flick works when you're just rocking back and forth in less than extreme angles, extreme being as often as not a state of mind. But what do you do when your kayak is apparently thrown up on its beam ends and you feel that you need to take more aggressive measures? You turn for support to that most yielding of surfaces—the sea beside you. Now, it's going to seem not only very strange but downright backward to lean out over something as soft and unsup-portive as water when every muscle in your body is screaming that you're falling abruptly in that same direction. The first brace you use will seem a fluke, the sec-ond a coincidence. With just a bit of practice, though, your muscles will come to rely on the brace.

If you think about it, the sweep stroke works because the paddle blade exerts tremendous resistance on the water. You stick the paddle in the water and with the blade as a fulcrum scoot your kayak around it. You can use that same stroke, with a few modifications in technique and direction, to brace a tipping kayak and rotate it back upright.

Just as with every other paddle maneuver you've learned, you have two ways to support yourself above the sea: with the power face of your paddle or with the back of your paddle blade. Both methods work well, depending on your position and need.

THE LOW BRACE

We'll start with a low brace. Low is a simple concept. The paddle is held below, or lower than, your wrists. Start in the basic forward stroke position and assume that you're toppling to your right. Hold your paddle so that it is at right angles to the keel line and horizontal to the water surface. With your control hand, rotate the paddle shaft so that the back face of the paddle blade is toward the surface of the water. Don't shift your grip, but if you have to, cock your wrists in order to bring the blade flat. Extend your right hand so that your elbow is about straight and keep your left hand more or less in front of your left hip. You do not have to rotate your body. Firmly and briskly, slap the surface of the water with the flat of your paddle. If you really smash down with a report like that of a terrified beaver,

In a low brace your paddle shaft is lower than your wrists, and you push down on the paddle shaft and the blade. Just like a push-up.

you've slapped a little too vigorously. If you can't hear the paddle hit the water, you've slapped too weakly.

Once the paddle blade is on the water, push down on it hard with your right hand. It takes a lot of force to push the blade down into the water, and what you'll end up doing is pushing yourself back up. You're using the palm of your hand against the top of the paddle shaft in a one-handed push-up. Since you and your kayak are one, the kayak will come with you. You're not going to be able to hang out on that blade all day. This is a momentary support, and so you'll have to help it along with a hip flick to rotate the hull back under you.

To be a tool in your paddling repertoire, the low brace has to be an instinctive reflex—as automatic as putting a hand out to catch yourself when you stumble. And that's all it is. A quick little whack on the water that keeps you high and dry.

The Skimming Low Brace

For a moment, let's play around with the variations on the low brace and how they can work alone or in series to stabilize your kayak. Start to slap the water in a low brace, but instead of whacking straight out from your hips, bring the paddle back with a little torso rotation and arm flex so that it is about 45 degrees or so from the keel line. You noticed that the "slap" version of a low brace gave you plenty of righting momentum, but that you could only apply this power for a relatively brief time. We're going to extend that time, using the motions you've practiced so far in learning the strokes.

Just before you bang the blade on the water (remembering to keep the back side of the paddle toward the water and the power face up), cant the front edge, the edge toward the bow, upward about 20 or 30 degrees. This is a good starting zone, and you'll instinctively find your own best angle after attempting this stroke a few times. We played in the river with the current to see how a blade reacted to moving water, and then we translated that to the back-and-forth swoops of a scull. We'll be working with the same concept now, with a few significant variations. You can see that you're in almost the same body position as you were in a reverse sweep. Once again, one stroke leads right into another.

Now, whack the water! As you do so, push down on the shaft with your outboard hand (the one next to the wet blade), just as you did in the first low brace. As you do this—and it should be in a smoothly combined movement and not first one and then the other—move your body and arms as if you were in a sweep stroke. The blade, canted up as it is, will skim across the top of the water through the arc of the sweep. You're putting plenty of downward pressure on the shaft, for sure, but this is being countered by the climbing force you created with the canted blade and the forward motion of the blade. The upward force lasts much longer and can be more precisely controlled than the simple push of a blade straight down into the water.

There is a danger, however. What if the blade trips during the arc, and its front edge dips? Unfortunately, the blade will then dive—just like your hand did when you were flying it outside the car window. If you keep the downward angle and keep your weight on the shaft, you're going to do a face plant on Father Neptune's roof. Odds are, you'll also do a deck plant.

The skimming low brace works when you are sitting still, but the forward motion of your kayak under way dramatically increases the lift during the sweep. The skimming blade, though, creates resistance, which does two things: It turns you to the paddle side, and it slows the boat. In fact, it will slow the boat until the forward motion is not enough to support your weight. By then, you should have flicked your boat back underneath you. If not, go ahead and start a sculling brace with the back side of your blade—no one said you can't. You've already practiced a sculling draw; the sculling brace is executed with the same motion, but your hands are above the paddle shaft and you apply power to the back face of your paddle blade. How much forward speed do you need, and how much sweeping motion from your paddle? It's a balancing act. With a lot of forward speed, you don't need to sweep at all. With no forward speed, you need a powerful sweep. Balance out the two, judging how much lift and stability you need in your particular situation.

Now, for the second variation on the low brace theme. Let's head on down the bay, just a few hundred meters in order to pick up speed, and we'll curve around behind that little skerry. As you and I approach the rock knob with its somewhat disgruntled-looking great blue heron staring at us, you see that I let my paddle trail back into a stern rudder. You do the same, but you wonder why I've left the turn so late. We're going to turn in an arc far beyond the skerry, and instead of catching the eddy made by the ebbing tide, we're going to have to paddle back against the tidal current. As you watch, I rotate the top of my ruddering blade out away from the boat, increasing the angle of the turn, and then, to your surprise, actually shift my weight out onto the paddle shaft. What I've done is to combine the stern rudder with a sweeping low brace, and in doing so put enough of my weight on the shaft to really crank my kayak around. As I sit, bobbing, in the eddy behind the skerry, you duplicate each movement and glide in beside me. We didn't practice anything new. We did, though, link together the strokes we've been practicing, and in doing so we've demonstrated the skimming low brace.

The skimming low brace is good for more than turning, valuable as that skill becomes. If you find yourself swooping down the face of a wave (at this part of your paddling career, let's hope it's a small one) and you have little faith in your ability to twitch your balance (hey, on your first ride your bottom is going to be clenching the kayak seat with muscles you'd forgotten you had), just reach over the top of the wave and rest your weight on your skimming blade sliding just a tad behind the top of the wave. You might be sliding sideways, but your paddle will keep you upright as you slip along.

The low brace, especially when linked to the sweeping motion that sends your blade skimming over the water, is your bomb shelter. When in doubt, even experts fall back to the reliable, incredibly stable, and remarkably easy-to-do low brace. Learn it, and learn to love it.

The low brace works best when applied in the arc from your hips (perpendicular to the keel line at the cockpit) aft. It is difficult to apply the needed downward push when the blade is in front of the cockpit. This isn't so bad, once you realize that the low brace is done with the back face of your paddle. Remember, you have a whole other face, which is prime for the bracing you want to do ahead of yourself.

THE HIGH BRACE

When you want to stabilize your kayak using the power face of your paddle blade, you'll use one of the most misnamed and often misdone strokes in kayaking. The latter is unfortunate, because the high brace is also one of the most useful tools you'll learn.

A high brace is high not because it is favored by high society nor because its practitioners belong to a high church. It isn't even high up in the air. When you do

In a high brace the paddle shaft is higher than your wrists. You stab the paddle blade into the water and pull on the paddle shaft as if you're raising yourself up.

a high brace effectively, your paddle shaft is merely higher than your wrists. A properly performed high brace is actually as low to the kayak as possible, and for health and safety's sake, never lift the paddle shaft so high you can't see over it.

There's a popular perception of a kayaker with arms extended far over his head just planting his paddle into an incredible brace. His boat is smashing through a wall of foam. But what this picture doesn't show is the fierce strains rippling through that kayaker's shoulders, which with luck won't result in the ripping sound of a shoulder dislocation.

With the low brace, you applied power by pushing down on the shaft and building resistance with the back side of the blade. With the high brace, you apply power by pulling down on the paddle shaft and build resistance with the power face of the blade.

Don't move your hands from their normal paddling position. You'll set the angle of the blade used in the stroke by rotating your control-hand wrist and, if needed, cocking up your forearm. You'll be tempted to cheat and shift your hand, but if you try it a few times, you'll find that the upper-hand position becomes viable. Not strong, and I don't think comfortable, but as long as you keep your upper hand close to your body, it will be sufficient.

Remember, the high brace works best in that broad arc from ahead of to perpendicular to your hips. Once your boat moves your hips ahead of the blade, the potential power and stability erode rapidly.

You're paddling ahead, and you stumble off balance—the reason why doesn't really matter. Reach out with the paddle on the side toward which you think you're toppling and whack the water hard with the power face of your blade. With a "normal" paddle of around 220 or 230 centimeters and an "average" kayak beam of 24 inches, you're going to reach out around 2½ to 3½ feet. You're not aiming at a precise target—you want to reach out as far as is comfortable to give you the best leverage. You should make a good bang with it, much like a beaver passing the word. If you forget to rotate your paddle and slam it into the water edge first . . . well, experience in this case is a very wet teacher. Your bracing-side arm is extended almost straight, and your upper hand is tucked in fairly close to your shoulder. Go ahead and do a one-handed pull-up with your bracing hand while your upper hand is locked into a fulcrum around which the paddle rotates. Don't punch out or up with your upper hand, despite an almost instinctive inclination to do so. You need the strength of that locked-in hand with its contracted biceps.

The first few inches, perhaps as much as a foot or so, of travel from the surface down into the water gives you the most righting motion. You can hang off the shaft and really twitch your boat back underneath you. As the blade goes deeper, you'll pull your boat toward the paddle shaft, but it will be more difficult to rotate your boat under the shaft. By the time you pull your boat right to the blade, you can either rotate the blade and convert your motion into a forward stroke or you can retract the paddle by pulling the blade aft—edge first—until it rotates up and out of the water.

A few pages back you were sliding broadside down the face of a wave, and you calmly reached over the top of the wave and planted your low brace on the back side of the wave. That works quite nicely . . . up to the point when you can no longer reach over the wave. You could just close your eyes and toss your paddle away—a technique I've attempted on more than one river. While your kayak has the inherent stability to ride through some pretty amazing water, however, I wouldn't suggest this abject surrender to natural forces. Instead, bend both your elbows until your paddle shaft is at shoulder height and then firmly stick your blade into the face of the wave next to your shoulder. You want to reach into the upper portions of the wave in order for this to work, but you can find quite a bit of support by attempting a chin-up off this shaft.

A high brace, though, doesn't have to be a static stroke. Begin, if you will, a forward stroke on the side to which you feel unbalanced. Instead of keeping the paddle blade vertical in the water, angle the top edge of the blade back toward your stern. As you pull on this angled blade, two things happen: You pull your kayak forward, and as you apply pressure to the angled blade, the paddle attempts to lift out of the water. There is no need to get involved in a long discussion of how much angle to dial into the stroke, or even at what point and speed the lift from the angled blade becomes effective. Practice the stroke a few times in placid water and change the blade angle with each stroke. You'll know more in a few minutes than we could discuss during a long day on the water.

The Sculling High Brace

What happens when you need a longer period of support than that offered in a high brace? You can scoot your boat directly sideways. You already know how to do it! You learned how when you combined a draw stroke with a sculling motion. All we have to do now is change the angle, so that you are pulling down on the paddle shaft rather than using the paddle shaft to pull your kayak toward the paddle.

Sit square in your kayak, with your back erect. Bring your paddle up to a line just below your shoulders, horizontally, with the midpoint of the paddle right at your PFD's zipper. Extend your hand on the bracing side so that your elbow is about straight and your hand is underneath the paddle shaft. Your paddle should be about perpendicular to your kayak's keel line. Think of holding the paddle shaft as if you were going to do a chin-up. Your upper hand should be in front of your shoulder and the zipper of your PFD should line up with the bow of your kayak. In other words, don't rotate your torso. Thump the water with your paddle blade, power face toward the water.

If you were starting a normal high brace, you'd pull down on the shaft and let the paddle blade sink into the water. But you need more support. Cant the front edge of your blade up, and sweep the blade forward. Once the blade is up around your knees, reverse the angle so that the stern edge is canted up and then sweep the blade aft. Switch the angle with your control hand, but don't shift your basic paddling grip. The motion should be smooth and continuous—no starting and stopping. You create a righting effort by pulling down on the shaft with your brace-side hand (the other hand at your shoulder is a fulcrum). At the same time, you keep the blade at the surface with its angle and the back-and-forth sweeping motion. If you're just rocked over a little, you'll use long back-and-forth sweeps.

If you're well over on your beam ends, your strokes will be shorter and faster.

How long can you keep this up? That depends on your attention span and your physical condition. If you're up to it, you can let your boat rock over until you're almost kissing the water and just hold your boat there all day.

The skimming low brace is a rock-solid brace, and one you need. But it works well only when your kayak is close to horizontal. When the world really starts turning sideways and the angle of lean gets scary, scull out of a high brace. You might be battered by a wind, tossed about by waves, or even washing-machined in the wake of a hot-rodding powerboater—it makes no difference. When you're on your beam ends and nothing else will help, you can scull your way out of trouble.

CHAPTER TEN

Linking Strokes: Making Your Paddle Work for You

Everyone, including me, keeps telling you that you can link all your paddling strokes together. The only problem is that none of us ever gets around to telling you *how*. Borrow a training tool from our whitewater cousins and take a few practice turns through an English Gate. Slalom drivers use English Gates as a way of honing their turning and balance skills—and the gates work just as well for quiet-water paddlers.

PLAYING IN AN ENGLISH GATE

The gate is simplicity itself. All you need is two marks and a little water. Slalom drivers use poles suspended from an overhead line. If you don't have anything to dangle a pole from, consider a pair of bleach jugs anchored about 4 feet apart. If you're in the mood for craftsmanship, start with a 4-foot length of plastic pipe for your pole. Tie a 3-foot line from one end of the pole to the handle of a bleach jug. Tie another 3-foot line from the other end of the pipe to a second jug. Fill two more jugs with gravel. Tie a line equal to the depth of the water less 2 feet from one end of the pipe to one gravel-filled jug and a similar line from the other end of the pipe to the other jug. Drop one anchor jug, and then paddle out a bit and drop the other. The jugs will stay in line and 4 feet apart, despite your wake. The plastic pipe should—if you measured correctly—be a couple of feet underwater and out of your way.

How do you use your gate? Here are a few routines that will hone your paddling (and because of the sharp turns and changes in directions, your bracing) skills.

1. The simplest path I know starts with you on one side of the gate. Paddle through the gate, make a left turn and return through the gate, and then make a right turn and pass through the gate again.

2. The second exercise starts with you just outside the gate with your stern toward the gate. Back past the gate without passing through it. Scull sideways until you are lined up with the gate. Paddle forward through the gate. Once through the gate, back down past the gate on the opposite side from your initial course and do not go through the gate. Once past the gate, scull sideways until you are again lined up with the gate and paddle through the gate opening.

3. A third exercise starts with you just outside the opening of the gate and with your stern toward the gate. Back past the gate but don't pass through it. Continue backward and make a left turn, which sets you to back through the gate. Make another left turn and back through the gate.

4. The fourth exercise starts with your bow pointed toward the opening of the gate. Paddle forward past the gate on the outside without passing through the opening. Scull sideways until you are lined up with the gate opening. Back through the opening. Once clear of the gate, paddle forward on the outside of the gate until you are completely past the gate. Stop. With a combination of sweeps, spin your boat end-for-end and paddle forward through the gate.

If you can Eskimo-roll your boat, that's great. Find a convenient point—say in the third exercise when you first back past the gate and scull sideways until you are lined up with the opening. Before you start sculling, roll your boat.

Paddle through each of the exercises a few times, looking for preciseness rather than speed. You want to be smooth, and you want to put your boat exactly where it should be each time. Once you have each and every exercise in your mind, combine them into one smooth whole. Speed and dexterity will come with practice, and as you practice, your muscles will learn the proper linking of each maneuver.

CHAPTER ELEVEN

Keeping It Straight

Most novice paddlers find, within minutes of first snugging down into their cockpit, that with a quick push of a rudder pedal they can turn their kayak and that with alternating pushes on each rudder pedal they can correct imperfections in their strokes to keep their kayak moving in a relatively straight line.

What they (and you) have done is paddle into one of the longest ongoing and unresolved arguments in paddle sports. One side says that a kayak should be designed so that it slips smoothly, gracefully, and in a straight line through the water without need of a conglomeration of levers and fins dragging off the stern. Paddlers should learn to control the direction of their boat with the precision and elegance of their paddle strokes. The other camp maintains that changing conditions demand flexibility of the total hull form and that rudders and skegs are significant control and safety factors that are vital to the sport.

Before you take sides—or maybe it's just me who leaps to conclusions—you should realize that both sides are absolutely right and both sides are using deceptively similar words to discuss really different concepts.

Rudders and their close cousins, skegs, aren't hanging off the stern of your kayak to help you turn. Quite the opposite. They're back there to help you go straight. Either one is simply a fin. The rudder is hinged so that it can turn from side to side. The skeg is held in a rigid frame so that it cannot turn from side to side but holds perfectly parallel to your keel line. Almost all skegs can be adjusted by how much of the blade is inserted into the water.

TRIMMING YOUR COURSE WITH A RUDDER

The most common way to adjust the angle of a rudder is by pressing on foot controls, which are in turn connected to the rudder by cables. Push ahead with your left foot, and the blade of the rudder is pulled to the left side of your boat. This makes your boat arc to the left. If you looked at the boat from overhead, you'd see that the angle of the rudder actually pushes the stern of your boat to the right and that your boat pivots at a point somewhere around the cockpit. Just like on a teeter-totter, when one end goes one way the other goes in the opposite direction; that's why the bow swings to the left. Foot pedals, though, are not the only control mechanism. Easy Rider, for example, has a special rudder control system that is controlled by one line snugged through a jam cleat. Pull it to set a rudder angle on one side; release the tension, and the elastics will pull the rudder back to the other side.

Isn't that a bias toward one side of the argument? Not really. Because you, the novice paddler who figured it out, and, not long ago, I myself were both wrong when we thought we should adjust the rudder angle in order to turn. What we didn't understand is that we change the rudder angle in order to make the boat go straight. To understand what either the rudder or skeg does, you have to understand that all kayak hulls—all boat hulls, for that matter—are a compromise. (Of course, if you're an airplane pilot, you've already figured out that rudders and skegs are the aquatic equivalent of trim tabs.)

Boat designers tell me it's not difficult to design a hull that will perform well within one specific environment. If the wind blew at a constant speed from one direction; if the sea conditions were always exactly the same; if the hull always went at the same speed, in the same direction, carrying the same weight, and trimmed exactly the same—if that never-never world existed, then a hull could be drawn and fabricated to perform elegantly and exactly. Right. I don't live there, either. Every hull is a compromise between the demands placed upon it and the varying conditions it will meet.

In a boat hull that is "balanced," with one combination of wind and waves, your kayak will glide effortlessly ahead. If the wind shifts, or if it picks up, the balance between the bow and stern, above and below the water, will shift, and the boat will swing into or away from the wind. If you were a small-boat sailor, you would identify this as a "weather" or "lee" helm, depending on whether your boat swung its bow toward the wind or away from it.

You're paddling along, and the wind shifts. Suddenly, the sharp vertical plane of your bow digs in a bit. The wind begins to push your stern downwind. What do you do? Lower your skeg into the water. Depending on conditions, this might be a little dip or it might be a bigger one. You'll know by how much your boat swings. If the beam wind starts to push your bow more than your stern, raise your skeg a notch.

But your boat has a rudder, so let's use it. Apply just a little rudder angle to keep your boat heading straight. You could paddle harder on one side than the other, you could take two strokes on one side for each one on the other, or you could start throwing in a few sweep strokes to correct your course. This irregular rhythm will make you weary in a short time, but you can do it. It's a lot easier to dial in a few degrees on the rudder.

I've been talking about wind as the principal reason for these controls, because wind is the principal variable in the cruising kayak environment. But lots of other factors can come into play. If you're tired, if your boat is unevenly loaded, if you're towing another boat and the effort swings you about—use your rudder or your skeg as a tool to keep you on the straight and narrow.

Rudders and skegs cannot be the only answer—you have to learn the strokes and how to balance in order to keep your boat on a straight line. Any mechanical device will fail, and the unfortunate rule of the world is that it will fail at the most inconvenient moment. Sand or grit will jam a blade, corrosion will eat away at a connector, and elastics will lose their snap. If you can paddle well without these aids, you'll be a better paddler and you'll be able to venture forth safely and with confidence.

CHAPTER TWELVE

Wearing Your Kayak

You wear your kayak, just like a pair of shoes. In order for you to paddle efficiently and with pleasure, your boat has to fit snugly and give you support at your feet, knees, hips, rear, and back. Fortunately, you don't have to lace up a kayak.

If you don't believe me, put in a few minutes of enthusiastic paddling in an ill-fitting boat. With every stroke you slide forward on the seat until your buns are weary from trying to hang on. A roll of pain settles in a band across your lower back from one hip to the other. The insides of your knees develop twinges. I wouldn't be surprised if your feet felt as if they were falling asleep. And this is after only a few minutes. With that kind of discomfort building, no wonder you're going to be dog-tired in minutes.

It doesn't have to be like that. Let's see what we can do to get you a good fit.

Right from the top, kayaks are not shoes. You can't buy a size 10E kayak. You can, however, read the manufacturers' brochures and spec sheets. Some boats are designed for relatively small people, others for bigger people. If you weigh 325 pounds and have size 14 feet, you're not going to be comfortable in an extremely low-decked, low-volume kayak. Likewise, if you're over 7 feet tall, you probably won't be happy (nor can you cram into) an extremely short boat. I'm belaboring the obvious, of course, but it is often the obvious that we do not see.

FITTING IN YOUR KAYAK

Kayaks are designed to accommodate a wide range of folks. We'll start with the basics.

Sit in your boat, with your rump fully on the seat (most seats are form-fitting, so you're really in them) and your back up against the back band of the seat. Adjust your back support so that you are sitting comfortably erect. As your mother used to say, don't slouch. To use your total body to paddle, you're going to have to sit up.

Your kayak can take you as far as your dreams allow. Here a Khatsalano folding kayak from Feathercraft cruises along the rugged coast of Greenland. PHOTO COURTESY FEATHERCRAFT

The balls of your feet should be lightly pressing against your foot pegs (or bar or rudder pedals, depending on your boat—we'll call all of them foot pegs). Not your toes, not your arches, but the balls of your feet. Your heels should be somewhat close together, depending on the width of your boat, and the toe ends of your feet should be splayed out toward the sides of your boat. Think of the angle of your feet and legs when you're standing with your feet comfortably close together and your body erect—and that's about the right angle your feet should form when you're in your kayak. Your knees should touch the underside of your deck. They should not be crammed and jammed into place, nor at such an angle that you have to stretch to reach the deck. You should have just enough pressure so that you know there is firm contact. The farther apart you can spread your knees and the closer you can comfortably rest them to the outside edges of your deck, the better control you'll have over your boat. If you have a light pressure on your feet and knees, you should have a similar pressure on your back.

Why all this concern with positioning? Because the power and control you create with your paddle are transmitted to your kayak through the points where you touch the kayak. Break the connection and it is just like pulling the plug on an electrical appliance. You might have plenty of electricity in the house wiring, but if you're not connected, nothing works.

ADJUSTING THE FIT

We'll start off using the adjustments built into your boat, and then we'll start modifying your boat until the fit is fine. We'll need some closed-cell foam, a *sharp* knife, duct tape, and glue. Open-cell foam is like a household sponge. It's great for compressing, putting in water, and releasing to sop up the spill, but it's lousy for sitting on, because it gets wet and stays wet. In contrast, closed-cell foam is like a whole pile of microballoons glued together. Liquids cannot seep from one balloon to another. Closed-cell foam, under a variety of trade names, is used in everything from backpacker sleeping pads to packing for delicate electronics.

The glue you select will depend on the material of your hull. For fiberglass, contact cement works pretty well. For other hull materials, talk to the dealer or the manufacturer.

Back to your feet, with a task more easily done on the back lawn than out on the water. About every kayak foot peg I've seen for years is adjustable. Some are mounted on a pair of bolts anchored to the hull, and you can change position by spinning off the nuts (usually wing nuts) and repositioning the entire foot-peg assembly. Some foot-peg assemblies ride in channels, almost like one side of a drawer, and spring clips hold the pegs in position. Release the lock and slide them into place. I have a rudder on my boat, and the cable that controls the rudder clips to the peg. I can clip the peg to the cable in almost an infinite number of places for minute adjustments. No single spot is best. What you want and need is a firm surface against which to rest your foot. Are your legs the same length? That's not a flippant question; many people's legs differ slightly in length. As long as your back and rump are square in your seat, nowhere does it say you have to have both foot pegs set at the same length. The boat has to fit you, not the other way around.

You have the balls of your feet on the pegs, your heels are angled in toward each other, and your feet are at a right angle to your lower legs—all is right in the world except that your heels aren't resting on anything. Your feet are just dangling off the pegs. Take a couple of squares of closed-cell foam and tape them to the deck where your heels should rest. (We haven't opened the glue can yet—and don't. Use some of that duct tape and tack the foam into position.) A couple of thin pieces may be easier to place than one thicker pad, but that's going to depend on what size of foam you acquired. My feet are long enough to reach the pegs when my heels are on the hull, but I like to paddle while wearing sandals— and I think that a square of foam feels better than the fiberglass of my boat. In my case, the pegs can be adjusted for a comfortable fit. If you have to extend your foot a little more than you like to keep the ball of your foot on the peg, go ahead and add a little foam to the face of the peg.

For comfort, I like a thin square of foam on the underside of the deck where my knees rest. I paddle in shorts much of the year, and I like the extra padding that foam gives me. From limited experience, I think I'd like foam on the inside of a plastic boat as well, and I know I would want it on wood.

You're not restricted to one thin piece of foam. If you need more depth in order to maintain good contact between your knees and the deck, add thicker pieces or more pieces of foam. I've seen a couple of people sculpt form-fitting hollows into which they place their knees, but I think I like to squirm around more than that would allow. These folks wanted to lock themselves into place for high-intensity workouts, so you may want to make your own custom mold if exercise is your goal.

Some boats come with molded-in hollows along the lower front of the coaming, to be used as thigh braces. You can pad these out with foam for comfort and a better fit.

You'll be surprised how much you use your back and hips in controlling and propelling your boat. If you slosh sideways on your seat, you lose a huge amount of power and control. You don't have to lay out a lot of money for a custom seat. Just add a little foam to the sides of the seat to keep from sliding from gunwale to gunwale. A few accessory manufacturers are making hip pads that can be strapped onto your seat, and these work well—plus the fabric outsides are comfortable and durable. Whether you buy a set of pads and strap them in or carve your own from foam and place them yourself, don't add so much that you are wedged in like a cork in a bottle. You should be able to slide your fingers down each hip and touch the seat when you're sitting in place. That means at least a half inch but not more than an inch of free space off each hip.

You need a back support on your seat. Period. Not a back rest, because you're not going to be slouched resting on it, but a support through which you can transmit power and control to the hull. You probably won't find one much higher than the top of your hips. Most back supports are adjustable. Some are a fabric band attached to the vertical seat supports up ahead of your hips, which you adjust by tightening or loosening the fabric. Others may be a concave plate, hinged to the rear of your kayak seat and adjusted by a line that runs from one seat support around behind this back support to a cleat on the other seat support. No doubt there are other models, as designers seek the most comfortable and efficient device. You can pad the support as necessary, but proceed slowly. It would be easy to add padding in the wrong spot and develop a nasty backache.

Last is the seat itself. The seat should be as low in the boat as possible for better balance, and the seat angle should match the angle of your thighs. I haven't seen any for years, but we once had a spate of kayak seats with a higher lip right at the front of the seat. That lip, within a quarter of an hour, would press against your sciatic nerve and send your feet and calves into tingling sleep and then temporary paralysis. To experience this feeling, just paddle with a wallet in your hip pocket. If you find a kayak seat with this lip, don't be afraid to modify it.

You have to be able to slip in and out of your kayak, but at the same time you don't want to skid all over your seat. You might want to put a thin layer of foam on your kayak seat, or you might want to pad the seat with a thin layer—say, 2 millimeters—of neoprene, fabric-side up. This might make it a little more challenging to get in and out, since the foam or neoprene will work like stickum on the fingers of a football player, but it may make your paddling more efficient. It's worth considering.

Up to this point everything has been held in place with tape, and you should plan on a fair amount of paddling before you change from tape to glue. Make sure the padding you've added is comfortable, and make sure that you can paddle efficiently before you glue the pads and squares in place. Remember the carpenter's axiom: Measure twice, cut once.

A properly fitting boat is a joy to paddle, and you'll be amazed at how many more miles will fit into the same day without your stretching the seams of your physical conditioning.

CHAPTER THIRTEEN

A Saving Grace: Rescues

I have to make a confession—one that I hope doesn't affect the relationship we've built up as we've paddled together. I can't Eskimo-roll my Klepper double kayak. My decked canoe is a snap to roll—an open canoe, stuffed with float bags, will slosh right back to sunny-side up. But you see, with my Klepper, I fall out. I've been experimenting by seeing how far up on its beam ends I could rock that big vessel, and I've fallen out only to have the boat ease back and bob right-side up as if laughing at me.

That's okay. I have a big old comfortable tractor seat in my Klepper, with no hip pads, and my feet are braced against the frame rather than on a set of pegs. I still can enjoy puttering around Lake Union and watching the shipyards, the fishing boats, and the houseboats. I'm also comfortable about loading the Klepper and heading out into the remote islands along the fringes of the North Pacific for weeks at a time.

What I'm trying to say is that you don't have to learn to Eskimo-roll your boat the first week you go paddling. It's a good thing to know. You'll build up your confidence and become a better paddler because of your increased abilities. Who knows, someday you might need that skill. On the other hand, I know people who have logged thousands of miles without once being upset.

What's their secret? They paddle within their own capabilities. They serenely consider their options before paddling ahead. They are in no hurry. Let me back up a step or two before you think I'm inventing these paddling paragons as we glide along. Yes, these perfect paddlers have been in the water. But they upset in controlled conditions, testing the limits of their braces, their boats, and their ability to get themselves out of difficulty.

They were exercising the muscle between their ears.

But to get to that point, you're going to have to learn to use some other muscles and to link together some of the paddling techniques you've already learned. Face it, the Eskimo roll is the quickest way to recover from an upset. Head pointing down? Brace your paddle, flick your hips, and you'll pop back upright.

Rolling your kayak, though, is a lot like riding a bike. Maybe only one out of a thousand, maybe only one out of ten thousand, can learn how to do it from words in a book. The rest of us do better (and learn far more quickly) getting wet in the hands of a teacher, whether in a formal class or in a paddling club training session.

You'll start by leaning over the side of your kayak until your center of gravity overwhelms your kayak's innate stability. A moment later you'll discover that a kayak is perfectly happy floating while inverted. I found it easier to wear a mask (or goggles) and a nose clip the first few times I *huli*-ed, *huli* being Polynesian for "capsize."

Relax for a moment and get comfortable. You have plenty of air in your lungs and you're already good at a wet exit. Hold your paddle in both hands, gripping it at about the power position. Swing the paddle until it is right along the seam between your deck and hull, with the blade closest to the stern parallel to the surface of the water. Your knuckles will be bumping up against the surface, and the aft blade will be just below the surface. Let your PFD float you up toward the surface, and as you bend in a C shape toward that side, swing your paddle easily until the blade that was at the stern of your boat is now sticking straight out from the side of your kayak, still with the blade just under the surface. Your paddle shaft should be closer to the surface than your wrists. You still have lots of air, so don't pop your head above the water. In the real world you can sneak up for a breath, but we won't do it while learning.

You're right! Your hands and paddle are in a high brace. Now, use your hips and knees to rotate your kayak until it is beneath you. Remember that hip flick we practiced? This is exactly the same.

Leave your head in the water. It is heavy, so let the water cradle it while you're rotating your kayak. Your head should trail your shoulders out of the water as your kayak and body come upright. Now your body will be bent into a C shape, but a mirror image of that first C. Now you know why they call it a C-to-C roll. Those folks who lead with their head usually topple back into the water.

Practice the hip flick and rotation at the edge of a pool or alongside a low dock. Position your kayak parallel to the side of the pool (or the dock), turn your torso so that you face the side, and just latch your hands onto the edge. Use your hips and torso to tilt your deck toward the edge while supporting yourself with

With a little hands-on training and a properly outfitted boat, an Eskimo roll becomes a valuable safety tool. Here a paddler rights a Khatsalano folding kayak with support from his paddle blade and a quick flick of his hip. PHOTO COURTESY FEATHERCRAFT

your hands. Hip-flick back vertical, then try it again but with more of a lean. Pretty soon you'll be past vertical, with your shoulders in the water and the bottom of your kayak pointing at the sky.

Practice with a club, practice in a class. You'll probably meet some super people, you'll be exposed to new ideas and new destinations, and you'll find friends to share the water with. If the first club doesn't fit you like a glove, take a look around and find another. But join a club. Trust me.

Now let's get back to thinking about how we can rescue ourselves from uncomfortable situations.

My guess is that no more than two or three cruising kayakers out of a hundred have a bombproof Eskimo roll. That's because no more than two or three kayaks out of a hundred have the hip pads, back braces, and thigh supports needed to lock the kayaker into the boat in order to roll back up. Anyone paddling one of the other ninety-seven or ninety-eight boats is going to do just like I do in my Klepper —when the boat goes over, the paddler is going to fall out.

The Klepper was a red herring. With its knee braces and foot pegs in place, it comes upright easily. My Pygmy Coho, a solo kayak, rolls right-side up almost without effort. Fortunately, falling out isn't the end of the world. I'm going to assume that by the second time you topple over, you won't have all sorts of loose gear in the cockpit or resting on the deck.

Sit-on-Top Self-Rescue Technique

1. Miscalculating your center of balance while paddling a sit-on-top is no big deal. Splash your way back to the side of your kayak, about even with the seat, and, if you have to, reach over the hull to the other side and flip your boat right-side up. Don't bonk yourself on the head. Again reach over the boat and grab the far side of the seat area.

2. By pulling with your arms and kicking with your feet, swim and squirm your way across the boat until your belly is over the boat right in front of the seat.

3. Roll over to drop your butt onto the seat, and while doing so swing your legs on board. If you're on a narrow boat, say like a surf ski or the like, and you feel a bit tippy, just put one leg in the water on each side of your boat. This will stabilize you just like training wheels on a bicycle.

PHOTOS COURTESY OCEAN KAYAK

Back in the boat now. Feel my hand on your shoulder, and feel the quick shove? You're a swimmer!

Now what?

There are a few relatively simple techniques for reboarding your boat—given a little forethought and training. And good fortune. If you think about it, splashing around in the water, I've shoved you over in a very calm, protected, and warm bay. If I could have, I would have capsized you in the relative safety of a swimming pool. For that matter, even though you didn't notice when we were talking, a third friend drifted up behind us just to add a little moral support and safety during our demonstration. If this had been cold, open water, wracked by waves and swept by winds, everything would have been a lot more difficult and potentially a lot more dangerous. The little practice we're going to do here is just a taste rather than the full banquet of rescue techniques.

THE PADDLE FLOAT

Probably the easiest form of self-rescue to learn is with a paddle float—but keep in mind that we're in calm water and with skilled support. It's a lot harder in the open sea.

Your boat will have to be properly rigged, and you'll need a spare paddle, a paddle float, a pump, and probably a loop of rope to use as a step as you scramble back aboard.

With this gear we're going to build a small outrigger that will stabilize your boat. Splash over to your cockpit (roll the boat right-side up if it's capsized) and look at the rear deck. You'll see two jam cleats (one off each rear corner of your

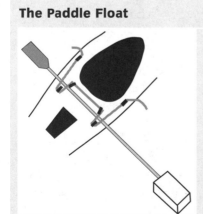

The Paddle Float

The use of a paddle float and a spare paddle is one way for a solo kayaker to get back aboard unassisted. This maneuver should be practiced in safe conditions until it can be done right.

cockpit far enough away so neither interferes with your spray deck), two tee cleats with their tees aligned with your cockpit and set on your flat rear deck just a couple of inches behind your cockpit and as close to the gunwales as I could fit them, and a pair of eye straps a couple of inches aft of each tee cleat. The eyes work well, but I could have mounted one-horned tee cleats with the horn facing aft instead. The cleats are not just screwed into your deck. Each is fastened down into a reinforcing pad fiberglassed to the underside of your deck. I've run a quarter-inch line from one jam cleat back to the eye strap, then forward to the tee cleat, where I've wrapped it around the outside of the cleat and across your boat to the matching tee cleat on the other side. The line goes around that cleat, aft to the eye strap, and then forward to the second jam cleat. Because I don't want to lose the line, I tied a stevedore knot into each end—which prevents the line from coming loose and being washed away.

Clip your paddle leash to a deck fitting, so that your paddle won't float away when you're thrashing about for the next few minutes. Slide your spare paddle out from under the bungee straps. (If it is a take-apart, as is logical, snap it together in an unfeathered position. If it isn't, or it is only feathered, don't worry.) Reach in behind your seat. I've tucked what looks like a plastic bag there. This bag is really a float, and you'll find it has straps to secure it to your paddle blade. Slide it over one blade of your paddle, fasten the straps around the paddle shaft, and puff a few lungfuls of air into the float. A big float could have 40 pounds of buoyancy. Earlier versions of the float were a seat cushion (with 18 pounds of flotation) or an empty bleach jug (with about 8 pounds of buoyancy). Loosen the line on your right-side up kayak so that it slips off the tee cleats, and lay your paddle across the deck between the tee cleats and eye straps in much the same position that you would have used to board your kayak off the beach (see how all our kayaking skills fit together?). The float is on the outboard blade. Tuck the line around the two tee cleats, and pull on the end through a jam cleat until the line is tight and the paddle is firmly secured to your deck. You'll need the buoyancy of your PFD, and you'll have to support yourself by hanging onto the boat.

This is an optional measure. Many folks find it difficult to squirm up out of the water onto the kayak, starting from just ahead of the paddle and putting weight on the paddle shaft and the float as they first slither up onto the rear deck and then flop over and wiggle back into the cockpit. This is hard. If you take a circle of rope that can stretch out to 2½ feet or so and loop that around the shaft, you can use the rope as a step.

Things aren't going to be easy. If you do it right, you'll be sitting in a cockpit full of cold water. If you don't, and you put your weight on the nonfloat side of your swamped kayak, the last thing you'll see before doing a face plant in the brine is your float arcing through the sky. Let's assume you did it right, and you're sitting in the filled cockpit. Get control of your paddle, and snap your spray skirt around the cockpit coaming. If, like me, you have a permanently installed bilge pump, get cracking on that pump handle. If you have a portable pump, get the sucking end down into your bilges and start moving water.

Why all this bother over breaking out a spare paddle for your float, rather than your regular paddle? Well, you were the one in the water. Something put you there. In most cases, that would have been a combination of wind and waves. Neither eased up while you were in the water. If they knocked you over once, they can do it again. You have to be able to brace your paddle with both hands while you are pumping, which also takes both hands. If I could, I might want to come up beside you and attempt to stabilize your boat as you pumped. Once your boat is relatively dry, pop the paddle-float line from the jam cleat and retrieve your spare paddle and stow all the components. Your boat will be almost awash while you are pumping, so if you don't put on a spray skirt, the waves will fill your boat as quickly as you pump.

A few caveats to using a paddle float: First of all, it's much harder than it sounds. The first time you need one for real, you won't be in a pool or protected bay, so you should practice until you can do it right. Second, although I have not seen it, I understand that some people have managed to bust their spare paddles while reboarding. My guess is that they had their step loop positioned right about where the ferrule is in a break-apart paddle, so you may want to watch out for that. (The ferrule is the joint between the two paddle halves.) Third, I do know folks who rolled right over again as they put their weight on the wrong side of the kayak and re-dumped. This is an example of good planning, but poor execution. Fourth, if you are in the water and being knocked about by waves as you attempt to right parts on a ton or more of swamped kayak, you're likely to get crunched. A boat is slippery, huge, and awkward—and will sorely try your patience.

Some people claim that a paddle float is inherently dangerous. While I believe they have a point, it still is the best way for a solo paddler to reboard a kayak unassisted. You should use caution and practice to minimize the risks.

SPONSONS

You might also consider sponsons as a rescue device. Sponsons are a pair of fabric pontoons, about 6 inches in diameter and 3 feet long, that strap on either side of your kayak. Straps go underneath the boat from sponson to sponson and straps over the deck fore and aft of the cockpit buckle from one sponson to the other.

In place and inflated, sponsons stabilize your boat to the point where you can

Always paddle with a buddy, or even better, in a group. First of all, there's a safety factor. If one paddler encounters a problem—a broken paddle, a lack of sunscreen, an inadvertent swim, or whatever—others in the group can be there to lend a helping hand. Second, it's a great learning experience. You'll share techniques and tips and watch how others respond to every paddling situation. Third, it will keep you paddling. The group will inspire you and sweep you along in group enthusiasm. You'll share drives to the water's edge, group equipment, the muscle power of carrying boats and gear, and the efforts in planning your trips. Lastly, it's simply major fun to paddle with friends. It makes the day brighter and the water warmer. PHOTO COURTESY OCEAN KAYAK

get up and stand in the cockpit. I have friends who use them when fishing—folks who paddle narrow kayaks and delight in the additional stability. I have never attempted to strap sponsons onto my kayak while I'm out on open water with waves kicking up, nor while in the water, but I don't want to hang around a swamped boat when it is being tossed in the waves. Given that, sponsons work almost like the side air chambers in my Klepper and some other folding kayaks and provide a lot of stability. One of my fishing friends leaves his deflated most of the time, with only the stern strap attached and the deflated sponsons tucked under rear bungee cords. With the second strap passed under his hull and then snapped into place, he can inflate the two air chambers in moments. My gut feeling is that, inflated or deflated, they will cause drag, but perhaps this is outweighed by the peace of mind they offer. You might want to install them before you venture into wind or waves. Sponsons look good in principle, but I have never played with them, and I may not be such a good judge of emerging technologies.

THE ASSISTED RESCUE

One safety procedure I have tried, which is harder than it looks, is the assisted rescue. You're in the water, overturned by wind or wave. I'm going to paddle up alongside and stabilize your boat as you clamber back aboard. The technique is to put my boat next to your swamped boat, with the paddles from both boats reaching from my boat to yours on each end of our cockpits. I'm to lean out with all my weight on the paddles and grasp your cockpit coaming. You string the stirrup loop over the paddle end on your side and climb into your swamped boat. On paper, with no waves, this method works. If actual conditions are bumpy? Well . . . it *should* work.

Another suggested plan is for you to stay in your inverted boat with your head under water until I paddle up alongside you, bow to bow, about 2 feet off your side. I place my paddle between my deck and your hull, you reach up from the depths between our boats and grasp the paddle, and with that as a lever, you pull yourself and your boat right-side up with a hip flick. Before you say, okay, this sounds like a snap, think of this: What prevents my boat and yours from crunching together as you roll up?

I've seen folks work together in a swamped double, with one of the partners stabilizing the boat with his or her own weight and paddle while the other squirms aboard. With one aboard and the boat pumped, a firm brace will support the boat while the other climbs in. Maybe. This is hard, hard work and demands super teamwork.

Has all of this discouraged you? I hope not. I simply wanted to keep you from building up false expectations. In a couple of decades of kayak cruising on saltwater, I have not had to roll my boat nor use the other rescue techniques mentioned in this chapter. And none of my friends and paddling companions have needed to use any of these methods. We have practiced them, against the day that something goes wrong. And we have huddled on the beach waiting for the weather to blow through. You don't have to paddle in the wind and surf. That's not in the contract.

There should be at least two separate rescue packages with each kayaking party—what if the sole rescue package you have is aboard the boat on its way into the depths? You should have a spare paddle, a stirrup loop, a portable bilge pump, and a floating towline at least 20 meters and preferably 40 meters long.

If land is nearby, in time if not in distance, consider having the paddler in the water clamber up on the rear deck of a kayak to catch a ride to the beach. It would be relatively quick, compared to other rescue methods, and the paddler/swimmer would have access to dry clothes, warmth, and shelter while others in the party attempted to tow the overturned kayak back to shore. For that matter, if it comes to choosing, it is a lot more important to bring a paddler ashore than a boat.

TOWING

First of all, if possible, right an overturned craft. It will tow more easily. To outfit a boat for towing, hook a carabiner into one end of the towline and snap the carabiner into the bow loop of the disabled boat. Run the other end of the towing line through a strap eye on the rear deck of the towing kayak, and secure the line in one of the jam cleats within easy reach of the cockpit.

Some folks believe in running the towline through the bow loop and back to the cockpit, where it can be secured to a deck fitting. Forget about tying a big loop into one end and passing it over your shoulder. There will be a surge and snub every time the two kayaks are out of phase in the waves, not to mention a side-to-side yawing of the towed boat. Your back doesn't need that whiplash crack! I suppose you might be able to run the towed boat tight under your quarter and tie its bow loop to your jam cleat, but this doesn't strike me as suitable. I've heard of systems where the disabled boat is rigged in front of the rescue boat, with the bow loop snubbed to the other boat's jam cleat and the rescue boat pushing the rescued craft, but I fear this would be like pushing a rope.

CHAPTER FOURTEEN

Tools of the Piloting Trade

It's easier to find your way around the water world if you have a few simple tools. The stress here is on "simple." If you want, you can load your kayak down with electronic speedometers, global positioning devices, sextants, and radio direction finders. All these high-tech gadgets will help you locate your position on this spinning globe. You can do just as accurate a job, however, with far fewer tools.

CHARTS AND THEIR SCALES

To locate where you are, where you want to be, and the path between the two, start with a chart: an accurate drawing of a particular area. These are not magic maps. There will be a note somewhere on the chart indicating its scale. One scale may be 1 to 80,000, usually written as 1:80,000. That means 1 inch on the chart represents 80,000 inches in the real world—which translates out to 1 inch on the chart measuring just about 1.1 nautical miles in real distance. A 1:40,000 scale means 1 inch on the chart equals 40,000 inches on the world, or 1 inch represents just a tad over a half mile. The scale on your chart should be a reasonable one. It would be absurd to make a 1:40,000 chart of the sea surface between Los Angeles and Hawaii—not to mention a waste of trees to produce all that paper. At the same time, it wouldn't be useful to produce a chart scaled to 1:800,000—or 1 inch equaling about 11 miles—of a terribly convoluted harbor with many small points and obstructions. Since charts are made for people in boats, it stands to reason that more detail is given to the water than the land. Some important land fixtures should be shown, of course, such as towns and harbors, as well as easily identifiable objects like church spires or petroleum tank farms.

But what else does a chart show? First of all, it gives a fine outline of all water and land. Usually, the land will be depicted in a beigy-yellow color, shallow water close to the land will be blue, and deep water will be white. The division between blue and white will vary with the scale of the chart.

Water depths may be shown in meters, or may be stated in fathoms and/or feet (1 fathom is equal to 6 feet).

All the "road signs" of the sea will be marked on the chart. On the water, cone-shaped buoys, called nuns, and can-shaped buoys, called cans, mark out channels; these buoys are color-coded as well as numbered or lettered. Some buoys have lights (occasionally flashing), while others have horns or bells. There may be lights mounted ashore, or large signs called range markers that may be lined up so that one appears directly above the other to signal you are right in the middle of a channel. Most of these signals are depicted on a nautical chart as little symbols that look just like what they're supposed to be.

The vessel lanes for commercial ships are also marked, and just as the high-speed lanes of freeways aren't places for Sunday drivers, these aren't good spots for small craft such as kayaks to dawdle.

If you fall in love with charts (it's easy; they're seductive with the promise of mysteries unfolding), you might want to buy *Chart No. 1: Symbols, Abbreviations and Terms* (published by the National Oceanic and Atmospheric Administration), an inexpensive, great little book that clearly illustrates every symbol on a chart.

In most, but not all, cases, the top of a chart is north, the left west, the bottom south, and the right east. There are strip charts, made for small boats, which extend along waterways rather than being oriented to the north. All charts have at least one drawing of a compass face from which you can align yourself with the world.

COMPASSES

Take a good look at the drawing on page 127. It's called, in boat talk, a compass rose, and it really has two sets of degree markings on it. The outer set of numbers refers to true north, which is the way mapmakers see things. The only problem with this concept is that the little magnet in a compass points to the big magnet up near the top of the world, which unfortunately isn't at the North Pole. There are all kinds of neat little tricks and mnemonics to let you convert from the direction your compass thinks is north to the direction of the North Pole, but you don't need to know any of them. All we're going to do is figure our directions using our magnetic compass and simply use that inner ring of degrees on the compass rose.

So you're going to need a compass. Probably the easiest type to use is a deck-mounted dome firmly attached a bit ahead of your cockpit. This type has a line

Buoys

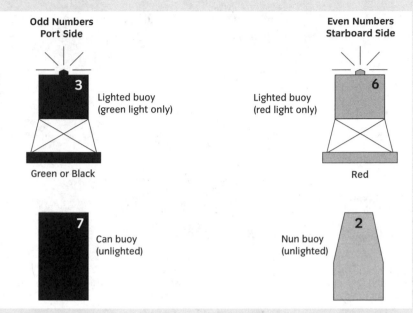

**Odd Numbers
Port Side**

Lighted buoy
(green light only)

Green or Black

Can buoy
(unlighted)

**Even Numbers
Starboard Side**

Lighted buoy
(red light only)

Red

Nun buoy
(unlighted)

Buoys are just another form of road sign. Green or black buoys mark the left side of a preferred channel when you are coming from the open ocean toward port, and red buoys mark the right side of the channel. Green or black buoys are odd-numbered; red buoys are even-numbered. Unlit green or black buoys are shaped like and are called "cans," while unlit red buoys are cone-shaped and are called "nuns."

Lighted
(white light)

Spherical buoy
(unlighted)

Some buoys mark the middle of channels or fairways. These are red and white. While they are not numbered, they may be lettered. Some are lit, and some are unlit.

This Suunto Pioneer and compasses like it are mounted to your kayak's deck with screws or bolts. You won't lose them overboard or to unscrupulous hands, but they are exposed to bangs and bumps when transporting or storing your boat.

down the clear dome of the compass (called a lubber line) showing the direction of travel; the compass turns underneath this line. You read your direction from the numbers under the lubber line. If you want to talk nautical, the stand that holds the compass is called a binnacle.

When we're paddling our solo kayaks, we use two different models of surface-mount compasses. Neither are permanently mounted, but use shock cord and snaps to hook into eyes mounted just ahead of our cockpits. (A permanently mounted compass is less likely to disappear from an unwatched boat; a removable compass is less likely to get banged around when you're transporting your kayak.) My wife likes a Suunto Pioneer, which is easy to read with fairly large numbers. Hers is bright yellow. I paddle with a Ritchie Sportabout. The compass can be slipped from its mount and used to check the bearing to any landmark. It also comes with wee chemical light sticks that can illuminate the compass for six hours or so when I'm paddling home in the dark.

I've been playing with a Silva compass, which is a bright yellow (for visibility) floating plastic box. You use the black marks on top of the compass to make a bearing on an object and read the bearing from you to the object and from the object to you on a floating ring within the protective case. This compass has a small red light for reading it at night.

Some paddlers prefer to use an orienteering compass. Think of a rectangle of clear plastic, usually with an arrow carved into the plastic, with a rotating dish or bowl mounted on the plastic rectangle. The outside of the bowl is marked off in 360 degrees. Within the bowl is the compass needle, swinging so that it always points to magnetic north. Keep the plastic rectangle and its arrow parallel with the keel of your kayak, rotate the outer body of the compass so that the needle points to the 0-degree mark (north; usually, there is another arrow inside the body of the compass and you can align the compass needle with this arrow), and you can read your course where the number on the compass body crosses the direction arrow on the plastic rectangle.

As a young oceanographer, I would ask an unsuspecting student to bring a nearly full cup of cocoa to someone on deck. The inevitable result as that young person attempted to balance that cup along a narrow passageway in any sort of sea was a stomach in revolt. Think about that when you try to balance a compass for long periods. And take warning. Staring fixedly at a half-dome compass on your deck will have the same effect. You'll concentrate so hard on holding a course that you'll be in danger of losing your last meal. When possible, take a bearing at an object on your course and look at that object while you paddle. Despite claims to the contrary, I know few kayakers who can hold a course within an arc of 10 degrees once the waves get a little sloppy. And so what? You're going to a place, not attempting to carve a razor-straight line on the sea.

There are little round compasses without base plates, there are great huge machines that have a circle floating in a thick liquid with degrees marked clearly, and there are even electronic compasses that read beeps and chirps from satellites

Compass Rose

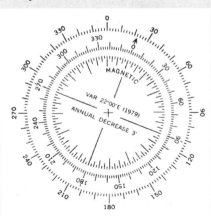

There are two circles in a compass rose, each marked in 360 degrees and noted with the cardinal directions of north (N), west (W), south (S), and east (E). The outer ring is oriented toward true north, or the North Pole. The inner ring is oriented toward magnetic north, as on a magnetic compass. At the center you'll see a note on the variance between the two. On many compass roses there will be a third ring, divided into quadrants but not marked with numbers. This reflects a bit of navigation history, when sailors steered by points (as in "north by northeast" or "west by southwest") rather than degrees.

Compasses such as the Ritchie Sportabout clip to the deck fittings on your kayak, making them both secure when they are in place and easy to remove and protect when you transport your kayak or leave it unattended.

or distant radio transmitters. But there are no best models. You'll probably find one that is simple to use, without batteries or gadgets, and that's the one you'll stick with. Remember, kayaks are a low-tech, keep-it-simple way of traveling. You don't need to clutter up your mind or boat with modern inconveniences. But whatever type you select, remember that compasses sink. Tie the compass lanyard to your boat against the day you will drop it—and believe me, someday you will drop it.

MEASURING DIRECTIONS

You'll need a pencil to draw your course, and you'll need a tool to move the course line so that it passes through the center of the compass rose. You could use parallel rules, which look like a pair of rulers hooked together; you could use a rolling ruler, which looks like just one ruler with a long roller hitched to one side so that it can be rolled from side to side of the chart; or you could use a single-armed protractor, which is a square of clear plastic holding a rotating clear circle marked out in 360 degrees as well as a long clear arm that reaches well across your chart. To use the single-armed protractor, put the clear arm right along your course and rest the center of the plastic square on one of the printed edges of the chart. Rotate the degree-circle until it's oriented to the north, and you can read your course right where the arm crosses the circle.

Or you might get a sheet of clear, flexible plastic about the size of the clear plastic bag you're going to get to hold your chart on the deck of your kayak, and scribe a whole series of parallel lines about a half inch apart from one side of the sheet to the other. Hold one of these lines right on your course, and you'll probably be able to reach a compass rose with another line on this sheet. The line passing through the center of the compass rose will show you your course.

My personal favorite is a square of thin, flexible plastic—about 4 inches on a side—with a circle marked out in 360 degrees on its face. A 2-foot-long black string dangles from a hole at the center. Stretch the string along the course you penciled on your chart, place the center of the plastic and the 360-degree mark on the right- or left-hand edge of your chart, and read the course right off the protractor. Yup, there's one slight problem. You might be reading the correct course, or the reciprocal, but that's an easy challenge to overcome.

MEASURING DISTANCES

A pair of dividers is handy to measure distances. If you don't have dividers, just use a scrap of paper, marking the two ends of the distance to be measured and then holding the scrap up to the right or left side of the chart. Each of the 1-minute divisions on the sides of your chart equals 1 nautical mile, which means you can read the distance marked by the ticks you penciled on the paper scrap. Dividers, which look much like the drawing compasses used to make circles, are more convenient to use than paper.

When you're paddling, you'll be happier knowing your cruising speed. A watch will come in handy, too. Sure, without one you'll still be able to tell day from dark and your stomach will tell you when it's time to eat, but if you know about how fast you're traveling and for how long, you'll be able to make an educated guess as to how far you went.

LAYING OUT A COURSE

Let's put all these ingredients into the pot. We know where we are, because we drove to our launch site and even as we talk we're standing under a sign that clearly says BEDFORD TOWN DOCK. And Bedford is clearly marked on our chart, even to the finger of the dock. We know where we're going, because we've already made plans to camp at Deer Island State Park.

With the edge of our ruler, we'll draw a straight line on the chart from Bedford to the bay at Deer Island. That's going to be our course. We might use rulers, or we might use that sheet of lined plastic. It doesn't matter. Then, using our rulers or the lines on the plastic sheet, we'll create an imaginary line parallel to our course right

Laying Out a Course

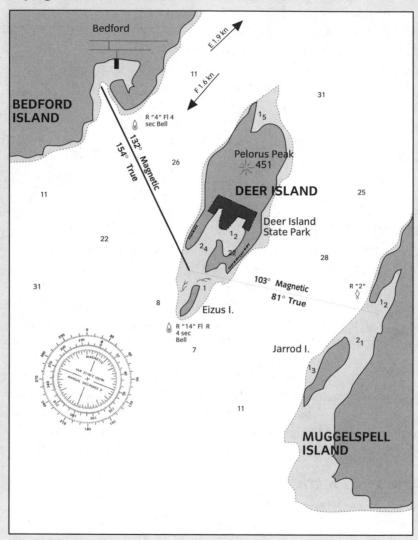

Current arrows indicate the maximum flow and the direction of flow. Remember that the current varies with each stage of the tide and that the current may vary at different locations in a channel.

You can figure your course using true north (T) and then convert this to magnetic north (M), or you can simply work with the inner circle of numbers on the compass rose and figure your magnetic course directly.

Finding Your Position

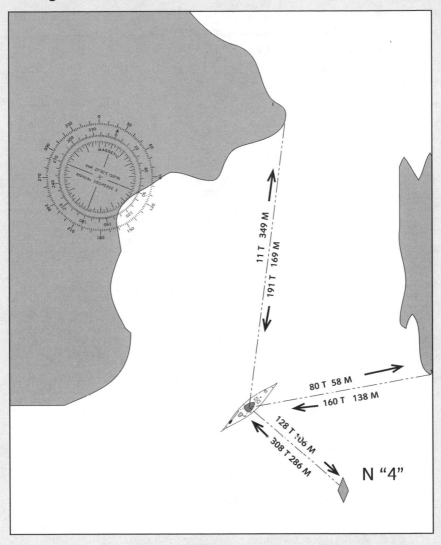

Finding your position is easy. Take a bearing on an easily identifiable object. Then, from that object, draw a line on the reciprocal (the exact opposite of the bearing you just sighted) from that object. Repeat these steps with another object, at quite some angle from the first. You are located where the lines cross! For insurance's sake, and because mistakes happen, try to use three bearings. Take your time and practice on shore a couple of times, and you'll be surprised how easy and accurate this method is.

through the middle of the nearest compass rose. We'll read the course off the inner ring of degrees.

When we start paddling, we'll line up the lubber line of the compass with the degree we just read from the compass and that's the way we'll head.

The imaginary course line will cross the compass rose at two points. One will give us the compass reading from Bedford to Deer Island, and the other will give us the course from Deer Island back to Bedford. We'll write these readings down on the course line. Then we'll put one point of our dividers at Bedford and the other at Deer Island. We'll move over to the scale, or to the minute marks that are part of the left and right sides of our chart, and count off the distance in nautical miles. It's 6 miles, and we paddle at 3 miles per hour (or 3 knots, if we feel nautical). We'll arrive at Deer Island two hours after we leave Bedford.

What if we want to go to Muggelspell Island, but Deer Island is in the way?

Just like with a lot of other things in life, the route is simple if we take it one step at a time. We'll start by drawing a course from Bedford to the point at the south end of Deer Island. Then, just like we did before, we'll copy an imaginary line through the nearest compass rose to find our compass heading. We'll write it down. With our dividers or scrap of paper, we can figure out the distance. "Hey," you say, "one simple course . . . I can remember that."

But we're not talking about one course. One course, or more properly, one leg of the course, only got us to the south point of Deer Island. With our ruler we can draw a second course from Deer Island to Muggelspell Island. We'll go through the steps we've already mastered, and now we have a two-legged course that will lead us from Bedford right to our camping spot.

"Why do we have to bother," you ask, "with all those numbers and lines and rules? All we're doing is messing up the nice chart I spent a few bucks on, and besides, I can see Deer Island. It's right over there. And I can see Muggelspell just beyond it."

You're absolutely right—*if* and *only if* you plan on paddling in a small bay in good weather with excellent visibility. What we're doing now is playing scales against the day we get to play a whole song.

Now that you've laid out a simple course, does it mean you know all there is to know about piloting and navigation? Only if you've just learned how to open up the wrapping on a bandage and you think you're ready to perform brain surgery. The art of finding your way in the liquid world is one in which there is no final examination, no diploma on the wall certifying that you know all there is to know about it. It's a constant aggregation of little skills. Later in this book you'll get a few hints on how to find your way across currents, through winds, and amid fog and darkness.

USE YOUR SENSES

Losing the moon below the horizon was no great loss. It was a day or so off new, and a thin ray of reflected light spilled off one arm only to be sopped up in the gloom of the narrow bay. This far away from cities I would have expected the stars to at least fracture the dense night, but all I could see were the wake and the paddle dips of the kayak just a couple of lengths ahead of me. My partner eased his stroke and blew a short blast on his whistle. A second later he surged ahead. Five times in the next ten minutes he repeated the shrill whistle.

"Are you worried about another boat not seeing us?" I finally asked.

"Listen." Another burst of sound, with an echo back on us immediately. "There's a cliff along the south shore. As long as we get a quick echo, we're still in the bay. Once we're clear, we'll swing around the headland and make for camp."

This was a new trick to me. I hadn't stopped to consider that bats navigate by echo-ranging and that the Dutch used to time the echo from the yip of their barge dogs.

We were paddling home another day late in the afternoon when the sea draped us in a low haze, and within seconds I was totally turned around. My paddling partner canted his head back, took a deep breath, and altered course 15 degrees to starboard. "Beach is right over there," he said and pointed into the haze.

"How do you know?"

"Open your nose. We just came downwind from the pulp mill."

You'll learn, in time, to trust your senses. Shallow water feels different from deep. You'll hear, and you'll see, more than you realize. You'll feel the wind, and—just as important—you'll feel the lack of wind. You'll have confidence that you can read your compass and paddle in a straight line.

To move confidently on the water, you have to know only a few things: where you started from, where you're going, the direction in which you have to go, and your speed.

SPEED

If you know how fast you're going, you'll know how long it takes to get where you're going. You could, if you were so inclined, install a hot, state-of-the-art speedometer on your kayak. At kayak speed, though, sightseeing and gunkholing along as we do, that hunk of battery-eating electronics is close to useless. All you really need is your chart and a watch. Find two marks that are visible and an easily measurable distance apart. There are measured miles and measured half miles near many ports, but you can use any distance that can be transformed into a percentage of a nautical mile. To make our numbers easy, let's assume that you locate two buoys *not* in a direct current that are precisely half a mile apart. If you want to do this on a lake in town, use your car and measure out the distance between a set of streets. Paddle on down beyond one mark and then come back in a straight line from one of your chosen marks to the other. As you pass the first, note the time to the second. Mark the time you finish the run.

For the sake of convenience, let's assume you took exactly ten minutes to cover that half mile. (If you took three minutes, trade in your cruising kayak and try out for the U.S. Olympic sprint team.) Ten minutes is 0.1666 hour. We figure speed as:

$$\text{Speed (knots)} = \frac{\text{Distance (nautical miles)}}{\text{Elapsed time (hours)}}$$

$$\text{Speed (knots)} = \frac{0.5}{0.1666}$$

$$\text{Speed (knots)} = 3$$

Sure enough, our speed is 3 knots, or 3 nautical miles per hour. That's two ways of saying the same thing, and knots is a bit shorter. Now paddle back the other way. The odds are your time will be a bit different, depending on the wind and currents. Add your camping gear, and you might go even more slowly. Change your paddle, and you could pick up a little speed. But if you make several readings, you'll come up with a fair approximation of your speed. You'll find that experienced paddlers will return to time themselves under different conditions, with different equipment, or even just to keep an eye on their technique.

There is no right speed. That's one of the flat-out absolute rules. You cannot go too slow, nor do you get points for going faster. All you're doing is putting together a very low-tech speedometer for your boat.

Incidentally, 3 knots is not far off an average cruising speed for many paddlers.

LATITUDE AND LONGITUDE

A nautical mile is 6,076 feet. This may sound like just another arbitrary measurement, but it really has a practical application.

We'll assume there really is a North Star, toward which the axis of the earth directly points. Actually, the star Polaris is almost directly over our North Pole and is usually called the North Star. If you stood precisely at the North Pole, this star would be directly overhead, and if you measured the angle between this star and the horizon, you'd come up with 90 degrees. If you stood at the equator, the angle between the horizon and the North Star would be 0 degrees—with the star apparently resting right on the horizon. Walk back north, up to around Eugene, Oregon, and the angle would be 45 degrees.

When you're figuring your speed, remember that your course drawn on the chart is a straight line, while you'll most likely be playing in all the little coves and inlets along the way. There's a big difference between the speed you could be making and the good time you're actually making.

Well, look at that—those angles are exactly the same as the lines of latitude. Let's remember this, but for now keep moving along to discuss the nautical mile.

We could divide the distance between the equator and the North Pole into 90 equal chunks—one for each degree. Why 90 degrees? Slice the earth right in half, through both poles. Each half will be shaped like a circle. And there are 360 degrees in a circle. The arc from the equator to the North Pole would be one-quarter of the total, or 90 degrees.

The only problem is that each of these quarter-circle chunks would be a pretty big stretch of real estate. To make these sizes more manageable, mathematicians like to divide each degree into 60 minutes. Why they chose to take a perfectly sensible name for a unit of time and use that same name for a measurement of angle is just one of those things you have to accept rather than explain. If there are 90 degrees between the equator and the North Pole and 60 minutes within each degree, doing a little multiplication shows that there must be 5,400 minutes of arc between the equator and North Pole. If you took your handy tape measure and counted the number of feet between the equator and North Pole (okay, you'd need a very long, handy tape measure), you would measure 32,810,400 feet. Divide that number by 5,400 (for the minutes) and you'll come up with 6,076 feet per minute of arc.

And that's where the nautical mile comes from. Why is it a number to remember? Because any time you use a nautical chart, the right- and left-hand edges are marked with degrees and subdivided into minutes—each minute equal to 1 nautical mile. That gives you an immediate scale. Remember that the right- and left-hand marks on your chart are lines of *latitude*.

The top and bottom edges of your chart are also marked in degrees and minutes, but these refer to lines of *longitude*.

Imagine the top half of our planet as a wedding cake. You could be more formal and call it the northern hemisphere, but it still looks like a wedding cake. If you measure from any point on the bottom rim of the cake to the peak of the cake, the distance will be the same as that measured from any other point on the bottom outside rim to the peak. Go ahead and slice a piece of cake. Look at the piece you just cut. On the lowest level of the cake, the piece may be 6 inches wide. On the second tier the piece may be 4 inches wide, on the third tier 2 inches, and at the very top just a sliver.

Let's measure your cake slice further. With a protractor (or a compass, because the compass also divides a circle into 360 degrees), you'll see that the pieces of cake from each layer all cover the same number of degrees of arc. But of course, they are not the same physical size. The piece from the bottom layer is the biggest. Another way of saying this is that 1 degree of arc at the equator covers more territory than 1 degree of arc at Eugene, and far more than 1 degree of arc just a few feet from the North Pole.

Now, back to the longitude scale on your chart. Those degrees and minutes on the top and bottom of your chart work just like the cake—they will differ in size depending on how far you stand from the bottom edge of the cake, or the equator.

So are these measurements useful? You need some more information before you can answer that.

There are 360 degrees in the circle of our planet, and we can draw 360 lines—one for each degree—down from the North Pole to the equator. It takes twenty-four hours for the earth to make one complete rotation, so it takes the earth one hour to rotate 15 degrees.

A long time ago, the English arbitrarily decided the prime meridian (that line from the North Pole to the equator that was on the 0-degree mark) went smack through the Royal Observatory in Greenwich, not far from London.

Now, set your clock to the exact same time as at the Royal Observatory. The sun should be directly overhead at noon there. But you're not in England. The sun is directly over your head when your watch, still on Greenwich time, reads 8:00 P.M. It's taken the earth eight hours to rotate from the point where the sun is directly overhead in Greenwich to where it is directly over you. We already figured that the earth rotates 15 degrees each hour. Multiply that eight-hour difference by 15 degrees per hour, and you find that you're standing somewhere on the meridian that is right on the 120-degree mark.

But you still don't know where you are. You could be at the equator or the North Pole and you would still be on this 120-degree mark. As far as you know, you're somewhere on an arc 5,400 nautical miles long.

Let's help you pinpoint your location. Remember when we measured the angle between the horizon and the North Star? After dark, get out your angle measurer (sailors use a sextant, if you want to talk technical) and measure that angle now. From where you're standing, it's 48 degrees.

Take your drawing of the earth and rotate it until you find the 120-degree meridian line. Then go north until you come to the latitude line on the 48-degree mark. Those two lines cross a bit east of Seattle, Washington, and that's where you're standing.

All the numbers are no big deal, when you look at things this way. And even if you never paddle out of your home bay, you'll know why there are lines of latitude and longitude on your chart—besides having a good tidbit of information to drop at your next party. Latitude and longitude create a handy grid by which you may locate a point on a globe and therefore are a convenient way to tell others of a precise location.

DISTANCE AND DIRECTIONS IN A MOVING WORLD

With your pencil and chart, you've already discovered how to find your way from one place to another. Compass bearings are easy to sketch in place and relatively easy to follow. But it's not always so easy to get where you want to go.

There are two vastly different distances in the water world, and because of this, two vastly different perceptions of speed: over-the-water speed versus over-the-bottom speed.

If we paddle with the current, we add our boat speed to the current speed. If we paddle against the current, we subtract the current speed from our boat speed. And if we forget, or do it backward, we're liable to end up miles from home.

Calculating speed is relatively simple. The next level of difficulty comes as we calculate directions. Let's cross a current as we attempt to reach a particular point on the far shore. Should we paddle directly at it? No, because we are going to be swept down-current and away from our goal.

Let's put some numbers on the chart. This channel crossing is just 3 nautical miles wide, and we have to cross it at the peak of a 2-knot current. Our compass

Plotting Your Course in Shifting Currents

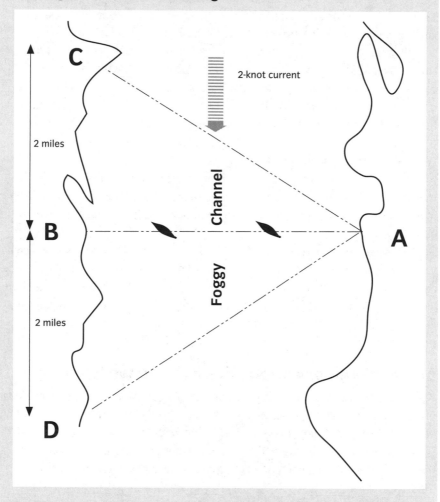

Paddling 3 nautical miles across the Foggy Channel with your cruising speed of 3 knots and with a 2-knot current running can be challenging, especially if visibility is limited. If you launched at A and paddled a compass course for B, during the hour it would take for the crossing you'd be swept 2 miles down-current! You'd really paddle the course from A to D. You could wait for slack water, but there is another way. On your chart, lay out the course from A to B. Then measure 2 miles up-current and mark point C. Draw a course from A to C, and use a compass rose to find your compass course.

Now, launch at point A and keep your bow on the compass heading you figured for A to C. Don't keep your bow heading for C, though. What you and I are doing is "ferrying" across the current, an art right out of river paddling. We're paddling up-current at the same rate we're being pushed down-current, and we're also making good our passage across the channel.

course is 90 degrees, or due east, while the channel runs exactly north and south. Our cruising speed is 3 knots, and in calm water it should take an hour to make the crossing. But it won't today. We're swept 2 miles away from where we want to go. Two long, long miles, and since we'll be paddling against the current as we work our way back to our original goal, it will take us another two hours of paddling.

Let's sit down for a moment and see if we can figure out an easier course. On our chart, draw a line from our launch to our landing. That's the base course, or the line we really hope to follow. But we will be blasted a couple of miles down-current if we follow it. Instead, measure up-current 2 miles from our proposed landing and make a mark on the chart. Draw a line from our launch to that second mark. Using the same tools we used in figuring our course in calm water, transfer that new heading over to the compass rose and figure out the new course.

What happens next requires an act of faith as much as paddling skill. Let's you and I launch our boats together, for company, and steer a compass course keeping the lubber line on your compass right on that bearing. We're not interested in looking at the point on the other side of the channel 2 miles up from our landing, and we're not interested in keeping the bows of our kayaks pointing that way. What we're going to do is crab kind of sideways across the channel in what a river paddler would call a ferry. We'll glide along the line between our launch and our planned landing, but our bow and stern won't be parallel to that line. It's also going to take us a little more than our planned hour to make the crossing. If you measured the line from our launch to that point 2 miles above our landing, it would be close to 3.6 miles long, and at a speed of 3 knots it will take an hour and eighteen minutes to make that distance. That's the distance we're going to make over the water, although we're going to cover just 3 miles over the ground. More importantly, we'll arrive at our original destination.

This is a simple illustration of plotting your course in shifting currents, and it has been simplified even further for your first shot at piloting. In the real world the current will not be constant from one shore to the other, and rarely if ever will the distances be so convenient. That's okay—once you realize that high school geometry can apply to the real world and you're willing to take your time in applying it, you can find your way anywhere.

Paddling down a Range

One of the basics of kayak piloting is the ability to paddle a reasonably straight line over a distance. Hardly anyone can stare fixedly at a compass and keep paddling (at least not without getting queasy), and lining up on a single reference point and paddling toward it does not take into consideration the effects of wind and current. You may be carried far to the side and only realize it when the point that had been due west of you is now due north. The point didn't move, but you were swept down-current and the relative bearing changed.

One of the best ways—one of the oldest, simplest, and most reliable, and that sounds like the best—of holding to a particular course over the bottom is running down a range. It'll take only a few seconds to learn, requires no fancy equipment, and can be used nearly anywhere. All you do is line up two objects that lie directly on your course. Line up a buoy on the water with a steeple ashore, a smokestack and a fir tree, the edge of an island and a lighthouse. As long as the two objects are lined up, you're on course. If it looks like the nearer of the two objects has moved to the right, what has really happened is that you've drifted a bit to the left. If the nearer object appears to have shifted left, you're to the right of your course.

This works just as well at night, when you can line up two lights. Be a little discriminating, though, when you choose your lights: Headlights from a car, the stern light from a boat, or a star will surely lead you astray.

Bearing Down

Paddling down a range will put you on a line, but it won't give you your location. Kayak touring is mostly preparation, not reaction, and this also holds true with your piloting skills. Using your chart, line up another set of markers that establishes a range that crosses your course. When you look ahead and see your first range marks in line and look to the side and find the second range marks also in line, then you're right where those two lines cross.

A meticulous paddler might want to set up three ranges, to precisely locate a position. Whenever I've tried three lines of position, I've been bouncing around in my kayak and either I've been off a degree or more in my sighting or the pencil has slipped—in either case the three lines come together in a small triangle rather than at a single point. The good news is that I'm inside that small triangle.

Here's a neat twist that will help you determine your over-the-water speed. As you paddle down your course, look to each side and arbitrarily establish ranges from clearly identifiable landmarks. As you pass each range line, mark it on your chart along with the elapsed time from your last cross-range line. That will give you an accurate record of time and distance, which translate into your speed.

The Blind Crossing

In the first problem we worked out, we had to paddle across a known current. But what if you don't know the force of the current? Ride along an azimuth (compass bearing). With your hand compass take a bearing on your destination. Just sight over the compass, and see what direction the campsite is from your position.

Then make a best guess as to the speed of the current, and calculate your kayak's heading based on that guess. Let's assume your destination lies on a bearing of 90 degrees from your launch and that with a current from the north you guess you'll have to paddle on a heading of 70 degrees to reach it. Swing your kayak so that the lubber line on your compass is at 70 degrees and start paddling. After ten minutes take another bearing on your destination. If that bearing is still 90 degrees, you're on course. If it is 80 degrees, you're being swept down-current and will have to ferry at a steeper angle (perhaps on a heading of 60 degrees). If the bearing is now 110 degrees, you've overestimated the current and you should reduce your heading to 80 degrees.

To complicate things, let's assume it's a foggy morning and you can't see your destination. On your chart, lay out your desired course; this will serve as your azimuth. When you start paddling, though, use the reverse azimuth—the reverse of your course—and sight back at your launch site. The reverse of 90 is 270 degrees on a compass (if your course is less than 180 degrees, add 180 to find the reverse; if your course is greater than 180, subtract 180 from it to find the reverse). If the bearing back to the launch is 270 degrees, you're on course. If it's more than 270 degrees, you're being swept down-current. If less, you're paddling too much into the current.

Going Wrong Makes It Right

Hey, you've done great. Let's take what you've reasoned out so far and mix it up with a real-world problem. We've been camping for a few days, and on the last night of the trip, we camped on Little Island, just a couple of miles off the mainland. Come morning, we'll hop across this protected channel to where we left the car. As we look across the channel, though, there are no distinguishing landmarks: The few scattered trees all look the same, and the dominant geographic motif is a series of identical dunes marching along as far as you can see in either direction. It is no help that weather conditions conspired to form a light haze, further obscuring things, and there is a fluky little wind. Oh, yes, you're pretty sure there is a current along the shore, but you don't know how much of one.

The good news is that we have a chart and an accurate compass, and while a few days of paddling through the islands has dimmed our collective memory of the mainland, the chart shows the spur road where our car is waiting. It is behind a dune, and we can't see it from the water.

Now what? If you chart a perfect course to the dune we think is in front of the spur road, guess the allowance for the current perfectly (as well as for any windage), and hold that course to the degree, we'll land in front of the car. Scramble a few meters over the sand, and there's the ride home. But what if we're a little

A small, removable deck rigged amidships supports the compass and the GPS receiver. The deck is a work in progress: The next step will be cleats for the mainsheet while sailing, and probably a jam cleat for the line that lifts the rudder blade clear of the water.

off—and with the variables of wind, current, and the ability to hold a course, we probably are. We land, and our car's not there. Which way should we turn? Flip a coin? It comes up heads and we trudge east. After all, there's a 50 percent chance we're right—or wrong. If we landed east of the car, we could trudge for hours through the dunes.

There's an easy solution. Paddle the wrong way. Plot a course deliberately to one side of where you believe the car to be waiting. It won't be the shortest course, and you'll have to take some extra steps, but at least you'll know in which direction your car waits once you land on the beach.

The (Not So) Boundless Sea

It's a fine, fair day, with just enough wind at our back to push us along and keep us cool and the great breast of the tide carrying us toward our destination. We didn't really load up our boats at the same speed, one of us poked along the beach for a few minutes trying for a photo of a fishing eagle, and we don't really paddle at the same rate. One of us wants to gunkhole in and out of the skerries paralleling our course, and the other wants to run right down the compass heading. You can't worry even a bit, with the beautiful weather and unlimited visibility.

How long is it going to take before we lose track of each other?

Remember, you're paddling on a globe and not a flat surface—despite what your eyes are telling you. With your eyes only about 3 feet above the water, the horizon is less than 2 nautical miles from where you're sitting in your kayak. You can barely see the head of a kayaker 2 miles beyond your horizon, with the rest of the paddler hidden behind the curve of the earth.

A paddle blade may rise 5 feet above the water during a stroke. At 5 feet the horizon is less than 2½ miles away. That 2½ miles plus the 2 miles from you to the horizon means you could just see a blade cutting above the edge of the sea at 4½ miles.

Raise a paddle directly above your head, and the top blade will be about 9 feet from the water. From 9 feet the horizon is less than 3½ miles away. That distance plus the 2 miles to your horizon means that you could just see the blade held vertically at 5½ nautical miles.

The sea may be boundless, but unlimited visibility comes in a very small circle when you're paddling a kayak.

GPS: A HELPING HAND FROM SPACE

The first time I crossed these waters it was dark, with just a fragment of a moon tossing little clumps of cream-colored light on the faces of the riffles following the wind from the north. We had a pole mounted on the rear deck and a lantern reeking of kerosene dangling from the pole. We paddled in a cone of our own light, following a compass course down a narrow channel. Somewhere up ahead the sheltering screen of islands to the north broke, and we would slide through the wind and current working their way across our course.

We were heading for a small bay, unlit in those days, more of an indentation in the sandstone walls of the island, with a gravel tongue tucked behind its rocky teeth. We paddled by compass and clock, guessing at our exposure to the push from the north—turning the bow up-current when our estimated speed and our estimated position said we had run from behind the shelter of the islands.

That was then.

Now, when you and I retrace this night crossing, you can key up a screen with the touch of a finger and reach out into space to pluck our position within a few boat lengths along this channel. It's all thanks to a little box, part of the global positioning system. This GPS receiver is easier to use than a microwave oven and costs less than a major trip through a grocery checkout line. Well, make that a very major trip. We're talking under $200 for a basic, battery-powered unit. I paddle with a Magellan Sportrak Pro, a waterproof GPS receiver set up for marine use. I'm not going to go swimming with it, not deliberately, but it's been splashed upon, rained upon, sprayed, and marginally dunked and kept right on searching out satellites in the sky. It even displays accurate nautical charts on its small screen.

The concept behind the global positioning system is simple enough. The U.S. government launched a fleet of satellites that broadcast radio waves. Your GPS receiver listens for those broadcasts, and when it can track at least three satellites, it can locate its position with pinpoint accuracy. If it can see four, it can also tell you your height above sea level.

Why is this so great?

Let's play with it for a moment.

We're camped on one of a host of small islets clumped into a bay on a low coastline. If we worked our way through the channels between the islets and paddled straight offshore, within minutes neither you nor I would be able to pick out the route back to camp. If we paddled only precise courses and marked each heading and distance down, we could make our way back—but let's face it, we don't paddle that way.

Instead, before we launch, let's ask the GPS to locate our camp and then ask it to memorize that location. Then we go paddling, and an hour later ask the GPS unit where camp is. It will give us a bearing from where we are to camp, tell us how far camp is (in a straight line), and, if we're paddling toward camp at that time, tell us how long at the present speed it will take to return.

That, by itself, is well worth the cost of the unit.

Let's take the next step. All GPS units don't have the same buttons, but this is how I work mine. On our chart I mark out the courses we'll have to paddle from camp to our destination. At every change in course, I make a mark and, by using the latitude and longitude scales at the top and side of our chart, locate each turn. And I give each point a name.

I put each of those names and locations into the GPS receiver's memory. You can call these locations waypoints, because they are points we'll pass along the way. Like street signs. At any time I can ask the GPS to figure where we are and in what direction and how far away the next waypoint is. If I take a detour into that little bay over there, the GPS unit won't mind—it'll just chunk along keeping track of where we are and remembering where we said we want to go. If we decide to trim a loop out of the day's paddle, that's all right with it, too. It will just home in on the next waypoint we ask it to find.

When we're paddling along, I can ask the unit to average our speed over the bottom—it doesn't concern itself with our speed through the water—and those numbers will pop up on the screen.

Last, but certainly far from least, it will track our course made good rather than limiting itself to merely the direction in which our kayak is heading. We're going to paddle down that same channel I started to tell you about back in the beginning of this chapter. When I'm paddling our Klepper, I have a compass mounted right on the centerline and the GPS receiver mounted off a bit to the side—far enough away so that when I turn on the electronics, they don't affect the compass. I ask the GPS to take notice of our course, and it will show the course that we're actually following. When the compass shows us on a heading of 270 degrees, that means we're pointed due west. If the GPS says 270 degrees, we're also moving due west.

"Big deal," you say?

Okay, we move down the channel a little bit. The compass is still rock solid on 270 degrees. But the GPS says 250 degrees. What happened?

We're still paddling on a heading of due west. But there's a current coming from somewhere off to our right, from the north, and it's pushing us south. Instead of actually moving west, our course made good is a composite of our westerly paddle strokes and the southerly drift of the water mass upon which we're resting.

At this point we have a couple of options. We can ignore the current and be dragged well to the south. Not a good choice. Or we can turn a bit to the north—we'll start by guessing that our compass heading should be 290 degrees—and paddle on that new heading. The GPS doesn't concern itself with which way we're pointed, only which way we're actually moving over the ground. If it says we're making a course of 270 degrees, then we're actually crabbing along on our desired course of due west.

We've paddled enough together, in this kayak with this load, to know we average just a shade under 3 knots. You turn on the GPS receiver and ask it for our speed over the ground. It tells you 3 knots, and all sounds well in the world as we continue on a heading of 270 degrees. An hour later, you check again and it says 1 knot. But we're working just as hard, paddling just as efficiently. We check in another thirty minutes, and the GPS says we're holding a speed of 1 knot, but on a course of 90 degrees. The compass still says we're on a heading of 270 degrees. What happened?

It looks as if we started paddling along this channel at slack tide, making good our average cruising speed of just under 3 knots. The tide, though, is against us. We really didn't tire an hour into the trip, but the current began to build against us. We were still moving at 3 knots through the water, but the body of water was moving in the opposite direction at 2 knots. This gave us a real speed over the ground of 1 knot. As the tidal flow increased, we were actually being carried backward 4 nautical miles for each 3 miles we paddled forward—leaving our speed over the ground 1 nautical mile per hour in the opposite direction we were pointed.

Why do I paddle with a GPS unit? Because it tells me where I am within a relatively small circle, it tells me the direction I want to go to my destination (either a checkpoint along the way or my final landing), it tells me the direction I'm actually moving rather than the direction in which I am pointing, and it tells me the speed I'm actually making toward that destination. And it will do this despite fog, the fall of dusk, or a horizon curtained with rain.

With a chart, a compass, and tide tables, you and I could figure out each of those factors. They're not hard; they're just common sense applied to a marine environment. The GPS is my warning light, a little alarm that warns me if things in my paddling world are not as I expected.

A GPS receiver is not infallible or indestructible. Batteries will die (my receiver uses four AA batteries, for about twenty hours of use), and the unit will stay alive for about twenty minutes when I'm changing batteries. (This is a common feature that can be found in anything from clock radios to computers.) I could paddle down a narrow fjord where it cannot acquire the satellites it needs for locating our position. I could fail to seat the battery case properly, and water could leak in. Heck, a meteorite could whack it. What I carry is simply one more tool that allows me to paddle with a bit more security.

Is there more to piloting than what we've covered in this chapter? Of course! But these are the basics. In time you'll be able to find your location by the depth of the water and the underwater profile, you'll find your bay by the composition of the bottom materials, and you'll take bearings on distant buoys to triangulate yourself. There are a number of outstanding books on small-boat piloting and navigation, as well as kayak navigation. Consider a U.S. Coast Guard Auxiliary small-boat class or a Power Squadron class as part of your kayaking education and absorb what you can from them. Contact your state's boating law administrator and get a copy of your state's boating education course. Most of these are aimed at powerboaters, but you'll find much to help you in your kayak.

CHAPTER FIFTEEN

Tides and Currents

Tidal currents sweep us willy-nilly down unexplored channels, and tidal waves threaten us with towering breakers. There's a rising tide of misconceptions about what exactly this surge of water within our seas is. Let's clear up a few points.

WHAT THEY ARE

Tides reflect the vertical movement of water. Supplying or draining the water to meet that movement causes currents, the horizontal movement of water. The two are closely related, but you and I in our kayaks have to deal with them in different ways. In a lifetime of study, one barely begins to understand the nuances of tides and currents, but in a few hours, you can learn more than you'll ever need to know. If you take your kayak to sea, you should have at least a rudimentary understanding of tidal movement and how you can use tide and current tables in conjunction with your nautical charts.

This vertical movement is caused by the gravitational tug of the moon. In most places there will be two high tides and two low tides each day. One high tide will be directly under the moon, the other will be on the opposite side of the earth. The low tides will be halfway between the highs. As the earth rotates through a full day, every place will pass through the alternating high and low tides. That's right—we move toward and away from the peaks and valleys of the gravity-influenced tides. When the earth, moon, and sun are in a straight line, the gravitational tug of the sun will pull the tides higher (and will cause the lows to go lower to make up for the water in the high tides). When the sun and moon form a right angle with the earth—at the quarter moons, when you see just half the face of the moon illuminated—the gravitational tugs of the sun and moon somewhat cancel each other and the tidal movements are less extreme.

You should have a few terms at hand. A rising, or flood, tide refers to that part

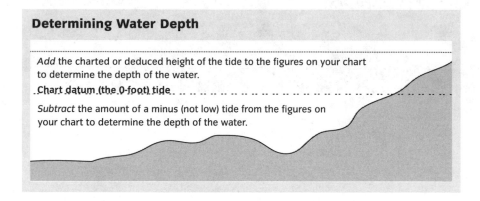

Determining Water Depth

Add the charted or deduced height of the tide to the figures on your chart to determine the depth of the water.

Chart datum (the 0-foot) tide

Subtract the amount of a minus (not low) tide from the figures on your chart to determine the depth of the water.

of the cycle when the height of the water column is increasing. A falling, or ebb, tide refers to that part of the cycle when the height of the water column is decreasing. Slack tide is the period of time between the flood and ebb tides, when for a brief moment the water pauses. Scientists and mapmakers invented the 0 mark on the tidal range to use as a benchmark. A minus tide occurs when the surface of the water falls lower than this arbitrary level—which is really like 0 degrees Fahrenheit on a thermometer. It really doesn't mean anything, but it is a handy reference point from which to measure. Expect to hear about spring and neap tides, too, which we'll explain at the end of this chapter.

TIDES: WATER IN VERTICAL MOTION

We'll start with tides. The one absolute in paddling on saltwater is that the liquid world is in a constant state of flux. Beaches advance and retreat. A rock is a tall landmark at noon, but by 4:00 P.M. is marked only by a rolling boil in the slosh of a wave. The open passage behind an island evaporates, leaving a thin-crusted mud-flat. Currents pause, reverse, and pause again. This is the world of the tide, with the oceans sloshing far up the beach and then drawing away under the relentless tug of the moon.

Tidal differences are least in the high northern latitudes and at the equator, but can reach 20 feet in the midlatitudes, which includes much of North America. Bays, channels, and inlets amplify the range, and the difference between low and high tide can top 40 feet.

How important can this be to a kayaker? After all, we don't have to stick to the deep-water channels. Well, if you visit me, you'd better know the tide. I live on a drying bay, which is a shorthand way of saying that for several hours out of each tidal cycle there's no water in front of my house. Around the point near my house there's an island—part of the time. The rest of the time it is a peninsula.

Let's go camping. If you land at high tide, you may be just steps from the ideal campsite. That's great. But you want to depart at low tide—not only has the water level fallen 15 feet but the shoreline is now a quarter mile away and the mud between here and there looks deep. Land on another gravel spit at low tide, pull your boat up, and doze off in the warm sun. A couple of hours later you're floating, and your boat has drifted off. I hope someone comes by to pick you up!

It's mid–low tide, and you land on the jagged rock shore of a perfect island. No reason to drag your kayak ashore. You drop an anchor off the stern of your boat with what you think is plenty of slack and bring your bow line to the rocks, where you tie it off. When you come back, stuffed and purple from a blackberry find, your kayak is doing a nose stand on a rigid bow line and you will have to swim to free it.

These things happen, because the water world is not a level place. We temporarily lost a campsite because when we launched, a wildly sculpted boulder was a perfect landmark. Four hours later the currents marked its position with a boil.

The tides may also make you believe in ghosts, as they did the old voyageurs. You paddle across a long set of flats one day, and you make good time. Another day, you struggle and fight to make the same speed, even though the wind is the same and the current is near nonexistent. Your kayak displaces a vertical wake as well as a horizontal one, and you may have to fight friction from the bottom while paddling in shallows. You'll use a third more energy maintaining the same speed in water just 1 foot deep than you would in water 10 feet deep.

So the tides are important. How can we use them to make our kayaking more enjoyable?

First of all, work with the tides rather than against them. Your primary tool is the tide tables produced annually by the National Oceanic and Atmospheric Administration. NOAA publishes time and height predictions of tides, both high and low, for a host of points all around the country. If you're not at one of the tidal stations listed, check the back of the book for height and time corrections at nearby locations. You might have to add or subtract time or adjust the height of the prediction. Before you do that, though, read the cover of the tables to avoid an easily made yet embarrassing mistake—make sure the tables you are reading are for the area you're in. The front cover will tell you. Check your watch, too. Most tables are figured in standard time, which means you have to reset your clock during a daylight savings time cruise.

The Rule of Twelve

I can tell by the look on your face that you just caught one of the problems of tide tables. You know the high and the low times, but if you're landing two hours into a flood tide, how high will the tide climb in the next two hours?

You can figure this out easily. About the time that people started going to sea and had a respectable notion of time, they discovered the rule of twelve. (This rule works for most bodies of water in most times, with Cook Inlet in Alaska and the Bay of Fundy being the notable exceptions. The walls of water that mark a tide there aren't under our general rule.)

The rule goes like this. The tide will rise one-twelfth of its total rise in the first hour of the flood. It will rise two-twelfths in the second hour, three-twelfths in the third hour, three-twelfths in the fourth hour, two-twelfths in the fifth hour, and the remaining one-twelfth in the sixth hour. Turn that around, and you'll see how much water will ebb away during a falling tide.

Let's apply the rule to a hypothetical easy-to-figure tide. There will be a tidal difference of 6 feet between high and low tide. That makes each twelfth equal to 6 inches. In the first hour after low tide, the water will rise just 6 inches, or ½ foot. In the second hour, the water will rise 1 foot, and in the third hour, it will rise 1½ feet. During the fourth hour, it will rise another 1½ feet. In the fifth hour, the water will rise 1 foot, and in the final, sixth, hour, it will rise ½ foot.

It doesn't take a lot of figuring to realize that not much water will move during those first and sixth hours and that currents will be at their weakest at that time. More water moves during the second and fifth hours, so expect more currents then. Currents should be at their most brisk during the high water rise of the third and fourth hours.

And that brings us to currents.

CURRENTS: WATER IN HORIZONTAL MOTION

Water isn't spontaneously created. Okay, during some of the Pacific Northwest rainfalls that point is debatable, but as far as tides and currents go, the water comes from somewhere and goes somewhere else. All this rushing about as the tide rises and falls creates currents. Because of the relatively slow speed at which you and I paddle, we are going to be affected by currents. The more we know of them, the more we can take advantage of them and the less we will do ineffectual battle with their muscle. Current tables tell us more about dashing hither and yon. Current tables are lists that predict current speed at specific times, for specific locations—just like tide tables.

Don't assume which way a current will flow. Direction and velocity depend on the profiles of the shoreline and the bottom, and the water pouring between two islands can be kicked into a totally unexpected direction by a reef. Start by comparing the little current arrows marked on your chart with the maximum ebb and flood noted next to each arrow, and expand that with the numbers from your cur-

Offshore rocks and reefs can give you the same breaking waves you'll find on an exposed beach. A rock that offers shelter when the tide is low may be washed over by waves at mid-tide. At high tide it may be invisible, until it trips a wave and the water bursts skyward as if part of an explosion. That's called, obviously, a "boomer." Your chart may show these submerged rocks, but since charts are made for larger vessels that can't probe near the shore, chartmakers don't always catch them. PHOTO COURTESY OCEAN KAYAK

rent tables. But remember that much of this work was done for commercial vessels that must stick to the center of the channels. In our kayaks we dance along the edge of the shore, we poke into bays, we sneak up on islands, and we paddle in waters where the main current is broken up into eddies and swirls.

Using the Moon's Muscles

Even if the tidal range is just a few feet, the resulting currents will affect your passage. If you're going with the current, you'll catch a free ride. If you're working up against the current, you'll expend your energy and make only a little headway. If you cross a current, you may be swept far from your intended landing.

Excuse me while I grab your kayak when you attempt to turn back to shore. What I said sounded like a bucketful of work and difficulties, and what you should have been hearing was that the movement of the waters is the best thing since free public transit. Which it is. A hundred or so years back, Native American paddlers could drift the channels all through the inland sea of the Pacific Northwest to wherever they wanted to go. Ride a current for a few hours, lie in the lee of an island, and then catch a connecting current across the sound. I assume that seagoing folks everywhere knew this same art of riding the currents to their destination—I know that the people of the rainy Northwest coast came close to perfecting the art of using the currents to help their travels.

Let's say that we want to paddle 5 miles down a particular channel. We already know that our over-the-water cruising speed is 3 knots. But, at the peak of the ebb tide or the peak of the flood tide, there is a 2-knot current flowing in the channel. If we time our launch so that we're going in the same direction as the current, we can make the trip in just one hour.

If we didn't pay attention to the current and launched when the maximum current was flowing against us, it would take us five hours to make good that same distance. We would paddle against the current at our cruising speed of 3 knots, but we would be swept backward by the current at a rate of 2 knots—which means that we would make good speed of just 1 knot over the bottom. With a "real" speed of 1 knot, we would work for five hours to make good that same distance. Whew!

I think I'll use the currents.

What if we have to force our way against a current? We can sneak around much of its force. The current will probably be strongest in the deepest and straightest part of a channel—a matter of friction. The drag of the bottom and the drag of the shore will slow a current. So don't paddle down the middle of the marine street. Sneak over next to the shore and glide along in the eddies formed by projecting points. An eddy is sort of like a shadow in the bright light of a current; it's a back current flowing into the low-pressure zone left behind an obstacle in the main current flow. Hop from the eddy behind one island to the eddy behind another. If the channel curves and you have an easy crossing, consider paddling the inside of the curve rather than the outside. If the current persists against you, no matter what you try, don't fight it. Beach at the first nice cove and brew up a pot of tea. Read a book, take a photo, or play your flute. Learn to enjoy the moments you snatch out of time.

If you must paddle from one large body of water to another through a narrow and constricted passage, expect turbulent water in that passage as the currents race through. Wait for slack water if you can. What I've done, on waters I know well, is to start into the channel just before slack water, with the last vestiges of the current on my bow, and sprint as far as I can as the waters shift direction. I can also catch the first few minutes of the beginning tidal flow on my stern. Do not do this without a lot of forethought, study, and plenty of local knowledge. The force of the sea in a constricted channel can be frightening—and if you're not frightened, you have little grasp of what's happening all around you.

Predicting Current Flows

Current flow is a lot like tidal movement—its strength builds gradually. The current isn't zero at slack time and 3 knots five seconds later, and it doesn't hold at 3 knots for the whole six hours of flow. Just like the tides' rule of twelve, we have a handy little theorem—the rule of three—that can help us determine the strength of a current throughout the tidal cycle. Don't bet your dinner on this, since local conditions can affect flows, but you will deduce a good approximation of the current. An aside: "Deduce" is a good word. You'll hear old salts talking about "dead reckoning" as they chart their position, and this has nothing to do with their life expectancy. *Dead* is a misspelling of *ded,* as in *deduced.*

To make the rule of three work for you, first look at your tide tables and the times for the high and low tides for the day you're planning your trip. The high and low tides will be about six hours apart, but for this illustration we'll assume the tidal cycle takes exactly six hours. The maximum predicted current speed is 3 knots. At the start of the tidal cycle—right at high tide or low tide—the water won't be moving and the current speed will be zero. One hour into the tidal cycle, the current flow will be moving at one-third of its predicted maximum speed, or 1 knot. At the second hour of the tidal cycle, the flow will have accelerated to two-thirds of its maximum velocity, or 2 knots. At the end of the third hour of the tidal cycle, the current will have reached three-thirds, or all of its maximum speed, in this case 3 knots. During the fourth hour of the cycle the current will begin to slow, until at the end of the fourth hour it will be at two-thirds of its maximum speed, which in our case would be 2 knots. It will continue to slow through the fifth hour until at the end of the hour, it will be at one-third of its maximum speed, or 1 knot. During the sixth hour of the cycle it will continue to slow, until at the end of the sixth hour—which is the end of the tidal cycle in our illustration—the current speed will be at zero.

You just divide the maximum current speed by three. At the end of the first and fifth hours of the tidal cycle, the current flow is one-third of the maximum. At the end of the second and fourth hours, it is two-thirds of the maximum flow. At the end of the third hour, it is at its maximum speed.

If you have to paddle against this current, it makes sense to paddle in the early or late part of the tide, when the current is at its slowest. When you have to paddle across the current, you can judge how far down-current you will be carried by the flowing water.

SPRING AND NEAP TIDES

When reading of the sea, you're going to run across the terms *spring tide* and *neap tide.* Don't confuse these old Saxon words with the seasons. "Spring" comes from *springan,* which translates as "to swell." Spring tides give you the highest high tides and the lowest lows during any month or lunar cycle. You'll find them when the moon is full or when it is new—in other words, when the moon, earth, and sun are all in a line and the pull of gravity is along that axis. Because the moon, although smaller, is much closer to the earth than is the sun, its relative gravitational force is greater—roughly twice that of the sun.

Neap tides also occur twice a month, during the first and third quarters of the moon. When the moon is between the earth and the sun, the face of the moon aimed at the earth is in shadow and the moon appears dark (a new moon). When the moon passes through one-quarter of its orbit around the earth, half the moon will be illuminated by the sun and half will be in shadow. In the second quarter the moon moves around until it is directly opposite the sun from our viewpoint on the earth, and it appears as a fully illuminated disk (full moon). In its third quarter it moves three-quarters of the way around its orbit and again is half lit and half shadowed. By the fourth quarter it has moved back between the earth and the sun, and the face we see is in shadow.

During the first and third quarters, the sun and the moon don't work together, and the gravitational pull of the moon can't quite tug up as much ocean water as at other times in the cycle. The high tides aren't quite as high, and the low tides aren't quite as low. The Saxons, who had a fairly good knowledge of the sea, called the tides during this time of the month *neafte,* which translates as "scarcity."

CHAPTER SIXTEEN

Resources and the Rule of Thirds

We paddle at the end of a long tradition, and the hard-won knowledge of those who have crossed the waters before us is ours for the taking. It is far better to use their knowledge than to re-create the mistakes from which they learned. One of the most important lessons of the past is that we should treasure our reserves of vital resources. These might be time, water, or food—whatever we need for the successful completion of our task.

One way to do this is to divide our task into two equal parts, and the resources we bring to the task into three equal parts.

Start off by marking the midpoint of your task. "Task" may sound like a disagreeable word, but there are pleasant tasks as well as the normal workaday assignments. We'll pretend that you're launching from the shores of Johnstone Strait high up on Canada's western coast and that over the next six days you plan to paddle around a group of islands and return to your launch site. The high point of your trip will be a stop at a Native American village with standing totem poles. You've already contacted the band that owns this village and they've granted you permission to land. The totems are exactly halfway around the chain of islands. Reaching the totem poles, then, is the midpoint of your task.

Now, divide your critical components into thirds. Critical components? Well, certain factors are critical to the success and safety of your trip. Food is one. Drinking water is another. Time, especially for the paddler, is a third. We'll start, arbitrarily, with time.

Build a paddling schedule that will bring you to the midpoint of your trip at the end of your second day—the first third of your time. Under ideal conditions, then, the second third of your time will carry you back to your put-in. With this great luxury of time in reserve, you'll not pace the beach early in the morning wondering if that rising wind will make the next channel crossing too arduous for your party, nor will you drive yourself late into darkness on the last day fearing that any delay will plunge those waiting for you into worry and anxiety. If you have time in the bank, you don't have to paddle out on the edges of the good-sense envelope.

You can also squander some of the precious time by poking into an inlet in search of rumored petroglyphs, or photographing the rich colors of paintbrush or fireweed against the bleached patterns of driftwood, or drifting over the shallows with row upon row of purple sand dollars canted up on their side. With time in your pocket, you can discover a new standard of richness.

The same goes for your food. Keep a reserve. Horde a few meals deep in the ends of your boat for a wind-bound afternoon. Some years back, my wife and I had only book knowledge of the Northwest Territories and the Mackenzie River when we paddled out of Great Slave Lake heading north, and the winds that pummeled us every afternoon shocked us. A wind that rolled in with rabbit-tail clouds at 2:30 P.M. each day? A little physics makes it all clear: The sun bakes Canada's wheat-growing plains, and the heated air over those plains rises. Denser, cooler air flows into the plains, and the easiest channels for it to flow along are the river valleys. The solar heating kicks in throughout the morning, and the air movements become noticeable right about the same time each day. That's why upstream winds in the early afternoon are common on rivers—like the Mackenzie—that extend from the ocean into a hot interior. (The opposite phenomenon can be observed while paddling in Chile, where you can feel a mass of cold, dense air pooled over the glaciated interior cascading down the mountain valleys toward the warmer sea. The fierce winds can overturn well-found yachts and send kayaks caroming over ripped-apart waves.)

The first afternoon, as we paddled across wide and shallow Mill Lake, the winds were a surprise and we scurried to shelter on a sandbar that was just attempting to grow into an island. This was mosquito heaven, and we had the tent up in record time as we watched the recently placid surface of the lake churn into some fairly respectable waves. By evening it was calm again, and we put in a few more hours of paddling. We had plenty of time in the bank, so we didn't have to force our way into the wind and the chop. We had a well-planned food reserve, including desserts and special treats, so that we could pamper ourselves without dipping into daily menus. And, most importantly, the knowledge that we had these reserves allowed us to enjoy the trip rather than forcing us to maintain an uncomfortable schedule.

Time, food, and water are the obvious critical factors. Carry more food than your minimum schedule says you'll need. Keep a store of potable water in reserve lest you cannot find the next spring.

The technique is, like many aspects of kayaking, easier than the implementation. But try to follow it. Divide your tasks in two, and your resources in thirds. The last third is your insurance.

CHAPTER SEVENTEEN

Taking Your Kids Kayaking

The lesson of this chapter is illustrated aptly by a classic little cartoon showing a horse harnessed backward to a cart with the driver (facing over the rear of the cart) saying: "I think I've found our problem." We have to put the horse in front of the cart; we have to determine if we are the kind of people our kids would like to take kayaking with them.

Let's imagine that I've been paddling for three or more decades, a lot of that in the wilderness, that I've been a professional guide and paddling instructor, and that I have a reputation for leading really fun trips. And I invite you to come on our next trip. But I'm going to treat you just as many children are treated as families paddle off on vacation.

Excited?

Well, first of all, we're going to leave at 6:00 P.M. on a Friday, after being up most of Thursday night rummaging through closets and the garage tracking down our camping gear. You're going to have to sit in the backseat, which is heaped with bags that we didn't get properly stowed. You can't really stretch out, even though we'll be driving all night, and no matter what you say, we're going to tell you to be quiet and we'll get there as soon as we can. Oh, yes, we haven't explained to you where we're going, but we have made it clear that you can't take any of your favorite things. And we're going to complain bitterly if you say you have to go to the bathroom. "Hold it," I think, will be the operative words.

Just after dawn on Saturday, we weave into our launch site, carry our kayak to the beach, and begin to shuttle that mountain of gear from the car to the boat. That's right, singular boat. It's a big touring boat with two cockpits and a center hatch, and as we cram bags into the center, we leave a dwarfish pocket for you—not quite long enough for you to stretch out your legs. As we push off, we advise you, "Don't move, this kayak is tippy!"

We'll land late in the evening, just after the light has gone to the point we can't find firewood, and we'll burn dinner as we fumble with the tents. My wife will tell you to sit down and stay put, you could get lost out here, and "Don't get dirty and for God's sake, don't go down to the water and get wet!"

Just think, you've got another twelve days of this to look forward to.

Are we having fun yet? No? Well, now that you've begun a kayaking trip from a child's perspective, maybe you've learned a lesson. Kids are willing to have fun and ready to go adventuring, if we adults don't work too hard to mess it up.

HOW TO MAKE YOUR TRIP FUN FOR ALL AGES

Let's start by asking some basic questions. Where do you want to go, when do you want to go, with whom do you want to go, and why do you want to go? A lot of adults don't really ask themselves these kinds of questions before they take a trip, and they wonder why they're not having wonderful experiences. If part of your family wants to voyage through high-latitude wilderness, say into iceberg-dotted LeConte Bay on Alaska's Panhandle or along the west coast of Greenland, and others want to loll on tropic beaches, languidly drifting from spa to resort, you may have some problems. Well before your vacation rolls up on the calendar, you should—as a paddling group—come to an enthusiastic agreement over where you're going. That especially means the younger ones in your party. You can make them go, but you can't force them to enjoy themselves, or to let you enjoy yourself. That's a group effort.

If your family has never taken a kayaking vacation, don't grab your seven-year-old and tell him camping is more fun than a week in Disney World. You will lose credibility the first time it rains. Sell your children on the fun. Sell them on the adventure.

Sell them on history.

A bottle of juice, a PFD, and a ride in a kayak—life just doesn't get any better.

Children do not live in the abstract. Tell them you're retracing one of the fur trade routes, and you'll be answered with a yawn. Make it live for them, make them live in the story, and you'll have an excited crew.

We planned to paddle down Canada's Dease River, across little blobs of lakes and along thin trickles of rivers that were well suited to the long sleekness of a cruising kayak. During the wet evenings of the previous winter, we pored over books and journals, seeking the stories of the explorers and fur traders who mapped this river. We were looking for, and found, the site of a Hudson's Bay Company trading post at the farthest stretch of the company's reach. It lay on a remote point of Dease Lake where the company had dug in its fingers for only one winter and then let it slip back into obscurity.

Could we sell that knowledge to a nine-year-old? Not likely. What we did was beach our fiberglass boats on the shore where the traders' birchbark canoes would have beached and hunt through the scrub for depressions where their cabin would have stood. We found it! We camped where the post had been, made moccasins as traders long ago had done before abandoning their post (okay, ours were from a Tandy kit), sang old voyageur songs, and cooked our version of the last meal the traders had cooked here. The traders had boiled the lacings from their snowshoes for their last meal before setting off downriver. We sat around the fire in our homemade moccasins and made faces, pretending the long strands of pasta were boiled rawhide.

Childish? Sure. But that's the point. Bring your trip into the environment and experience of the children. Find a real person from history, and follow that person's steps. Make appropriate costumes, reinvent meals, learn the songs. Make it a game.

Learn a coyote call, and see if you can have a coyote answer you. Look for fossils. We made a game of finding old log cabins and seeing who could find the most ways in which the pioneers joined the logs at the corners (we've found more than twenty). Is it important to do this in order to learn to paddle? No. But if you can invent games that include children in the party, you'll find your days in the kayak are much more pleasurable.

How old should a child be before you begin kayak tripping? You might ask: "How long is a ball of string?" The answers to both questions depend on a number of factors.

I have acquaintances who started boat camping with their son when he was barely a year old. It has worked out well, and now they have camped with both an infant and a toddler—but it takes more than a modicum of forethought to camp comfortably with very young children.

My opinion? Giving up daytime diapers is the watershed, forgive the pun. That

Match the voyage to the capabilities of the paddler. Finn, at five years old, loved to paddle (even though here he had borrowed an adult's paddle rather than use his smaller one), but a 200-meter trip to the far side of the bay was a major expedition requiring two breaks for snacks and at least one for a frolic in the water.

is not only a logistical mark—a diaper bucket doesn't pack well—but also is about the age (usually around two or three) when you cease to be the totality of a child's world and can join him or her in discovering the universe. Children at that age are still small enough so that a kayak can be both a playpen and a high chair. They're old enough to join you on easy hikes above the beach in search of petroglyphs, old cabins, and camera viewpoints.

Even without diapers, toddlers may create problems. It is difficult to find comfortable PFDs for them. Kids will fuss and fidget, and you'll be tempted to strip those bulky PFDs off them so they may play. Don't.

KIDS AND PFDs

My suggestion would be for you to wear a PFD anytime you're in a boat—hot or not—and use this as an unspoken illustration of what to do. If every time you are in a boat, you wear a PFD, your children will assume that this is the way of the world and will don theirs. If you live in a "Do as I say, not as I do" world in which you demand standards of your children that you don't in yourself—well, you're going to be worn down by a long trail of bickering. There are some great safety products available for kids, including equipment made by Englehart, Extrasport, and Sterns.

Don't buy a PFD that your kid will grow into. A couple of years ago, in Connecticut, we ran a very simple demonstration. We coached three little girls with long blonde hair and put them all in adult PFDs. All three had been carefully (and secretly) coached to grasp the bottom edge of their PFDs, and all three bobbed around in the pool. All the parents and grandparents in the audience patted themselves on the back for having the right number of life jackets on their boats. Then, at a secret signal, the three girls released the bottom edges of the PFDs—and all three of them dropped until their arms caught on the lower edge of the armholes and all you could see of them was their blonde hair floating on the surface. You wouldn't believe the rush on kids' PFDs that followed.

PFDs have to be beyond the essential. You don't have to nudge a paddling partner and ask: "Did you remember to bring your heart?" Your PFD falls in the same category.

CLOTHING AND GEAR

Every child and adult in your party should carry a whistle—the louder the better. Put one on a lanyard around your neck and one around each child's neck as well. The human voice can fade away in the bush or on the water, but a full-lung blast on a good whistle can be heard for a mile or more. Listen to the awe-inspiring blast from a Storm or a Fox 40, both of which are loud even when wet, and use them as the criteria for the whistles you'll carry.

Children are not little adults. Parents sometimes forget that. Kayaking can be hot, can be cold, can be spray in your face or the sun beating down on you. Children have neither the body mass nor the acquired stoicism to cope with weather not far out of their comfort range. Yes, you'll see a child demanding to frolic in an October surf, or wearing a down vest in July, but you'll also see a child who is almost instantly transformed from comfortable to miserable.

Let's start at the top. Like you, a child needs a hat. It seems to me that most children enjoy hats as well as require them, and if you give them a voice in the selection, they'll sport the headgear until it's a ragged ruin. Look for something with a brim or bill to shade their eyes (and shelter their face from the rain and spray). A floppy fisherman's crusher will also protect their neck from sun and water.

Trousers and tops—one word only. Layer. You may be in shorts country, or floating among icebergs, but conditions can change quickly. If it is hot enough for shorts, remember that sooner than you expect it will be chilly enough for long pants. What is true one way is equally true the other. Most children will be in a constant flurry of changing clothes, and that's perfectly all right. Set a few basic rules, such as that every item has to be repacked once doffed, and keep a weather eye cocked. You'll find that most children have no idea of when they will be too cold or too hot, and your counsel will be appreciated, even if they don't admit to it.

Foul weather gear should be readily at hand. And I use the term "foul weather" rather than "rain" deliberately. Foul weather includes rain, but also means wind and spray. Look for a stout jacket that works as an outer layer of personal armor. It has to allow for freedom of movement (even over layers of clothing), it has to ward off the bite of the wind, and it has to protect vital core heat from the robbing fingers of spray and rain. Don't settle on a thin plastic garment because your child will soon outgrow it and because you'll never paddle under conditions where your child will need the extra comfort. Excellent paddling clothing for children and adults is made by such companies as Kokatat. Even if the price is outside your recreation budget, you should be paddling with others, and odds are at least one of your companions knows where to buy used gear at an affordable price.

I believe in bright, fluorescent colors and am not overly concerned with color coordinating. Why? No matter how firm the rule, some article of clothing will be dropped and forgotten. Camouflage patterns or drab colors blend into the background and may be overlooked. On the other hand, you're not likely to miss international orange and lime green. And although we might rather not think about it, bright clothing is also easier to spot if someone wanders off from camp and gets a bit dislocated.

Footwear for kids? Go poke a stick in a wasp nest and you'll stir up less controversy. Generally, what works for adults also works for children, but children sometimes have an absolute sense of style. If you can, go along with their desires—they go along with yours. Inexpensive sneakers work, but they will get wet and they will stay wet. Some folks prefer Alaska oxfords—stout rubber boots with laces to snug them tight. Still others swear by river sandals—Teva, Merrill, Reebok, Nike, Alps, and Sports Cruiser are all well known, and there are many copycats—worn with or without socks. I like the sandals-and-no-socks approach, with a pair of warm and dry socks all set to put on when I'm off the water for the day. Since I've equally supported sneakers, boots, and even wetsuit booties in the past, I suspect that I may well switch my footwear preference at some time in the future.

THE BOX

There are two other absolute essentials in kayaking with kids. These are just as important for adults, but we sometimes forget to offer children the same considerations we expect for ourselves. The first is their box. That's BOX, and it is personal, private, and absolute. They can bring *anything* on the trip with them, as long as it fits in the box. A Power Ranger action figure, a battered toy car, a set of tiny dishes—whatever eases the transition from a secure and well-ordered home into the confusing, stimulating, and surprising world of the kayak is perfectly fine. You might have ideas on what's proper, and in that case you can put what you need in your box. If your child wants to take a tattered stuffed bear along to keep away the night creatures, that's his or her right.

THE BOX

The second absolute is THE box. THE box is slated for opening at predetermined times. Those times are not based on how people behave, nor on the emotional state of the boxee. When it is time, THE box is opened. Make it the responsibility of the children to know when THE box is to be opened, to bring them into the drama and excitement of the opening.

THE box was born during a quiet-water trip in northern Canada, when our paddling companions placed a large wrapped and taped cardboard box in their boat with the smug announcement that it would be opened on Tuesday evening—two full days away. Despite cajoling, threats, and some outright begging, not a hint was given for two days. Come Tuesday evening, the box was presented with all proper ceremony and carefully unwrapped, and there packed in dry ice and insulated with wads of newsprint was a selection of Popsicles.

Why this effort? Because we all deserve treats. Never, ever, say that we can't open the box because someone hasn't been good, or someone hasn't helped gather firewood, or even that someone hasn't cleaned a plate. So what? The box and its supply of treats come from a universe beyond our failings or successes, and we simply take pleasure in what is offered.

The Popsicles started THE box, and in subsequent voyages we've found fudge, glow-in-the-dark Frisbees, and even the fabric dome and instructions for a do-it-yourself sauna.

SHARING THE FUN

Think back to that imaginary trip when we crammed you in the center hole of our big cruising kayak and made you sit by the hour. What was the worst part of it? I'll wager the most frustrating aspect was the knowledge that you were merely luggage, a spectator while everyone else was a participant. Would your children feel any differently?

A young child, just out of the toddler stage, is not going to be a significant motor on your voyages. That said, they'll only learn by doing. They need a paddle. What they don't need is an adult paddle. As an adult, you're comfortable with an oval paddle shaft somewhere in the range of 1 by 1⅛ inches to 1⅛ by 1¼ inches

Kids love to go paddling, as long as you as an adult are as smart as they are about it. Keep each leg of a kayak voyage—the time in the boat—at a reasonable length from the kids' viewpoint, let each participate to the extent of their interest, and include toys and snacks as part of your mandatory boat equipment. PHOTO COURTESY PYGMY BOAT

thick and with a length of around 220 centimeters. How would you like a paddle shaft 2½ inches in diameter, on a paddle 300 centimeters long? Your hands would be exhausted just trying to wrap around that big cylinder, and your shoulders would ache from attempting to twirl that log. Not to mention the fact that the blades would be so huge that you couldn't manipulate them in the water.

And you're going to hand that giant piece of equipment to a child and urge him or her to have fun?

A child doesn't need a "good" paddle, but a youngster does need a practical-size paddle. We made our first kid's paddle with the blades from an inexpensive raft's oars and a shaft from a piece of carefully sanded and varnished doweling. Efficient? Not in the slightest. But the kid could comfortably grasp it and could mimic the paddling actions of the adults. As his paddling skills increased, he acquired better paddles.

We found two ways to encourage his participation. One, when he was of an age to be in a cockpit safely by himself, was to team him with the strongest paddler and let him paddle in the bow of a double. He'd paddle when he felt like it, and he played with his toy trucks curled up in the bottom of the hull when he didn't.

The second method developed in our three-holer cruising boat, as an absolute rule. Two of us paddled and one rested in the center hatch. Whoever was paddling could ask for a switch at any time, or whoever was resting could ask for a switch, and we would make it—at the first available beach. Not at a preset time, not with a "We'll paddle for an hour and make up some time and then you can paddle" and not with a "We just switched, be patient!" Instead, "I want to paddle" or "I want to rest" meant an immediate detour to the beach.

The first couple of trips were a closely linked series of launches and landings. I suspect that the adults were being tested as to the commitment of their promises, but that's not the kind of question I could gracefully ask. Besides, now when I want to rest, the rule is still in effect, and now in his thirties, my son is willing to beach the boat and let me loll amidships.

Children realize there don't have to be "chores" in setting up camp. Chores are work, and most of us will avoid work or at least be slackers. Make it a cooperative game, or at least a team play, and be willing to switch tasks.

When our son was seven and a week out on a long voyage, he announced that he was tired of collecting firewood while the two adults put up the tent, built the fire, and put on the coffee. He wanted the tent and fire duty.

Putting up the tent is complicated and far more suitable for the knowledge and experience of an adult mentality than the mindless scurrying about in search of firewood. I don't know if that was his opinion, but it was certainly mine. But we agreed to switch jobs, nevertheless.

The first few times he put up the tent, he certainly took a long time. Not only that, he pointed out to me what kinds of fallen twigs and branches were needed to build and maintain a good cooking fire and how I had taken the lazy way rather than collecting what was necessary.

Switching tasks can be humbling.

Washing up comes at the end of the meal, and the person who is washing the dishes feels left out of the camaraderie as everyone else lolls back with a full belly and comfortably tired muscles. Everyone gets to take a turn at cleaning up. Don't delegate it to just one person, nor to the kids. Rotate the roles, and let everyone learn to enjoy them.

If you're willing to share the best, be willing to share the rest. We created a rotating roster, with one person (two, in a larger party) responsible for planning, preparing, serving, and cleaning up all the meals in one day. You may have difficulty imagining having to eat a meal concocted by an eight-year-old. But it's an eye-opener to find out they think the same about you. And in my case, the eight-

Larger people—grown-ups—can paddle all day with pleasure. Smaller people—kids—need a place to play, a place to rest, snacks, and frequent breaks to shake their sillies out. Which only goes to prove that smaller is smarter. PHOTO COURTESY BRIAN HENRY/OCEAN RIVER SPORTS

year-old planned some pretty good meals. Here's the dinner menu he prepared and presented, with the only adult help being the buying of the materials (we were within a day of a store).

Red wine, Tang, or coffee before dinner
Tossed green salad
Macaroni mixed with canned chili
Peas
Rolls and butter
Dessert: Canned chocolate fudge topping heated in a double boiler, served with fondue forks and a selection of marshmallows, orange slices, apple slices, and banana sections
Coffee

Breakfast had been cold cereal with tea, while lunch was pilot crackers with peanut butter washed down with Tang and sweetened with candy bars.

After our son washed up the dinner dishes, he had no kitchen duties until the rest of us in the party had taken our turn behind the stove. The combination of several days off and the (well-deserved) praise for his meals made his tour as chef a fun and positive experience, rather than a tail-dragging chore that it would be better to avoid.

Is it easier for an adult to share these duties? The four most popular words in the English language might be "Let me show you" or perhaps "Let me do that." The most supportive phrase in the English language (and the most difficult for me) consists of the words not spoken as I sit with my mouth shut. We must help when help is requested, and offer support that is absolute and invisible as our children try new things, but we must also painfully and honestly sit back and let them do what they try.

KIDS AND BOOKS

We were huddled up under a rain fly, bundled to avoid the bite of an ice-chilled wind, the evening the dragon attacked and the kids had to flee for their lives.

Well, actually, we were cruising in the Alaska Panhandle, with the end of each day marked by reading aloud a chapter from the book we had brought along. It takes no great skill to read aloud, and while many of us look back with fond memories at being read to, that seems to have been something our parents did *for* us—we think of ourselves as the readees rather than the readers. We were several families on that trip, with a handful of kids who had never read *The Hobbit* nor had it read to them. The first night, when we ventured into Tolkien's world, the kids thought themselves too sophisticated to listen, so they sat out on the fringes and pretended not to pay attention. During the reading of the second chapter, the kids circled right around the fire and the adults lurked in the fringes—too old in their own minds to listen to a fable but unwilling to miss a word.

On the one rainy evening of the two-week trip, the kids put up a rain fly and built a fire so we had a place to read. As drizzle finger-tapped at the lean-to fly and waves groaned against glacier ice, we read of Bilbo finding the dragon's hoard and of the dragon soaring unexpectedly around the cliff and lunging at the Hobbit and the dwarves. Just then, a nervous girl nudged a fire log and overturned the coffeepot into the glowing ashes. As the eruption and steam settled away, there wasn't a kid to be seen!

You don't have to be a skilled and evocative reader. You just have to be open enough to enjoy the book and to draw comfort from a small body pressed up against your side as the dragon stalks your heroes. While reading is fun, don't forget to share the entertainment. Pass the book to a child after a while.

Don't take the advice here as gospel. What worked for us may not work for you. These memories are not an assembly kit for joyous expeditions, but they may get you started building your own.

A FINAL WORD

There's a terrible disease running rampant among adults, and one of its side effects is the ability to ruin just about any paddling vacation. I think people catch it at work, or from watching exercise infomercials. It's called "Neffie." Spelled NFE,

Kids are attracted to kayaks like bees to honey. It's a personal boat, to their scale, and a child can move and maneuver a kayak easily. But don't tell them that a kayak is an excellent learning platform for responsible judgment and physical growth—that would make it sound like work. PHOTO COURTESY WILDERNESS SYSTEMS

which is the acronym for Not Far Enough. Most of the adults I know, myself included, want to jump into a kayak and paddle and paddle. And paddle. A kid—and kids are smarter than adults because their brains haven't been worn down by a lifetime of demands to work harder and faster—knows that somewhere between three and five hours is long enough to be in a kayak. Big people want to paddle for ten hours or more, to make some more distance. And even then, it's Not Far Enough.

The kids are right. If you want to make speed, take an airplane. Writer Bob Pirsig said once, "We were making good time. We just weren't going very fast." Every kid knows that a kayak opens up the world because it gives you plenty of time to see that world. It doesn't pass by as a blur outside your window.

If you see a beach, stop. If you see a big rock in the middle of a slow stream, swing into the eddy behind the rock and enjoy the swirls of water and the turbulence along the eddy lines. You'll share more of the world with your child, and that's one of the reasons you went paddling. Your blood pressure will go down and you'll live longer. And maybe you'll get a chance to see how neat little whirlpools are curling out from a rock.

Three to five hours in a kayak? That means maybe 9 to 15 miles. It's enough.

CHAPTER EIGHTEEN

First Aid and the Paddler

This is going to be a short chapter. To learn about first aid and paddling, look up the telephone number of your local Red Cross chapter and sign up for a class. Once through the basics, take the CPR course and every advanced class they'll let you take. First aid is worthy of several books, and you're not going to become proficient from a chapter in this one.

I can give you a few pointers to get you started. The most common minor injury from kayaking is a blistered hand—which, since that's your engine, isn't all that minor. Try paddling after the fact. It's a good idea to apply a chemical such as Tufskin ahead of time to build up an artificial callus. A severe blister may mean you'll have to be towed, and then the blister is both painful and embarrassing.

The sun burns. You can blister, bleed, and inflict serious, long-term, and possibly fatal damage to your skin from overexposure. Use a strong, waterproof sunblock found at a dive shop or surf shop—and don't believe that once you tan you won't burn. One of the nastiest burns I remember was on an African-American girl who thought she was immune from the hammer of the sun. She won a trip to a doctor but fortunately didn't scar.

You could also develop sore wrists. Don't paddle, and see a doctor if pain persists. You could have a case of inflamed tendons. It's my belief that this happens to worried paddlers who grip the shaft too hard or those who paddle with feathered paddles of more than 80 degrees.

It's hot, you're working hard, and water is in short supply. That's an invitation to disaster. Drink plenty of liquids. Bike racers say you should drink before you're thirsty and eat before you're hungry, and this advice applies to paddlers, too. If you're dehydrated or have low blood sugar, you won't make good decisions and may become faint. On a day trip or longer, take note of your urine. If it's dark and pungent, you aren't drinking enough water. Sweets will not provide you with energy. You need complex carbohydrates, and plenty of them. Think about keeping spaghetti or noodles on the menu.

If you find yourself with a severe headache, a likely cause is that you forgot your sunglasses. Wear them when the sun is strong, along with a hat or cap with a deep bill.

If you find yourself with back pain, I mean, deep, I-hate-to-move pain, probably you don't have proper lumbar support. You're also likely slouching as though you're in a chaise lounge. Depending on your stomach, take along an over-the-counter pain reliever to ease the discomfort of overused muscles.

Paddle wisely. Don't go out for a three-week trip at the beginning of the season. You probably can't paddle 50 miles a day. For that matter, you can't drive for ten hours and paddle for ten hours the same day. Lightly stretch your muscles before you put them under pressure. The whole idea of kayak cruising is to have fun. Don't punish any part of your body in the process.

Remember sunblock, and plenty of it, on the water. It takes very little time for the sun to turn you crispy. Good sunglasses are a must, a hat would be a good idea, and frequent applications of a waterproof sunblock are necessary. PHOTO BY DOUGLAS PEEBLES/OCEAN KAYAK

CHAPTER NINETEEN

Water, Water Everywhere and Not a Drop to Drink

Many cruising kayakers live under a host of misapprehensions about the availability of pure and fresh water.

First of all, the tale goes, look for running rather than standing (or stagnant) water. Second, look for water that is running through or being filtered by rocks rather than dirt, loam, or duff. Third, look for water that is bubbling up out of the ground rather than in a stream or pool.

There's a small problem about getting water through these methods, a problem so small that it's microscopic. It is a wee creature, a protozoan called giardia, which is endemic in all the waters of North America. Let him find a home in your intestines, which is virtually guaranteed if he's in the water you drink, and you'll be wracked by diarrhea, weakness, and aching muscles. He's only one of a host of nasties that reside in water of all descriptions and that may cause discomfort, severe illness, or even death. Even that clear, sparkling stream cascading brightly down a cliff side can be filled with a soup of nasties, along with pesticides, herbicides, heavy metals, and the rest of the chemical world that does us no good.

Water coming out of a faucet is not necessarily better. It can also contain a host of things with which your system is not prepared to deal.

So if you don't want to drink that soup, you have four options.

1. Carry your water with you. On many arid islands that's your only choice.

2. Boil any water used for washing, drinking, or food preparation. Heat works to kill most of the pathogens that are lurking out there, but it's going to take you some time and fuel. Bring the water temperature to a minimum of 150° F to kill most of the bugs and nasties. You probably won't have a thermometer with you, so figure that bringing the water to a rolling boil is sufficient and is really the minimum. But you'll gain nothing by boiling away for more than five minutes. Consider your time, fuel, and the heat generated by your stove: When you're still planning where to go, try timing just how long it takes to bring your big camp pot to a boil with your camp stove. Using that number, determine how long it will take you to boil the one to two gallons of water each person will use in a conservation-conscious day.

3. Treat your water with chemicals. You can lace all your water with pills and liquids. Expect to have your water taste of iodine or chlorine, depending on the chemicals you use, and don't plan on treating great quantities of water. The chemicals will kill off the nasties—or at least most of them—but they won't remove waterborne solids or the soup ingredients such as pesticides, herbicides, or fertilizers. It's an unfortunate irony that in a pristine paddling environment, we have to be concerned about the industrial fallout from our modern way of life.

4. Use water filters. You can pump out a liter at a time using a small pump and special filters. These work, and in fact may be the only practical way you can process the amount of water you need. Katadyn, General Ecology, PUR, MSR, and Sweetwater are units that work well and are somewhat convenient. You'll need to consider whether you want a ceramic filter that can be cleaned, an enclosed filter that can be backflushed, or a unit with a chemical purifying unit and a carbon filter to remove the chemical taste. There are pluses and minuses to each of them, and in all fairness, it would take a book larger than this one to explain the differences. One note of warning that applies to all these devices: Most of the purifier instructions will tell you how many liters of water each will pump before the filter starts to clog. Ignore that information. The amount will vary with the pollutants in the water you're attempting to cleanse. (*A hint:* If you're attempting to purify water from a muddy or murky source, wrap a bandana around the pump inlet. The bandana will strain out much of the big chunks that otherwise would quickly clog your filter. Most filters come with a prefilter at the opening to your intake hose, but I'm a believer in using both belts and suspenders. If nothing else, the bandana won't hurt anything.)

In an emergency, and just being a little thirsty doesn't constitute an emergency, you might dig a small pit on the beach right where the moist sand and the dry sand meet. Fresh water is lighter than salt, and a layer of fresh water may often be found at the top of the water table. This is not pure water, and you may well pay a miserable price for drinking it.

CHAPTER TWENTY

Nattily Attired

"Beware," cautioned Henry Thoreau, "of enterprises which require new clothes." It was good advice on the shores of Walden Pond, and it is good advice when it comes to kayak cruising. You don't need new clothes to go paddling. Don an old pair of pants, a flannel shirt, and a pair of sneakers and you're set to go. That is, you're set to go in comfort in the middle ranges of the paddling environment. There have been a few advances in clothing technology since Thoreau shuffled off to Walden, however, and these can make your paddling experience more enjoyable.

First of all, a bit of advice for women paddlers. Don't wear a one-piece swimsuit while paddling. Or a jump suit. There is little privacy in the water world, and when nature calls, you'll have to strip.

THE CHALLENGES OF KAYAK CLOTHING

What should you wear in a kayak? Let's get out of the kayak for a minute and go for a long trip. You'll need to select the best single set of clothes you could wear for a one-day cross-country airplane flight, a brisk scramble through one of the city's parks, and then a long afternoon of very high-pressure business meetings. Staring at your closet? You've just discovered the principal challenge facing your kayak wardrobe. You have to plan for a variety of paddling environments. Your lower body is sheltered from the wind and waves. Your upper body is in the full grip of the elements. Paddling is going to keep you warm—sometimes too warm. The sea is fractions of an inch away and can precipitously chill you. Since you're in a damp environment, the air constantly erodes your body temperature.

Fortunately, on most day trips in mild weather, you won't have to be concerned about all the possibilities. After a few seasons of paddling, you'll have so many opinions on what to wear and bring that you'll be a source of advice to others.

What do I wear? Paddling in the Pacific Northwest, I wear shorts most of the

Treasure your hat! One like this Seattle Sombrero from Outdoor Research will keep you warm by insulating your head, keep you cool by protecting you from the beating rays of the sun, keep you dry, keep those nasty little drops of water from running down your neck, and will shade your eyes. And a lanyard will keep the wind from snatching it away.

year. I'm inclined toward Predator paddling shorts made in Vancouver. Matt Kelly designs competition clothing for Predator, and it is comfortable. I wear their Lycra shorts with a padded crotch (similar to cycling shorts), which are great in hot weather As the mercury slides down, I'll shift to shorts with a Lycra front and neoprene rear, and then to all neoprene. Shorts made of all neoprene tend to be a bit clammy. If you're not into that look or feel, check out the river shops for guide shorts—quick-drying material with a mesh liner. Kokotat, Chums, ExOfficio, and Patagonia all make good shorts, and I'm sure there are a lot of others on the market.

When the temperature drops a bit, I might also slip on cycling tights. They add some warmth, don't cut off the circulation, and pad out my knees against the deck. Some folks like wool military surplus trousers.

LAYERING

Topside, I start with a polypropylene T-shirt—short-sleeve for warm days, with a long-sleeve T in the bag. Atop that I'll go with a synthetic pile fleece vest. Under most conditions I'll complete the ensemble with a long-sleeve, water-resistant, loose-cut paddling jacket. I get warm paddling, and I want ventilation, not water-proofness. I want the sweat to evaporate, not to be trapped inside a waterproof jacket. If it's chilly, I'll pull on a dry-suit top. I have a Mountain Surf top with neo-prene cuffs and a neoprene neck. Equally good tops come from paddling stand-bys Patagonia and Kokotat. Cotton clothing is great in some environments, but it gets damp and stays wet on the beach.

A big hat, with a floppy brim, is essential—but it has to have a lanyard to keep it from being blown away. Baseball caps are fine for keeping the sun off your eyes, but you also want the rays and raindrops off your neck.

If you are sensitive to the sun, or worried about being so, consider sunblock clothing. Most materials barely slow UV radiation, but some manufacturers make clothing that is as effective as SPF50 sunblock.

Footwise, either water-sports sandals or rubber boots work well. Your choice will depend on what's comfortable for you in your kayak and still protects your feet from sharp objects when you step ashore. In cooler weather I wear sandals with breathable waterproof socks over a light pair of wool socks. Old sneakers are fine, too. I used to wear wetsuit booties with a semirigid sole, a holdover from river days. I still like them, but after a few days my feet wrinkle up, and the booties—well, they need a good deodorant.

WETSUITS AND DRY SUITS

If the water is really nasty, I stay on the beach. I'm not in enough of a hurry to go anywhere to have to attire myself in ultimate survival gear. If I think I'm potentially going to get wet, I might put on my dry-suit pants. Wetsuits, especially in the thinner weights, are a practical safety item with a few drawbacks. One, you have to don your suit ahead of time; I've never met a person who could put one on in the water. Two, they trap your body heat very well, and you'll toast under most conditions. Three, they also can become rank (at least mine can). I would wear a Farmer John, a wetsuit with long legs and a bib overall–type top, to keep the most flexibility around my shoulders. My wife prefers a "shortie," which is the same suit but cut off at the knees.

If you like high-tech clothing, remember that a dry suit keeps you dry—you may need insulating layers under it if and when you go in the water. A wetsuit doesn't keep you dry, but it does keep you warm. As for me, you can see I'm very traditional. I favor layers of clothing that I can shed or add depending on the temperature, and I can adjust my insulation to fit conditions.

Last, but not least, when the temperature dips into the forties with a wind nibbling at me, I like pogies. A pogy is a combination of bag and palmless mitten that wraps around your paddle shaft. Your hand fits into the wrist opening, and you can grasp the paddle shaft inside the bag—while the nylon or neoprene fabric keeps the cold wind and spray off your hands.

In my dry bag I keep heavyweight sweatpants, a wool sweater, and a pair of stout walking shoes. And, to absorb perspiration as well as precipitation, a thirsty towel.

No one has ever asked for my opinion as a fashion consultant, and please don't accept these opinions as carved in stone. They work for me. They may be a springboard for you in finding your paddling comfort zone.

CHAPTER TWENTY-ONE

Rack 'em Up!

If you live on a protected cove right on the beach, on a body of water so wonderful and diverse you can and will spend the rest of your life exploring it, and the kayak shop from which you bought your boat will deliver it right to your dock, and your kayak is so well-equipped that you'll never have to bring it to town for another gadget or doodad, then read no further.

For the rest of us, though, paddling isn't that simple. Our water universe expands with the speed and convenience of our vehicles, and in the course of our cruising, we roam from the orca pods cavorting in British Columbia's Johnstone Strait to the lure of pirate treasure in the sand-rimmed cays of Florida's 10,000 islands.

CAR RACKS FOR CARRYING KAYAKS

You could, if you were so inclined, toss your kayak atop your car, open the windows, and thread a rope through the windows and over the top of the car and the kayak. Loop it around a bunch of times, tie the rope ends together with a granny knot, and off you go. You'd beat up the top of your car, you might get rained upon and certainly couldn't listen to your tapes, and you'd probably hang a significant bend right about the middle of your boat. Fortunately, there's a better way of transporting your kayak.

After you've selected the model of kayak you want, and probably before you start nailing down all the incidentals such as color, tear yourself away from the enticing accessories shelves and amble over to the rack department. Brace yourself, because unless you're already into outdoor sports, you're going to be whammied with a severe case of sticker shock. "That much? Just for some little vertical posts, a couple of crosspieces, and a pair of little slings to hold a kayak?"

In a word, yes. It's easy to start by putting a couple of hundred-dollar bills on the counter, and then piling on more when you begin adding all the bells and whistles to the rack. Remember, though, that what you're doing is not just buying a conglomeration of aluminum struts. You are acquiring a carefully engineered system that will support the thousand-dollar (at a minimum, and probably a lot more) kayak that you want to transport, and in doing so will keep it firmly attached to your vehicle. In any paddling group there will be someone who is all too familiar with the wry and bitter joke of the driver looking out the car window at a kayak in free fall and saying: "Boy, that boat looks a lot like mine."

It happens.

If you aren't fairly knowledgeable about racks already, you're best off sticking to one of the two major brands: Yakima or Thule. After all, they became the dominant players in the car-top transport game for the good reason that they both work well. Let's look more closely at your kayak rack. The towers are those posts that extend more or less vertically from your vehicle. They come in pairs, one for each side of your car. They also come in various heights, depending on the profile of your roof. You mean you didn't notice that all vehicle roofs aren't flat? Some cars (regrettably few these days) have rain gutters that extend along both sides of the top above the windows. One style of tower clamps right to these gutters. Another tower style has a broad foot and rests atop the car roof with clamps that extend around and grip the top of the door frame. Still another clamps to the factory-mounted "luggage racks" atop some station wagons and minivans.

The crosspiece, no great surprise, is the horizontal bar that extends from the tower on one side to the tower on the other. The crosspiece actually fits right through the top of the tower and is clamped into place.

The cradle is a U-shaped metal bracket that supports a fabric or rubber "sling" upon which your kayak rests. The cradle is mounted on the crosspiece. If you want to carry a pair of boats, most crosspieces will hold two side-by-side cradles, and the longest crosspieces—which as often as not may protrude well out beyond the sides of your vehicle—could even hold three. It's easier to slide your kayak onto fabric cradles, a plus when loading a kayak by yourself. On the other hand, the rubber cradles don't slip around—which may add a minuscule safety margin when you're on the road, and some paddlers feel that the rubber does a better job of cushioning and protecting the hull. You'll need two sets of cradles, one for the front end and one for the back end.

Fortunately, you (and I) won't have to figure out the proper tower foot, the proper tower height, and the proper crosspiece length. Both Yakima and Thule have installation guides, and all you have to do is look for your vehicle make and model and you'll find the dimensions you need listed in the book.

As much as I would rather not think about this, go ahead and spring for a set of locks. One set of locks will hold the towers to your car and another (usually a cable lock) will hold your boat to the rack. One thief—whom I hope suffers from a disgusting and untreatable itching rash forever—stole the boat in which one of the United States' best paddlers won the U.S. National Championships. The thief took it right off the roof of the paddler's parked car.

At the risk of offending both manufacturers, let me explain that the significant design difference between Yakima and Thule is that Yakima has a round crosspiece while Thule has a square one. This means that parts and accessories are not interchangeable without special adapters. If you have relatives or friends with whom you normally boat, you might lean in the direction of whatever rack they have. On the other hand, my son has a Yakima rack, I have a Thule rack on my old hippie boating bus, and I have a Yakima rack on my four-by-four. One friend has a Barracrafter.

Let the shop set up your rack, fitting it to your vehicle and showing you how to adjust and fasten the towers. Beforehand, you might want to mount eyebolts on your front and rear bumpers. A kayak properly lashed into the rack cradles is perfectly stable. I know people who have dropped their kayaks onto the cradles and then absentmindedly driven off and onto the freeway—without losing their boats. Despite all the claims of absolute boat security and safety, I still tie a line from the bow of my kayak to the eyebolt in the front bumper, and do the same on the stern.

You can get by with a set of gutter clamps bolted to a 2 x 4, with maybe a little rug for padding. That's the classic homemade canoe rack. And for most canoes, resting upside down on their gunwales, it works pretty well. But kayaks don't have a broad, flat surface on which to rest. If you cinch down the lines holding your kayak to a flat bar—such as a 2 x 4—you can stress-crack the hull of a fiberglass boat or deform the hull of a plastic boat.

Ropes work perfectly well to lash a boat onto your rack. I'd suggest a soft synthetic, such as Dacron or nylon, just to protect the finish of your boat. Better, though, is the synthetic and low-stretch fabric webbing offered by both Thule and Yakima. Loop the webbing through the slots on both sides of the cradle, and cinch it down snugly through a cam fastener. I suspect that if the rack would hold to the gutters, you could lift your vehicle with those straps, but I'm not about to check.

If you have a pickup, look at the rack systems from Jemb or Rail 'n Rack.

LOADING YOUR KAYAK

Loading a kayak, if you're substantially shorter than your vehicle, can be a struggle. There is at least one commercial self loader—a Solo—for canoes and kayaks, which involves a vertical post topped by a free-turning tee that can be clamped to your trailer hitch. Lift one end of your kayak to the cross tee, temporarily lash your kayak to the tee, and then lift the bow and walk it around to the front, where you can lower it into the cradles atop your vehicle.

A boat cart is nearly indispensable in moving your kayak to the water's edge. This Farring-ton Chariot comes with a long tongue and special clamp that allows you to trail it behind your bicycle. For a double boat, what's more appropriate than a tandem bicycle? Look for a cart that is over-engineered for strength and durability, will fold up to fit inside your kayak, and has wheels large enough and wide enough to roll over bumps and soft spots.

Another method for loading a kayak was demonstrated to me by an old codger with a pop-top VW camper and a heavy boat that I would have been challenged to load. He did it without breathing hard. His technique was simplicity itself. He had a 3-inch pipe, about 3 feet longer than his car was tall, with a 3-foot horizontal extension at the top. Think of a tower crane at a construction site, and you'll get the idea. He had a ring with a short rod, which he inserted into the jack opening on the side of his VW. The long pipe fit into the ring and would swivel within it. A second ring clamped to the crosspiece of his rack. He suspended a block and tackle from the end of the extension atop the pipe, and would hook this into a sling within the boat cockpit. He could easily lift the boat with the mechanical advantage of the blocks, and could then swivel the pipe to place his kayak right over the cradle. The parts could be quickly disassembled and fit within the camper (the long pipe on the rack), and off he would go.

These methods will get your boat from your home to the launch site. You and a friend can lift your kayak with the tee-grips at the bow and stern and easily pack an empty boat down to the water's edge. Kayaks aren't shaped for a balanced load, however. You'll kind of shuffle, and tilt to one side, and if the trek is more than a few dozen meters, you may well want to stop and switch hands.

BOAT CARTS

Humping a kayak from where you are to where you want to launch can be a strain on your back, your legs, and your patience. Unfortunately, there's just no easy way to carry a kayak—empty or loaded—for more than a few steps. Fortunately, you can just let the good times roll by resting your kayak on wheels.

For long carries—or if, like me, you live in the Pacific Northwest where kayaks are welcome aboard ferries—you might want to investigate one of a half dozen or so small folding boat carts. Basically, these are a pair of wheels, a small frame incorporating a simple cradle, and webbing to lash the kayak to the cradle. Fasten the boat cart just behind the cockpit, pick up the bow tee-grip, and take your boat for an easy walk. My Farrington Chariot can also mount a long tongue that fastens to the seat post of my mountain bike for close-to-home shuttles.

Boat carts take terrible abuse, even though you wouldn't think so. If the cart is not strong, it will fail at the worst possible moment. But then again, that's the reality of many machines.

Air Yedo. For moving any distance over reasonably good ground, balance your boat on a center-mounted cart such as the Air Yedo by Paddleboy Designs. It breaks down into a couple of aluminum struts and two 10-inch wheels that will fit through most hatches or cockpits. There's even one model that will hook onto a bike for moving to the water.

Seattle Sports. Faced with soft sand, loose gravel, or sloppy going? Pick up the optional 8-inch-wide beach kit wheel for Seattle Sports' Deluxe Beach Kit. It "floats" over a lot of soft going. Packing is more problematic, but you can flip the cart upside down on your rear deck and paddle with it parked there. The Roleez Canoe & Kayak Cart (not shown) has a pair of wide flotation tires that gives you a smooth roll over soft going, and can be parked upside down on your rear deck.

Kayak Kaddy. If you're cramped for room (or weight) and are moving on manicured lawns or well-maintained trails, the Hardy Kayak Kaddy is minimalism at its best. It's a stainless steel axle linking two 6-inch wheels and supporting a small vee notch that grips one end of your boat. Pop the wheels off, and the center slips through a 2- by 4-inch opening.

CHAPTER TWENTY-TWO

Let's Go Voyaging

You've been busy up to now. You've practiced the basic kayaking strokes, you've learned fairly well how to get yourself out of trouble, you've figured out how to find your way from place to place, and you've even given some thought to how to paddle with kids. But so far, all your paddling has been in this sheltered bay. You're ready now for a more adventurous trip.

Let's put it all together and take a trip out to the islands. If you want, we'll take it easy. No driving a great distance, no attempt to see who can carry the most, and no sprinting for the buoys. Just an outing on a pleasant day.

I'll warn you, though. I'm going to follow you. You're the leader on this trip. Are you ready? You've already done the basics. You've checked the weather, you have charts and a tide table, and you've looked to see that we have rescue equipment (including a spare paddle) and first-aid supplies. Great. I noticed that you even checked that I have my PFD, and I'm glad to see that you wanted me to wear it rather than just stash it away.

LAUNCHING

Starting as we did in a sheltered bay, launching was simple. Paddling isn't always get in and go, though. We could have been on an exposed beach, with waves crashing down on the packed sand. Sure, there are paddlers who feel that you should be able to leap off tall rocks into the foam, and others who demand that you should be able to smash through 6-foot surf on your way to the open water, but I'd just as soon sit in the sun and enjoy the day. Time may come, though, when we don't have an option.

First of all, let's put a few parameters on what constitutes paddling surf. If the surf is less than a couple of feet high and just slides up on sloping sand, your launch is going to be more on the simple side of the equation. "Simple" is a relative term, however. We're talking about a huge coil of cyclical force rolling across the ocean with more energy than a schoolroom full of second-graders. The smallest wave can chew you up and spit you out. Let's make this personal: The smallest wave can completely control me and my paddling skills if I let it. Illustration: I launched at a mid–Puget Sound island/park heading for a ferry landing where friends waited. A ferry heading in the same direction kicked up a wake of no more than 3 feet (as far off the channel as I was), and I sprinted to get atop this wave and hitch a free ride. I was riding just over the crest, hula-hipped into the face of the wave, and with a high brace nuzzling just over the crest and into the tight water of the back. There was spray flying back from the bow, and the boat was shivering in pure joy. So how do you get off the front of a wave? The surf and I were heading for Manchester, and 45 degrees away was Southworth and my friends. After two or three eternities of high anxiety, I just tossed in a couple of back strokes and slithered up over the crest onto the placid back of the beast and that was that. Those few moments on the front of that wave lasted a very, very long time!

On a rising tide, launching is even simpler. Set your boat down just higher than the dark mark of the incoming water and wiggle into your boat. As the tide climbs, the water will start to work under your boat and soon you'll be afloat. Sand appears to be the neatest surface, but take a little care. Each grain grabs hold of your hull, and it is hard to break loose. The easiest beach has sand the size of pea gravel, with each little pebble acting like a ball bearing.

For that matter, the flatter the beach, the easier it is to break off and go floating. On a steep beach, where the angle between the beach and the water cranks over to the higher digit side, you'll end up with your bow in the water and your stern high and dry. So you'll be balancing on the sharp ends of your boat with 71 percent of the world's surface tugging at you, and you'll be rocking back and forth—stable you won't be. The steeper the beach, the more of an angle you're going to have to put into the alignment of your boat. You'll be playing a delicate balancing game, though. You want to move straight off the beach, you want to move directly into the waves, and you want to be at the best angle to get your bow and stern off the beach at the same time. As with many aspects of the water world, you're going to end up compromising among the three different demands.

SURF

If the surf is from 2 feet to about 5 feet high, you can get off the beach with care and planning. With smaller waves the odds are you'll rise up and over each crest. In that mid-range you're likely to have a wave slosh over you, and if you're not careful, that could be two or three waves.

To work our way out through a set of waves, we try to hit each wave as close to perpendicular to its path as possible. Remember to keep paddling clear through the wave. If it looks like you'll get spray in your face, lean forward and drive through the froth. PHOTO COURTESY MARK W. LISK/AIRE

If the surf is 6 feet high or more—well, kick back and enjoy the show. Launching your boat isn't worth risking your hide and hair.

How can you determine the height of the surf? Go stand by the waterline. If you can just see over the tops of the waves, the surf would be about 5½ feet high if you are a 6-footer or 5 feet high if you stand 5-foot-6. If you can easily see over the waves, kneel down. That puts your eyes about 3½ to 4 feet up. If you can still see over the waves, plant your rear on the beach and look out—your eyes are now around 2½ feet above the water.

Take a look at the surf. Some waves will march up to the shore and seem to let the top of the wave spill down the front face in a long, controlled slide. These are the easiest to work through. Other waves seem to curl over and let the top of the wave fall or collapse in the front of the wave. These are harder to manage. What you'll face in these short, steep waves is water falling directly upon you, and as you struggle up through the foam, you'll wade right into the circular energy form of the wave body.

Surf is not uniform. You might have bad dumping surf at one end of a crescent of beach and small spilling surf at the other end. If that's the case, I know where I'm going to launch. For that matter, doesn't it look like the surf is only ripples up there beyond the point, where the kelp seems to form a breakwater and the little

If crossing a significant surf line is in your future, the first thing you need is patience. Wait until you see a pattern in the waves and are able to predict the least aggressive set. The second thing you need is commitment. Once you decide to go, just put your head down and drive through the waves. Hesitation in the surf is not an option. PHOTO COURTESY FEATHERCRAFT

offshore rocks break up the oncoming energy patterns of the waves? Take your kayak in that direction—a carry on the beach is preferable to a thrash in the surf. Also look beyond the immediate surf line. Is there a clear passage you might follow once you're through the first waves?

We'll start our passage through the surf by getting in the slosh just at the beach line, with paddle in hand and our spray skirt already around our midsection. Watch for a pattern to develop in the size of the waves coming in, and ready yourself. Some people count the seconds between each swoosh of water rumbling up the beach, while others look for the visual pattern of towering waves versus waves that are smaller and more friendly. Your goal is to be in your boat, your spray skirt snapped into place, and your paddle driving just after the largest waves in a set have slid up the beach. Keep your hands out in the low-gear end of your blade, and drive ahead with plenty of power. The first time you try this, you'll want to keep the slop out of your boat and you may try to get in too far up the beach . . . which means you'll sit there and try to scoot along while the beach holds you firmly. Until the big wave comes and grabs you. Commit yourself with vigor and élan.

If you are high and dry, try scooting yourself forward with each wavelet that piddles away under you. Use a hand on one side and the knuckles of your other hand wrapped around your paddle on the opposite side. Yes, you can lean back and really pry on your paddle, but if you do so, think about how much you paid for your lightweight cruising stick. Now, if you'd only asked for more heft on the blade . . . ? Use your hands instead.

With luck, you'll slosh through the foam and maybe have to climb a swell or two. The idea is to charge at right angles (or perpendicular) into the oncoming waves. This approach may or may not put you at right angles to the beach. Push your weight aft to bring up your bow as you start into a swell, and then shove forward as you pass over the top of the wave.

Well, you made it unscathed, but I didn't. I'm going to get popped by a small wave—one of those 2- to 3-footers that were lurking. I'll plant my paddle blade in the most solid part of the wave I can find and pull myself forward (with my chin down). One school of thought is to shut your eyes and hold your paddle over your head. This method depends on the same kind of aid that parted the Red Sea, and most of us do not have that kind of communication system or influence. With one of the big graybacks, your best bet is to hunch forward (to prevent the wave energy from grabbing your chest) and power ahead with everything you have. A 5-footer will thump you hard, and in all honesty you can get a bit disoriented under the froth of a breaking wave. The absolutely worst thing you can do is cower down and hope nothing will happen if the wave doesn't notice you. It doesn't even know you exist to begin with. A wave is merely programmed to whoosh up the beach. If it grabs you and flings you over on your back and drags you upside down up the beach, it isn't even aware of it.

Many novice paddlers fall victim to one of two basic mistakes when first attempting to launch into surf. Fortunately, there are remedies for each one.

Mistake number one is to paddle through a small set of waves and then sit up to relax. There's a bigger set all primed to grab you.

What if you don't have time to get your spray deck snapped down before the wash from a wave grabs you and you're willy-nilly in the soup? Go for it! If you don't do anything, you're in major trouble. That's the ultimate rule in paddling. If you're doing *something*, even the wrong thing, you can always correct yourself. Your strokes will help stabilize your boat. If you do nothing, you will wallow in disaster. You have no stability, no power, no maneuverability . . . and no chance.

You might have heard that you should deliberately roll your boat and let the bottom take the full force of a dumping surf. Right. That puts your head hanging down from the other side of your boat, and the reason the surf is dumping is that the wave has tripped on the shallows. So guess what part of you is closest

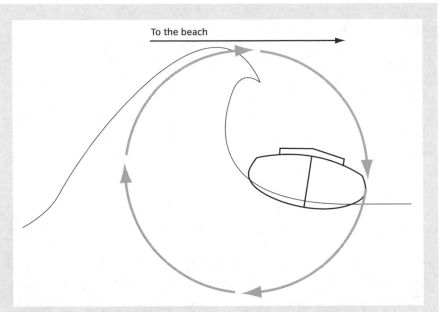

To the beach

A wave isn't a mass of water rushing horizontally across the liquid surface. Rather, it is caused by a rolling cylinder of energy in which individual particles of water rise and fall vertically as the circle of energy passes through them. If the energy is "tripped" as it collides with a steep beach or a reef, it cannot lift the water particles to fill its circle, and it collapses—and in collapsing creates a breaking or "dumping" wave. These can be quite dangerous and should be avoided by all but experts, who should have enough sense to stay away anyway.

to the bottom? In my opinion, if you find yourself upside down with anything less than a bombproof roll—and if you had one, I'd be at your knee, learning from you—try a fast roll followed by a wet exit. If you can hold onto the offshore end of your boat, great—it will be easier to work it inshore. But don't get your hand tangled in the grab loop, and for your own sake don't get between your boat and the shore. You're going to feel like a lost sock in a clothes dryer, turning around and around, and you definitely don't want a ton or more of sodden kayak smashing down on you.

Now for mistake number two, which may be even bigger than mistake number one. It is a lot easier to get off a beach than it is to get back on. Where will you land? Waves are a creature of wind, and if our destination is downwind, you might as well figure that we will be landing with the wind at our backs. I hope that you looked at your chart and found us a place to land out of the prevailing wind and waves.

LEEWARD AND WINDWARD

I'll pop in another couple of nautical terms you should know; they both refer to the position of an object in relationship to you. Anything *windward* is upwind of your boat, or in the direction from which the wind and the weather are coming. Anything downwind of your kayak is *leeward*.

Remember, these are only directions relative to you and are not locations.

When you're going to land, it is usually better to do so on a shore that is windward of you. The wind is blowing from the land, over the shore, and out across the water. As you paddle into the wind and get closer to the shore, wave action will usually decrease. If you paddle downwind toward a shore that is leeward of you, the wind will impart more energy to the wave system and the wave action at the beach will be more intense.

It gets confusing if you forget that "windward" and "leeward" are only as significant as their relationship to you. If you are on the island of Hawaii, the "windward shore" is upwind from where you are standing. Keep the wind in your face and walk across the island until you come to the shore, and you'll find a shore battered by high surf and wind. If you are in your kayak just a quarter mile farther upwind, the relative direction of that shore is dramatically altered. From your kayak, that shore is now described as a "lee" shore and lies leeward of you. It hasn't changed—you've moved. Now its position, relative to the wind you're experiencing, is different.

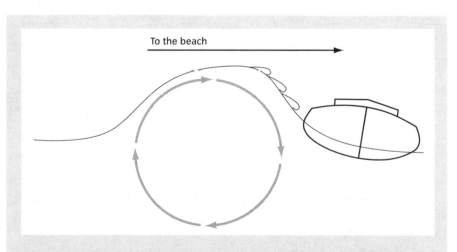

To the beach

Some spume will spill down the front of a spilling wave, but a kayak may glide easily up the slope of the wave's face as the circle of energy passes under the kayaker. A small spilling wave offers a fun and quick ride to the beach.

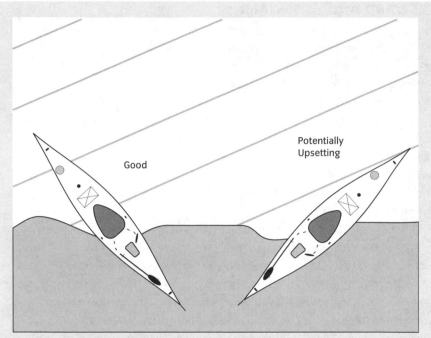

Launching in a surf is a challenge. While it is often easier to launch at an angle of 45 degrees or more to the shoreline (depending on the steepness of the beach), it is even more important to launch the bow into the oncoming waves. Don't try to launch parallel to the waves, where you can get caught in a trough. Likewise, it is more important to land with the surf than to attempt to cut across the waves for a better approach to the steepness of the beach. Use your head—like most aspects of kayaking, launching and landing in a surf mean balancing *all* the needs.

As a rule of thumb, it is easier to land on a shore from which the wind blows rather than on a shore toward which the wind blows.

Is there a protected beach from which to launch, and will there be a protected beach upon which to land? Finding those are part of the planning process. And we don't have to be in the wilderness to take advantage of them. I like to paddle around Lake Union in the heart of Seattle, which offers a banquet of houseboats, shipyards, parks, and commercial fishboat marinas as well as yacht races. I can launch from an exposed point where I get bounced around or in a sheltered nook that is as quiet as my bay.

COLLIDING CURRENTS

You lead me down the bay and through the narrow entrance that dumps into Puget Sound. It's a couple of hours after high tide, and the ebb is in steady flow so we make good time. However, you tell me the water looks all swirly right in the entrance. Good call—it is. You're paddling right into the confluence of two tidal flows, and you'll find swirling and disturbed currents where they meet. You could find some good chop and sharply defined eddy lines. Be ready to brace. You'll also see some waves reflect off the northern point and set up sharp, peaked waves that seem to rise and fall in jagged mountains. You might see these off any point, caused by the reflected waves moving in and out of sync with the wind-driven waves. The reflected waves pass through the pattern of the wind-driven waves, and where they coincide, special waves called *clapotis* can seem to explode from the water's surface. Some folks might choose to sneak along the beach to miss the major collision of the two tidal streams. Beware, though, because that might put you in the surf zone below the confluence. You'll have to call this on a situation-by-situation basis.

Where would you look for wildlife? At the break between two kinds of habitat. That's true for birds, that's true for elk, that's true for whales, and that's true for fish. All of these creatures live in one habitat and hunt in the other. The confluence of tidal currents is a pretty good spot to fish, although you need to consider bottom structure and water temperature, too. Most bottom-dwelling fish—including the whole family of rockfish that are the best eating of any marine creature—don't like to battle swift currents, but they do like new crops of food to come drifting in like clouds of manna.

RIDING THE CURRENTS

We're still in a narrow channel, and the current here can build to a brisk 4 or 5 knots. But that's in the middle, and we could probably sneak back against it by working along the shore. However, I hope you looked at the chart before leading me this way. Right in the narrowest part of the channel ahead, a big ridge sticks up out of the seafloor. While it doesn't pose any danger to us, or even a big ship, it does block the current stream—which in turn can create a series of breaking waves called an overfall. I'd just as soon skirt by them.

THE NEAREST SHELTER

I have my hand-bearing compass out, taking sights, and you drop back to ask what I'm doing. Simple enough. If anything goes wrong, I want to know the direction in which to paddle to the most available safe landing. Not necessarily the nearest—if I had to paddle 2 miles to a protected beach right into the teeth of the current, it could take me a couple of hours. With the current, wind, and waves at my back, however, I could cover 6 or 7 miles easily in just an hour.

Assuming fog closed in, which is possible any month of the year, I know which

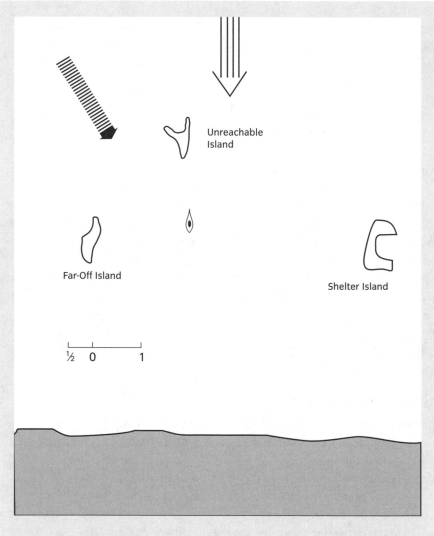

Unreachable
Island

Far-Off Island

Shelter Island

½ 0   1

Distance is a relative term in the winds and currents of any large body of water. If the arrow at the top of the drawing represents a 15-knot wind, the paddler will find it difficult to make good the mile and a half to the nearest shore of Unreachable Island—with its only sheltering bay open to the wind and current.

If the bold arrow represents a 2-knot current, then it will take at least an hour and a half to reach Unreachable, and with the wind that's probably closer to three hours. Far-Off is only 2 miles away but would take at least two hours to reach at a paddling speed of 3 knots. The mainland, at the bottom of the sketch, is an unprotected shore open to the full force of the wind-driven waves. Shelter Island, 3½ miles away, can be reached in forty-five minutes with the paddling speed added to the current.

way to head to get to the nearest landing. It's a habit I fell into long ago. You're not worried, because you know I'm taking care of this. But on the other hand, what if we get separated in the fog?

WAVES

Sliding down the front of a big roller is an intimidating experience, and one that will test your bracing and other boat-handling skills. No matter how you cut it, a cruising kayak is not an ideal surfing machine. You're also offering the wind even more distance in which to build up the waves and surf. While crashing through the surf on a lee shore ranges between embarrassing and dangerous, it may be preferable to dumping far at sea. Scooting right next to an islet, cranking around into a sharp turn across the eddy line behind it, and then making a soft landing is . . . well, it sounds easier than it is. Ocean rollers are not necessarily a hazard. The period of the wave is so long that you'll have a hard time really looking at it. You'll be in a trough and the horizon will be close in, and as the grayback passes underneath you, the horizon will magically spread out. You may not even feel the slow climb and dip as it passes, and you'll barely register that sometimes you'll see your fellow paddlers nearby and sometimes you won't.

Think of a big hair curler just rolling around in the open water. The energy pattern in a wave looks something like that, with the energy coil moving along and the water staying horizontally in place. Water at the leading edge of the wave will be forced down, and water on the back of the wave will be lifted up, but you won't see a lot of horizontal displacement. Problems arise when the water is shallow enough so that the bottom of the energy coil trips on the seafloor. The wave

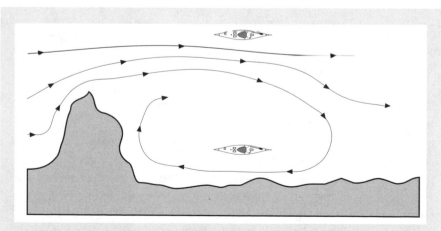

Don't fight the full force of the current in the main channel. Work along the shore, using the back currents in the eddies to make your passage easier and quicker.

Flying across the face of a wave can be an exhilarating ride, with a bit of experience and gear. There's a whole school of paddlers that take to waves just like snow skiers take to moguls, and for the same exciting rush. This paddler is leaning slightly into the wave, which gives him a more stable ride, and is reaching over the top of the wave with his paddle if he needs to brace in the less aerated water behind the foaming and unstable crest. He's also wearing a helmet, mandatory for playing in the surf, and a paddle leash secures his paddle to his boat. You can see his knees hooked under straps, securing him on the boat. In a conventional kayak, the paddler would brace his knees and thighs against pads mounted under the deck on each side of the front of the kayak. PHOTO COURTESY OCEAN KAYAK

runs out of water needed for the front end to dip and the back to lift, and instead of a smooth pattern moving along, we suddenly have a breaking wave with the front face eroding away.

Our plan is to turn west at the bottom of this channel and head up to a secluded little anchorage for lunch. Good plan, but as we make the turn from this channel into the other one, we'll have the current right on our bow. We could charge straight into it for three hours, or until the tide changes, but neither of us wants to work that hard. You cling tightly to one shore. Again, a good call. The current will be the strongest in the middle and in the deepest channel—so let's avoid those places. Instead, we'll sneak up behind the points jutting out into the channel and take advantage of the eddies behind each. We'll have to be on our toes, because we'll have to cross those lines where the main current is flowing one way and the back current of the eddy the other. With plenty of speed and caution, we'll slide right through. Plus, since we're ready to stabilize our kayaks with a bracing stroke, we'll be alert enough to avoid the situations in which one is required. We'll look more closely at eddies in a couple of paragraphs.

FERRIES

This channel arcs in a graceful curve through most of its length, and right now you have us on the outside of the turn. And to the outside is where the current will be directed. If we stay on this shore, we'll have the current pushing us right into the beach . . . not to mention we'll have to overpower the current even to move ahead. Why work that hard? We'll have to ferry across to the other shore. We could wait until we pass by this little cloud of islands, but maybe we should share the work of crossing the channel with the natural assistance of the eddies. If we cross behind the islands, we'll manage either to be in an eddy or at least to be sheltered from the full thrust of the current as long as we are in the islands. We won't have to work as hard, and we won't be shoved back down-channel.

Our plan is to ferry over behind one island, paddle up its eddy as far as we need, and then ferry across the narrow cut between that island and the next. River paddlers learn about eddies right away, because that's how we use the incredible power of the river to move from place to place. So now we're tucked in behind a big rock at one end of an islet, and it's time to really understand eddies.

Look right off the edge of the rock. There's a swirly line in the water peeling off from the rock. If we had the wings of a seagull, we could look down on this channel and see the water pouring out the lower end. The islet we're sheltered behind breaks up the smooth flow of the water and directs some of the current to each side. The current doesn't immediately close around the islet. In fact, it takes quite a distance for the two pieces of current to join again after being split. You don't end up with a true hole in the water behind the islet, but you do end up with water flowing back into this area from downstream where the current streams join together. The water molecules might see the hole, but it takes them a little time to peel off from the main current and work back into the hole. As a result, you literally have a reverse current flowing into the hole behind an obstruction.

At the same time, since water likes to cling to itself, you have two currents in opposing directions rubbing up against each other. I've seen the wall created between strong currents rise to an abrupt 6 or 8 inches, which is nearly cockpit-high on a cruising kayak. From a cockpit that wall looks huge!

What happens when you attempt to cross this line? One current will grab your bow and send it one way while the other current will send your stern in the opposite direction. If you're not prepared, the sudden jerk of the water can spill you right over!

Look just beyond the paddler, right where he is looking. Water is pouring over a rock barely awash, creating a swirling hole on the lee side of the rock. Currents flow in reverse along the edges of that hole. If you cross that line, and it is easy to see, do so with speed and with a brace ready, as the currents will grab at your stability. PHOTO COURTESY OCEAN KAYAK

How do you get across safely?

Your first weapon is speed. Hit the line with vigor! Keep moving!

Your second weapon is angle. Depending on the relative velocity of the two current streams, you want to pierce the line at an angle of 45 to 70 degrees to the outside current. If you try too steep an angle—if you try to just ease across the line—you'll get tossed back. If you try too broad an angle—say, straight across the eddy line—your bow will be twisted about and you'll head down-current. If you mean to do that, that's all right, of course. This is called a peel-out, whether you do it on a river or on the ocean. But if your goal is to ferry across the current to the next islet and eddy, you have to be able to hold your angle.

Your third weapon is your lean and bracing stroke. At the least, cross the eddy line flat and paddle on your down-current side as you cross the line. Even better, tilt your boat a bit so that you're showing a bit of bottom to the outside current. You'll skid over the grasping fingers of the current rather than dipping your up-current gunwale and letting the sea get hold of your edge. If it does and you can't rock back in a great down-current brace, you're about to become a swimmer. (I learned that in more than one river.)

That was some hard work. I'm going to rest for a second by sliding up on this kelp. Kelp is neat. It works just like the old fishing-boat trick of putting a bag soaked in thick oil upwind of a vessel. Oil leaking from the bag would coat the water surface and quash turbulent waves. Kelp, a more environmentally safe substance, has the same effect with its thick fronds.

Ferrying is not easy work. And I'm tired of trying to keep my boat on the right heading. What I'll do is lean the boat over a bit on the down-current side to change its underbody shape. Each stroke I use to drive the boat forward will then

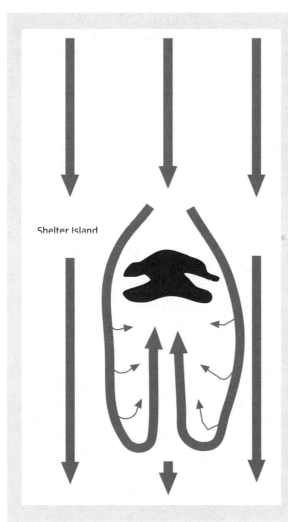

Shelter Island

The current splits around Shelter Island, as shown by the arrows, and in doing so creates an eddy behind the island. The flow of water within the eddy is opposite the main current and can actually form a line where the opposing water flows pass. While the eddy can shelter you from a current, it can also be difficult to cross into—a skill you need to develop.

slightly turn the kayak's bow into the current. As I glide ahead, with the wind off my bow, the combination of the wind and waves will attempt to push my bow down-current. As a result, I'll go along in a straight line without paddling a lot of corrective strokes and putting a lot of strain on one arm. What I've done by lean-ing my boat is to create an underbody in which one side becomes straighter—or nearer the keel line—while the other side becomes more curved as the gunwale is lowered into the water line. Think of a capital letter D. Your kayak will turn toward the straight side of the D and away from the curved side.

WIND

As we come clear of the islands, the wind is right on our bows. Wind is no friend to the paddler on the water. Few of us can paddle for any distance into the teeth of a 15-knot wind, and once the wind starts knocking the tops off the waves, we're in difficulty. Sure, master mariners know how to cope with this, but the rule of prudent seamanship is to avoid as many challenges as possible. Experienced kayakers are humble when they venture onto the water, and for good reason. We're small, we have limited stamina, and we're fragile.

If we have to climb up the face of each wave, and then get stopped by a blast of wind at the top, we're going to tire pretty quickly. Let's head to the shore that will give us the most protection. But if we went right for shore, we'd be in the trough of the waves, and we'd not only be rocked about but we'd also be carried down-channel by the current. After all, the tide hasn't changed yet. Instead, we'll turn so that we're at an angle of around 45 degrees to the wind and waves. I haven't been saying all our maneuvers tie together for no reason. We're ferrying across the wind and waves. At some point we'll find wind and waves that aren't rolling out of the same point, and then we'll have to angle across the waves and accept the wind. What we've done, in effect, is to take a long switchback across the face of the waves instead of a short and steep climb. Quartering doesn't work, though, if it merely leads you farther out to sea and away from shelter.

A SHELTERED LANDING

As much as possible, you keep us in the shelter of small islands and points as we work up-current, and you've found us a tiny bay on the lee side of an island in which to land. And I'm proud of you. We're coming into a steep little beach, but one that trails off from a relatively steep sand and gravel surface into a very grad-ually sloped mud surface. At dead low tide we would have faced a long trudge through the goo.

How did you know about the slope? Simple enough. You just looked at the depth numbers on the chart. The numbers changed quickly near shore, but then stayed the same for a long and tapering distance. On the chart, the drying por-tions of the beach were marked in green, and you could easily pick out the poten-tial problem. The chart also indicated the *sndy* areas of sand and the *mdy* areas of mud. You picked that up from Chart No. 1, the key to all our navigation charts.

Landing on an Exposed Beach

I'm glad you planned ahead, because I hate landing on an exposed beach. First of all, you can't see much from the outside of the surf line. You can't see if you'll be landing on a smooth beach, rocks, or logs. That's right, logs. Which could be churning around at the surf line! I told you I don't like this. We could be faced with spilling waves or a harsh, dumping surf. Your first option and your best option—okay, I'm biased—is to go somewhere else.

I don't think just stooging around outside the surf line waiting for conditions to improve is a viable option for cruising kayakers. If you're waiting for the current to slow coming out of a bay at the turn of a tide, or overfalls to subside in a tidal race, then yes, you have a point. But wind-driven waves on a beach probably have more endurance than you do.

Heave to (that has nothing to do with seasickness—it means to turn your bow into the wind and rest while you more or less hold your position) and let's con-sider our options.

We might not be able to see over the backs of the waves as they advance toward the shore, but we do have the tools to give us a reasonably accurate pic-ture of what's happening at or beyond the wave break: our charts and our tide tables.

As you remember, a wave is a circular pattern of energy rolling through the water. When it runs into the bottom, it trips—with the release of all the energy imparted to it by the wind. If the bottom slopes very gently, the energy of the wave is going to stumble along and dissipate slowly. Water will spill off the top and front of the wave in a rather gentle break. If the bottom shelves rapidly, if it is steep, the energy of the wave is going to trip as it abruptly hits the seafloor, and the wave is going to come apart with sound and fury.

How are we going to know the bottom profile? Look at the chart. If we have a long, shallow gradient working into the beach, we're probably going to have a spilling-type wave. If we have a bottom identified as mud or sand, we're probably going to have a spilling-type wave. If we have a bay with outlying rocks or reefs that can trip a wave, we're likely to find protected waters inside. That's also an alert: Rocks, like toadstools, rarely appear alone; an outlying reef or rocky islet may indicate more rocks within the bay. Check the tide tables. Most sandy or muddy bays will have a gently sloping bottom, with steeper inclines at the beach line. If we land during the lower part of the tidal cycle, we'll be on the flatter bottom rather than the steeper beach. For that matter, if we land lower on the beach profile, we'll have less chance of coming ashore on or in the driftwood—which can include logs.

On the other side of the coin, if we have an abrupt transition from deep water to a very narrow shallow zone (the blue area on most charts), we can be suspicious of the potential of breaking waves. If the cove bottom near the shore is identified as rocky, or we see the symbols for rock along the intertidal zone (the green area on most charts), we can suppose the beach profile is steeper. Yes, you can land on a steeper, rocky beach, but you face the risk of sliding back down the beach into the next incoming wave. Lee Moyers, an outstanding paddler as well as kayak designer, puts the best face on approaching such a beach. He calls them not so much a challenge for the paddler as a great photo opportunity for friends safely on the beach.

The chart and a little common sense offer other safe landing hints. If the beach is an absolutely straight line, the bottom profile is absolutely uniform, and the waves are coming in perfectly perpendicular to the beach, there's little to choose from. That's highly unlikely in the real world. We'll probably want to land in a cove or bay, which from overhead will look much like a crescent. The further the crescent shape of the bay is carved into the shoreline, the more likely we'll find smaller or more gentle surf near the outside edges, or horns. The waves will come straight into the center of the crescent, unabated. However, the waves will curve from their straight-in approach to slide up the side beaches, and this will dissipate some of the energy.

We're more likely to see the waves approach the overall beach at an angle, however slight. All other things being equal, the end of the crescent that makes the waves turn the most will have the least surf.

These are all hints and indications rather than absolute rules. You have to use a lot of common sense, a good deal of forethought, and the ability to first plan for alternative landing sites and the self-confidence to look at a particular beach and say, "Nah, that's not for me today."

After all that, I have to confess that with a proper boat and the right beach, surfing is simply a kick. Kayak touring is the water equivalent of cross-country skiing; surfing is running the slalom gates.

When I said that waiting around wasn't much of an option, I meant just splashing around with no plan and hoping. You *should* be patient. Come in reasonably close to the surf line (go ahead, back in if you are nervous and have your getaway ready) and focus on the pattern of waves surging to the beach. Your plan is to come in with the smaller waves that seem to follow in the shadow of the big guys.

Landing on any beach is a compromise. Your ultimate approach will be determined by waves, wind, obstacles, and the configuration of the beach itself. With all that on your mind as you approach the shore, you also have to remember that the beach slopes down to the water's edge. If you come straight into the beach, you'll have to drive your bow up that slope, and you'll spend at least a few moments with your bow on the land and your stern bobbing in the sea—with you suspended in the air between the two. If you can, approach the beach at an angle for a softer and less wobbly landing. PHOTO COURTESY SPLASHDANCE

Surfers like to fly down the front of the waves, their bodies arched in the curl and their smiles primed for any passing camera. I, however, have no desire to send 17 feet or more of cruising kayak down the front of a wave! Earlier in this book we found that some boats are made to turn and some are made to go straight—well, kayaks go straight and surfboards turn. The front of a wave is possibly not the best kayaking environment.

Really put your muscles to the paddle and try to climb high on the back of one of the smaller waves as you approach the shore. Too far forward and you run the risk of being part of the falling water on the front. Too far back and the backwash will pull you into the following wave. Those two dragons should be enough to keep you on the wave's back—but the fact remains that even with a wave nipping at your heels, you won't go much faster than 5 or 6 knots, while a wave can double that velocity. Ride one wave as long as you can, and as it surges ahead of you, pick up the next. You could very well ride through the surf on these waves and then slog through the slop to shore.

You want to come in at right angles to the motion of the waves. At the same time, you want to hit the beach at an angle. Remember, the beach slants up at an

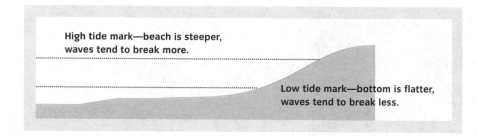

High tide mark—beach is steeper, waves tend to break more.

Low tide mark—bottom is flatter, waves tend to break less.

angle to the water surface (even though the water doesn't appear very level in the surf zone). By coming in at an angle, you decrease the apparent steepness of the beach and you'll be less likely to hang up suspended by your bow and stern. For that matter, you'll be less likely to bury your bow in the beach and have the next wave slew you about and send you tumbling.

A very experienced paddler—or one who has no choice but to attempt a landing on a hostile shore—can angle across the waves to a fast ride ashore. Work your way into the trough and turn until you're just about parallel to the movement of the waves. Paddle forward to hold plenty of speed (and if possible away from the first break of the waves), and as the wave starts to pick you up, use a stern rudder to angle your bow down and across the wave toward shore. Don't come straight in! If you bury your bow, you face at best an uncontrolled broach and possibly even a tip stand that leads to a flip. This can be anything from very uncomfortable to very dangerous.

Now convert that stern rudder to a low brace (remember how these moves work together). If the wave face is steep, lean into the wave and grab a high brace with your paddle high into the foam. The wave will eventually break, but a good brace should keep you surging toward shore.

If your angle allows it, drive right up on the beach. The backwash from each wave will attempt to suck you back out, so ready yourself for a quick exit and a full-muscled tug of your boat up the beach. The waves will chase you, demanding another chance at you and your boat.

Here's another landing technique. I've never done this, but I've seen it done. *Gingerly* back toward the beach. This is one of the times you should have your rudder or skeg out of the water! Work your way in toward shore slowly and carefully, looking back over your shoulder. What's the advantage of sneaking up to the shore this way? If things look bad, you're in the position for a quick getaway. I wouldn't do it in any degree of surf, say over 4 feet, and I'm not certain I would do it then, but some paddlers like this technique.

When the best-laid plans run afoul of reality, you need a great brace, the confidence to keep paddling . . . and sometimes the knowledge of how to swim in surf. Kayaking, for the most part, is a reflective, contemplative passion allowing you to choose the excitement of the day or to avoid it. But life is uncertain, and you should have alternative courses of action open to you. PHOTO COURTESY BRIAN HENRY/OCEAN RIVER SPORTS

In the Water

What follows is the information you don't need, about an event that will never happen to you under circumstances that will never come together. It's a kind of Halloween tale, and though you may find it scary, it shouldn't frighten you off the water. Paddling a touring kayak is 90 percent or more preparation and a small bit of reaction to changing circumstances. With forethought, caution, and a healthy respect for the environment in which we play, you may never find yourself in a situation more uncomfortable than wet feet and a damp behind. But in the worst of all worlds . . .

Okay, so something went wrong and you've had an upsetting experience. After this is all over, you should sit down with a cup of something warm and attempt to reconstruct the series of events that put you in the water. In doing so, you'll discover alternative courses of action that might have avoided the flip. But for now you're in the water—in the surf zone or in water churned by big waves hurrying to join the surf—and you've misplaced your kayak.

Be very clear on this. What we're talking about is a very narrow set of circumstances. You should be paddling with someone else, and that other person should be able to pick you up. Even if you get churned up in nature's version of a washing machine, you should keep in contact with your kayak. You've already practiced Eskimo rolling, paddle-float self-rescues, and air-bag rescues. You should be able to return to your boat, get back in, pump it out, and resume your journey.

But you can't. You've lost your kayak, and you have to swim.

Most of us don't think about our breathing. It happens, almost automatically. When you're swimming in rough seas, though, that's a luxury you no longer have. When you're pummeled by a breaking wave, when you're twirled about in the energy core of a wave until you're disoriented, you have to hold your breath. When you bob to the surface in a trough, you have to breathe. Controlling your breathing, and knowing that you're able to control your breathing, are the first steps in regaining the serenity to extricate yourself from the water's grasp.

Once you've gotten over the confusion of being tossed about in the energy patterns of the waves and have a fair idea of where shore and safety lie, it's time to swim. In swimming, though, you could run into one of two currents—both frightening, both frustrating. You can't outfight them, but you can outthink them.

Let's start by looking at what happens on a beach exposed to wave action. Following the uprush of water onto the beach after the breaking of a wave, the seaward backrush occurs. The returning water is called a backwash. Waves approaching the beach at an angle produce a current parallel to the beach within the surf zone. The speed of this current

A mug of tea, a good book, a Crazy Creek chair . . . and the afternoon sun to soothe those tired paddling muscles. How much better can it get?

rarely exceeds 1 knot, but can reach up to 3 knots.

Concentrated energy from the wave front can form barriers to the backwash, which is deflected along the beach to areas of less resistance. The backwash will accumulate at weak points and will pour seaward as it forms rip currents through the surf. The large volume of returning water retards the incoming waves. The waves on one or both sides of the rip, not being retarded by the backwash, advance faster and farther up the beach. From there they move along the beach as feeder currents, increasing the volume of water flowing out at the rip. The rip may form at an indentation on an otherwise straight beach, along underwater obstructions such as a shoal or bar, or where the energy of the wave fronts is refracted and diverged. Mind you, that's a simple explanation of a complex phenomenon, but fortunately when you're swimming, you really don't have to remember all the root causes.

If there are higher waves to both sides of you, and they're advancing to the beach while you're being swept away from the shore, odds are you're in a rip current. If you attempt to swim to shore against the current, you'll tire long before the water. And you'll go inexorably through the neck of the rip, where it punches through the surf, and wind up outside the breaker line where the current dissipates.

What to do? Swim parallel to the beach, more or less across the current. Once clear of the outrushing current, use the energy of the shore-bound waves to paddle your way in.

What happens if, as you attempt to swim toward shore, you get the feeling that the world is whizzing by you? Basically, you're going for a ride in a longshore current that parallels the shore. You might even find that you're being carried at an angle away from the shore.

Don't fight this current. Ride with it, swimming with the current but at an angle toward the shore. You're going to find yourself fixating on a particular shoreside feature, and you're going to want to reach that feature, be it a point, a rock, or even a beachside tree. What can happen is that you'll be swept past the object of your desire and you'll fruitlessly battle the current to reach that one ideal spot. But remember that your goal is to get to shore, not to a particular point on the shore. Even if you could swim just as fast as the force of the current, the net result is that you'd stay in just one place until you were exhausted. Me, I can't swim that fast. Olympians may hit 5 miles per hour in a short sprint; the average swimmer is pressed to top 2 miles per hour. Tired, clothed, bashed about in the waves, I doubt I could manage 1 mile per hour. I'd just as soon save what strength and body heat I have and ferry out of the current to shore.

Let's say you are caught in the seaward current at the mouth of a river. While it may sweep you a ways off the beach, it will dissipate rapidly. React just as if you were in a rip current and ferry your way out of the current.

Tides sweeping in or out of bays can generate very strong currents; I've seen 11-knot currents in restricted passages such as British Columbia's Surge Narrows. That's hauling. You can't fight a current like that, but you can beat it by ferrying with the current and stroking toward a reachable shore.

You're shaking your head. You, of all people, would never venture near smoking mountains of water crashing onto rugged shores. First of all, who's talking about 20-foot-tall cliffs of foam poised above the beach? Surf can also be a couple of feet high, on lakes as well as the sea. Secondly, currents will push and tug at your kayak just as they do on a swimmer. You can take advantage of currents at the beach, or you can waste your time and energy fighting them. The choice is up to you, but only if you've invested the time to understand the how and why of currents in the beach zone.

On the Shore

As we look around the sheltered bay you guided us to, you judge that the beach is safe and suitable. That's an important step, one that many people overlook. Too many people commit to a plan and forget to check reality. While kayaking, a plan is the general framework from which you hang your actions as suitable for the moment. I'm fairly sure that the wind isn't going to change while we're ashore and create a flock of monster waves crashing right on this arc of welcoming crescent beach. But I don't think I'm willing to bet the farm on my hunch. So I'm paddling over to the west end of this little bay, where a ridge of rock hooks out and offers a curling arm of shelter. It's the old belt-and-suspenders theory again—I want a double safety net. If there is a turn in the weather, I think I'll be able to launch in the shelter of the rocks and make a comfortable swing into the water beyond the bay rather than have to fight my way off the beach.

Let's enjoy a well-deserved lunch and plenty of exploration and recuperation time. We'll drink plenty of water, because we both used up lots of fluids on the way here. We've also dug into our energy reserves, so we need to refuel for the rest of the trip.

Be polite to the island. When nature calls, dig a small hole—maybe 6 inches or so in diameter and just a few inches down through the topsoil and humus. That's where nature's treatment plant lives and operates. If you go deeper, you're building an insulated, sterile box for your wastes. If you leave them unburied . . . well, I doubt if you'd be that rude.

Heating your food presents a dilemma. If you build a fire, you scar the soil and leave an unsightly carbon ring. If you use a butane or liquid fuel stove, you're burning petrochemicals. I'm inclined to go with a small liquid fuel stove for cooking, but

Knots

There are just about a bazillion knots described somewhere and known to someone. Many are great for a particular purpose and at least an equal number are purely for show. Here are four knots that will suffice for the vast majority of lashings you'll ever have to do.

The bowline is the mother of all knots, offering a jam-proof method of shaping a loop in the end of a line. It is indispensable.

The square knot, also known as a reef knot, is designed to fasten two lines together without jamming fast. It's suitable for lines of approximately equal size and stiffness. Because it was designed not to jam, it won't—and that means that under the right (or wrong) circumstances, it will release. Try holding one of the lines at each side of the knot and tug, and you might be surprised to see the knot disentangle. That's valuable if you want to free a line quickly, a disadvantage if you need the knot to hold under all circumstances.

The sheet bend is in the same family as the square knot, with a couple of important differences. First of all, it's best for lines of dissimilar diameter or stiffness. Secondly, it's much less likely to relax if one of the two lines is suddenly extended straight.

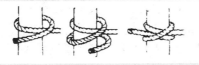

The clove hitch is a quick and easy way to attach a line to a pole or spar. It's strong and easy to untie.

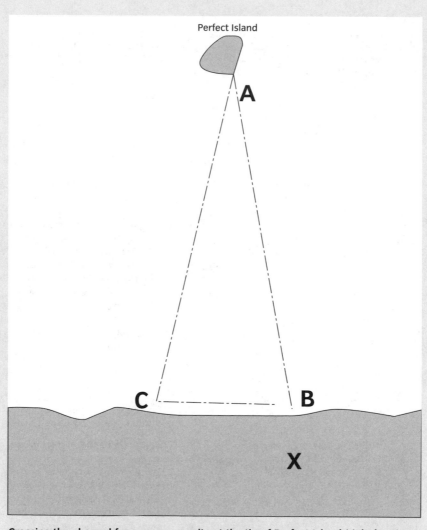

Perfect Island

A

C   B

X

Crossing the channel from your campsite at the tip of Perfect Island (right by A) to where you'll be picked up at B can be a snap—providing you can pick out the right landing spot on a featureless shore, the wind doesn't blow you willy-nilly along the shore, and currents don't pick you up. And providing the weather cooperates with good visibility. Otherwise, your course from A to B may be more of a hope than a plan. If, however, you plot a course to C, knowing you'll be well off to a known side, you can run down your bearings from C to B as you keep an eye out for your destination. Deliberately factoring in a gross error is an old navigation trick, and one that pays dividends in the slow and imprecise world of kayaking.

in an area with lots of driftwood, a fire may be more appropriate. Whatever you do, remember the advice of the old frontiersman. A big fire will make you sweat, not because of its heat but because of lugging all that wood. A small fire will keep you just as warm because you may approach it more closely and because it is far easier to cook upon.

PLOTTING THE COURSE HOME

I fell asleep when you were off exploring, and now it's late afternoon. Our take-out is on an almost featureless beach off to the west, and as near as we can tell, the beach looks the same for miles and miles. Should we lay out a compass course right to the beach and paddle that line? Well, there's a wind coming from the north, and so we'll be set to the south. We will also be crossing shallows and meandering channels, so the tidal currents are hard to predict. Over on the other side of our island, in the deep channel, you can forecast the current, but it's going to be devilish on those flats. Do you trust your course?

Just use the neat trick that we learned in chapter 14: Paddle the wrong way. If we land just south of the take-out but get confused and trudge south in search of the car, we could walk for miles. If we overcorrect and land on the north side of the car and hike north, same story. Only if we land to one side of the car and hike in the opposite direction will we find our way home. That means our odds of reaching the car are two out of four, or 50 percent. But by going the wrong way, we can improve those odds to 100 percent. Chart a course well to the north of the car. We can then hike south, and there's the car. As we get better at this, we can cut the error factor down, but a lot of navigators habitually set their course to land on one side of their goal and then run down the beach line.

As we work our way south along the beach line after our landfall, you spot the notch in the sand dunes that marks the trail, and the end of our trip. Though you don't mention it, I've seen a change in you. When we started paddling together, you would have doubted your ability to plan out and paddle a trip like this. Tides, currents, wind, and waves. And a route. It would have been too confusing. Funny how you can start with a few simple skills, and by using them one step at a time, you reach your goal.

CHAPTER TWENTY-THREE

Kayak Camping

Earth, air, fire, and water: The old Greeks thought they had figured out the basic building blocks of the universe, but if nothing else, they defined the four factors that are critical to camping out of your kayak. You need earth as a place to pitch your tent, fire to cook your meals, water to drink, and air to blow the bugs somewhere else. As we're paddling along together, let's chat about what makes these four factors work together.

If you're the kind of person who likes to squirm around with a tape measure, you'll soon compute that a touring kayak has at least three times the cargo area of a typical backpack. By the way your eyes light up, I'm sure you just figured out that a kayak is as close to a perfect people-powered camping vehicle as you're liable to find. You're right.

But before you start stowing everything but the kitchen sink through those hatches and in your deck bags, slow up for a moment.

Yes, you have a great amount of space at your disposal. And, no, you don't have to use all of it. We both know that stuff expands to fill the space available, but we also know that the more we pack into our kayaks, the more we're going to have to push through the water and the more we're going to have to carry up the beach. Comfortable camping is an exercise in simplicity, and it's almost true that the less you take along, the more comfortable you are. The opposite side of that is the fact you have the ability to carry along those things that are truly valuable.

Certain items we'll accept as givens: a tent with rain fly and ground cloth, sleeping bag and mattress, cooking utensils, a tarp to protect your kitchen. I cherish a chair to rest in of an evening. I pack along a Crazy Creek Lounger, which is a fabric cover with side straps that form a back. Inside it is a self-inflating mattress, which at night goes under my sleeping bag.

A CHOICE OF FIRE

Unless you want to eat only raw food, you're going to be faced with cooking, and cooking presupposes fire. Both campfire and stove have environmental impacts, and if you're going to travel gently on the land, you should consider the benefits and drawbacks of each.

I admit that I'm atavistic enough to really enjoy the flickering light, the smell, and the crackle of a campfire—to lean back in a chair with a mug of tea and a dulcimer, and to play the stars out of the deepening hues of the evening sky. But a fire is not suitable at all times and in all places. To use an open fire, for enjoyment or for cooking, mandates certain requirements. There must be a plentiful supply of down and dead wood. You have to be in an area of limited human use, both to ensure that supply of wood and to give the area a chance to heal the scars from

Packing your gear into your kayak is not, as it sometimes seems, a confused effort to shoehorn as much as possible into every nook and cranny of your boat. First you balance the weight—light objects in the far bow and stern, heavy objects as low and close to the centerline (the keel) as possible. You also have to plan your load so that the gear you'll need first is closest to the hatches or cockpit—so that you won't have to strip every bag out of your boat in a frantic search for the noon lunch bag. These folks planned ahead: When they beached for lunch, tools and ingredients were right on top. Food was in a SealLine dry bag, dessert was soon baking in an Outback Oven, the main dish was simmering in nonstick Evolution cookware, and clean water was ready in folding Platypus bottles. These brands aren't meant as a catalog, but are typical of good-quality outdoor gear. PHOTO COURTESY CASCADE DESIGNS

Many cruising kayaks have a high, peaked foredeck that, although great for shedding water, forms a mini-attic with little use. Some paddlers have glued a short section of 4- to 6-inch-diameter PVC pipe in this "attic" to work much like the glove compartment of a car. The size of the pipe was determined by the amount of space under the deck, allowing plenty of room for slipping into the kayak. A handy commercial version of this is the under-deck bag—a zippered fabric contraption mounted on slides—made by Mark Pack Works.

the fire. You also have to be willing to eradicate the marks of the fire before moving on. You might use a fire pan or confine your fire to an existing fire ring.

If your camp can't meet those absolute requirements, you have no choice but to use a stove. With a stove you won't have ashes or a fire ring, nor will you burn the silvering chunks of driftwood or fallen limbs. But you will be using a machine that took substantial amounts of energy to fabricate, and you will be burning non-renewable fossil fuels. On the other hand, you'll have an almost instant source of easily regulated heat despite rain, wind, or dark of night. With a stove you can concentrate your skills on cooking rather than on the art of fire tending.

After that as a warning, what's your real choice? Accept the best of both worlds, and tailor your kitchen to the resources available.

When it comes to stoves, you have a lot of choices. Fuels include white gas, kerosene, propane, and alcohol. Stoves range from one to three burners. I've found white gas (or Coleman fuel) to be the most universally available and a single-burner pressurized stove to be quite adequate for small groups. They are light, compact, easily regulated, and convenient—all big pluses for a lazy camper such as myself. I'm willing to trade off their noise (and they do roar) for their clean heat.

PORTABLE KITCHEN

My kitchen is fairly simple. I pack two- and three-liter pots with nonstick lining and add a 10-inch sauté pan with nonstick lining, oven, teakettle, pot gripper and hot pad (odds are you'll use both), plastic cutting board, wooden or plastic spatula, good knife, measuring cup, and a couple of 2½-liter water bags. Don't underestimate the value of a sharp knife. I've found that a Blackie Collins–designed Gerber knife holds its edge well and locks into a sheath.

The Outback Oven revolutionized camp cuisine. It is essentially a small convection oven that you perch atop a single-burner camp stove. With one, you can bake up biscuits, pizza, or a plate of brownies. For breakfast or dessert slice up an apple or two, top with brown sugar and cinnamon, dot with a couple of teaspoons of butter, and bake for twenty minutes. Take one of these ovens along in its compact package, and you'll expand your meal horizons and at the same time save fuel.

If you want, you can eat those meals where someone has to ask whether they're eating chicken or broccoli. But you don't have to. Spice up your meals, and camp meals will turn from drudgery into delight. A basic collection of spices includes basil, bay leaves, cayenne, chili powder, cinnamon, cumin, curry, dill, nutmeg, oregano, rosemary, pepper, salt, and thyme.

Tempt your taste buds with a few more condiments: brown sugar, garlic cloves, mustard, mushrooms, oil (corn oil, olive oil, peanut oil—match your palate and enjoy), salsa, soy sauce, dried tomatoes, and wine (decant into a Platypus water bag and use in a pasta sauce or in a dip for mussels).

For the do-it-yourself set, collect a set of plastic 35-millimeter film containers to hold your spices and buy a few plastic screw-top bottles for oils or other liquids. (Those refillable squeeze-type tubes seem to be a good idea, but I can't work them.)

If you're like me, you're going to find it easier to keep all the spices, condiments, and can openers in one place. A pouch made by Outdoor Research, called the Outdoor Kitchen, comes with a dozen or so bottles for condiments, a few bottles for oils, pouches for your kitchen tools, and mesh pockets for scrubbers, towels, and soap. Unzip it, hang it near your stove, and half your kitchen is in place.

There are a couple of ways to pack your food, one of which is convenient and efficient and one that builds character. You can cram everything into the largest bag you can find. When it's time to cook, you paw through the entire bag and end up by dumping it on the ground. It's also interesting when you attempt to push this big bag through a small hatch into your kayak.

The other way is to collect a series of smaller, color-coded bags. Well before you launch, prepackage all the ingredients for each meal into separate bags. One group of paddlers insists that you should put all your lunches in a blue bag, breakfasts in a red bag, and dinners in a green bag. The other group believes just as strongly that you should have a meals bag for each day, with one breakfast, one lunch, and one dinner in each bag. Both work. The first gives you an easy opportunity to vary your meals for a day, with a bit of random choice. The second trades off prepreparation time for camp cooking convenience.

Whatever method you adopt, remember that you're going to be exercising fairly vigorously and you're going to be eating more than you expect. Increase portion sizes, don't skimp on foods with a higher fat content, and remember to bring along desserts and evening snacks. Our rule of thumb is that we'll eat one more meal per day than we do at home. We've tried simply increasing the size of each of three meals, but we do better with a good breakfast, early lunch, dinner, and supper.

Oh, yeah: Remember to label each meal. I've found it handy to include ALL cooking directions inside each meal bag and to identify each component. When I'm packing, everything is distinguishable, but a few days out and I can't tell one from the other.

A REAL-WORLD CAMPSITE

There is, somewhere in our collective subconscious, an archetypal campsite on the banks of a trickling brook where we can dip pristine water from the stream and loll on the sandy beach.

In the world through which we really paddle, there is no pristine water. Virtually all the streams are filled with little nasties. And when we stop to fill our water bottles, we find that they are surrounded by a horde of slightly larger nasties: mosquitoes, biting flies, no-see-ums, and other flying appetites.

Appreciate streams for their beauty, but pump your water supplies through your water filters. Read the specs for your filter carefully. The filter that will remove 97 percent of the biological contaminants sounds great, but it still lets you sip 3 percent of the bugs. The closer you get to 100 percent filtration, the more comfortable you'll be.

There's an imaginary perfect camp, and there's a real-world camp. In most cases we're better off carrying water with us and choosing a spot open enough to let any breeze disperse the bugs and flat enough to pitch a tent or two. Sand, especially fine sand, will work its way into every nook and cranny of your gear.

Also, most of the little nasties are dense creatures. You might find an attractive little waterfall tumbling into a small pool, but the creatures bouncing down that waterfall are going to hit the slower water in the pool and sink to the bottom. Eventually they're going to wash on through, and the pool will not turn into a biological soup, but think where the greatest concentrations of contaminants will congregate in a stream. Few filters will weed out chemical or heavy-metal concentrations, so you're potentially better off avoiding still pools at the bottoms of quick stretches of moving water.

In a world in which the sea will creep up to float your boat away, it's important to lift your kayak well above the high tide mark—and to tie it to the shore as well. Something floated those logs high up the beach, so don't put your faith in distance from the water alone.

With your water containers filled, move on away from the favored habitat of all those biting and stinging creatures and look for a more habitable campsite. If you have a choice, you're going to find a gentle gravel beach tucked in behind a point. A large log tossed above the high tide line during a severe winter storm serves as a table and kitchen. Gravel? Sure. Our culture seems to put a high value on sand beaches, but sand gets into everything. On the ridge of the point itself, exposed to any breeze, you'll find a flat place for your tent. Cherish that breeze, because it will keep your camp free of those flying, biting creatures. A small bowl is not as comfortable a campsite: It will shelter the mosquitoes and flies, it will pool up with cooler air, and in most cases it will be damper than a more exposed spot on the ridge.

I have a nightmare that I'll rise in the morning to discover a bare beach where my kayak had been the night before. When searching out a campsite, consider where you'll secure your kayak. A steep beach will be harder to land on, and you'll have to carry your kayak up the slope above the reach of the tide. A flat beach means a long carry across the flats if you land at less than high tide or a long carry to the water if you want to launch before the tide comes back in. I've camped on slopes that were easy to land on but were impossible to launch from at most stages of the tide. Whatever beach you discover, I'd suggest carrying your boat well above the reach of the tide and then tying it securely with the bow and perhaps even the stern painter. And after all that, check it during different stages of the tide.

Remember, the farther your boat is from camp, the farther you'll have to carry each and every bag. The idealness of a campsite quickly fades with repeated long carries.

Packing and unpacking your kayak each day as you move camp takes time. You might, if your schedule allows and you planned ahead, make a base camp and paddle out from that for day trips.

Scratch out a latrine a discreet distance from both tent and kitchen. Scratch is an operative word. If you dig a deep pit, you've excavated down into a sterile soil environment, and the contents will be preserved for a long, long time. The active biological agents are in the top few inches of the soil.

When you and I are out here on the water, we're going to be guided by the moon and sun. The tides will determine our days, and the winds will establish our courses and distances. Those are truths we just have to live with, and in the real world are no more confining than gravity. What we can do, within those boundaries, is set our own schedules so that we're off the water relatively early on a paddling day. It's going to take an hour to two hours to land, unpack the kayaks, and set up camp. It will take at least that long to repack and launch when we're ready to push on.

When we can, it's often easier to make a long passage on a traveling day and set up a base camp as a home for several days. We can then set out on day mini-expeditions from this camp in boats that are lighter and more responsive, without the budgeted time for establishing a camp each day.

I've mentioned a few brand-name products. These are ones that have worked very satisfactorily for me. Don't rush out to equip yourself the same way, but you might use these as standards against which to measure the items you choose for yourself.

We've put in enough work setting up this camp. I'm going to take a break, get out my chair, and see if I can entice the evening stars out with my dulcimer.

CHAPTER TWENTY-FOUR

Waves, Wind, and Weather

Wind and waves: They are the boundaries of our paddling environment, and without understanding just a bit about how they interact, we're going to be paddling by the seat of our pants. And eventually get caught out in the weather.

WAVES

Without plunging into technologies, suffice it to say that in most cases waves are the direct descendants of wind. Waves are created by wind blowing across the surface of the water and setting up long coils of energy, much like a hand rubbing cat hair off velvet. As you rub, the cat hair forms long cylinders that pass over the velvet. The velvet might wrinkle at any one point, but doesn't move. Think of the water like that velvet, and the energy of the wave like the cat hair.

The size of a wave is determined by three factors: how strong the wind is blowing, how long the wind has been blowing, and the distance over the water the wind has been blowing. A strong wind will kick up big waves. A wind that has been blowing from the same direction for three days will produce bigger waves than a wind that has been blowing for only half a day. The farther downwind you go, the bigger the waves will become.

You'll hear weather reports giving both sea and swell, and before you nod off, you should know the difference. Sea refers to waves directly created by wind. Swell refers to waves still in motion from wind despite a change in direction (or even dying away) of the wind that created them. You can have a sea coming from the west and a swell from the south, and if nothing else, you've going to have confused, bumpy, and uncomfortable water where the two collide.

Catching a wave and swooshing toward shore is a major rush! However, learn the ride with an unloaded boat and a paddler skilled in rescue standing by just in case you miscalculate. Surfing with a fully loaded touring kayak is a graduate-level test of water skills. PHOTO COURTESY OCEAN KAYAK

Our paddling world is defined by wind and water, and the more we understand how the two interact, the more pleasure we will receive from our kayak.

Why should you know the two? Because you can judge that the wind is coming from the west and therefore the waves should also be coming from the west. But if waves were set in motion from a wind system that for one reason or another has not touched you, those waves could turn your careful plans into frothy garbage.

Enough about that.

WIND

Wind is simple enough. It's air in motion. But when you hear of a 20-knot wind from the west, don't be misled by the illusion that it is a uniform force pushing toward you. If it was a flat world, it would be—but our world has bumps.

Let's paddle up this shore, which is protected from the wide-open spaces of a big channel by a string of islands. You listened to a marine weather forecast earlier, and you learned that we should have 20-knot winds coming right across the 10-mile-wide channel toward us.

You've been paddling a fair bit recently, and you're confident that we can work our way across the narrow slots between the islands safely. The force of the waves will be broken by the islands and rocky reefs, and while 20 knots is a weight of wind, we can glide from shelter to shelter.

Whoops! The forecast was right in projecting 20-knot winds. What it didn't say was that when the wind funneled down in the narrow slots between the islands, it would increase in velocity. In a steep-walled gorge, it could hit 40 knots, and that's a bit of excitement. Not only that, it doesn't have to be a sea-level slot for the wind to reach high velocities. If the next island has two peaks with a low saddle between them, we could be hit by the same force of wind.

Let's say the next island in line has a long, high wall with a cliff on the lee side. Could we shelter under the cliff? Well, the wind can whip over the top of the cliff and fall out of the sky, hitting us with near explosive force. I once sat on a ridge in Glacier National Park and peered down onto a lake, and it looked like a giant was taking large handfuls of invisible wind and compacting them into balls of energy. He'd lob them over the ridge and they'd fall right to the lake—and burst with scudding streaks of foam in all directions. Totally unpredictable, from the cockpit of a kayak.

Because of reefs ahead, we're going to have to paddle out of the lee of the next island and work along the weather side. Here, the wind is striking the bluffs of the island at a slight angle. The wind doesn't hit and stick. Instead, the wind is reflected almost parallel to the face of the bluff. Depending on the relative angle of the wind and cliff, we could have the wind in our faces or at our backs as we sneak along. The apparent direction of the wind will also shift near the entrance to a slot or channel, with the wind turning to follow the shores of the surrounding islands as it feeds into the channel.

Now we're going to add the sun into the picture.

In the morning, most days, the sea surface will be cooler than the land and the air over the sea will be dense. Water, in the volumes we're talking about, is much more temperature stable than land. The sun will begin to heat the land and the air over the land. As the air is heated, it expands and rises. The denser air from the water flows in to replace the less dense air. That's why there is generally a breeze from the sea in the early afternoons, after a temperature differential builds up.

Come evening, the land cools more rapidly, and with it the air cools and becomes more dense. The air over the water is relatively warmer and less dense, so the heavier air from the land moves toward the less dense air. That's the land breeze that blows through the night and usually dies away before dawn.

Imagine that we're going to paddle across the mouth of a river or fjord penetrating the coastal mountains from the sea to the interior. You got it! The air movement created by the temperature differential will funnel down the opening, and we could be trapped by strong winds. That's strong, as in up to 25 knots, and with that much air cascading down around your ears, a pleasant paddle can turn into an arduous challenge. Fortunately, these localized winds are fairly predictable, and you can avoid them by transiting potential channels early in the morning or in the evening.

There's a fierce wind that in the North Pacific we call a williwaw. You probably will never run afoul of one, but better forewarned and forearmed. It occurs when a great quantity of cold air is dammed on the windward side of a mountain and then spills over suddenly and violently down the other side. Speeds in some of the fjords can reach hurricane strength.

As air high on a mountainside cools, it becomes heavier and denser and tends to flow downslope. The beach is the farthest down the slope you can get, and this wind can be strong enough to attempt to push you offshore. In nautical talk this is a katabatic wind.

If the wind and the tidal current are flowing in the same direction, waves tend to be longer and lower. If the wind and tide oppose each other, the waves will mound up in shorter, sharper, and nastier pieces of work.

WEATHER

If you've planned our voyage to be within an area covered by the National Oceanic and Atmospheric Administration, we can pool our resources and spend $20 or so on a radio receiver tuned to accurate marine forecasts. They're great. But you don't have to listen to a forecast to know whether or not it's raining. All you have to do is slip your hand out of the tent in the morning.

With a little common sense and a few jingles from our folklore past, we can predict the weather in our immediate vicinity accurately and easy. Let's rock, not around the clock but around the compass, for a bit of folklore about wind and weather.

When the Wind is in the north
The skillful fisherman goes not forth.

Izaak Walton penned that couplet three centuries back, when he was more interested in the cold, blustery winds that come from the north than in literary expertise.

When the Wind is in the east
It's good for neither man nor beast.

As a front passes by, and in the northern hemisphere these move from west to east, the east wind will often bring rain.

When the Wind is in the south
The rain is in its mouth.

The east wind is the child of the south wind, which also often brings rain in summer.

When the Wind is in the west
There it is the very best.

Walton summed it up. Weather riding on a west wind tends to be best.

One thing is certain. Weather changes come with a shift in the wind. If the wind has been steady from the same direction for a number of days, you can expect whatever weather you've been having to continue.

Cirrus clouds are the high, wispy ones that are often called mare's tails. Cirrocumulus clouds are a series of small puffs that come in waves and look (with a little imagination) like mackerel scales. They are often the first indications of high-altitude winds that could bring in a storm.

Mackerel scales and mare's tails
Make lofty ships carry low sails.

In other words, they hint at wind.

There's a general progression of clouds, from high to low, that bring rain.

Altostratus clouds (which look like a thick, gray sheet through which the sun and moon look kind of fuzzy) and altocumulus clouds (clumpy patches of cloud with gray centers that can group into lines) are the midlevel clouds that often come in after the high clouds with the promise of rain. When these start to form or thicken, keep your rain clothes at hand, because you can expect rain within eight hours or so.

The lowest clouds to blow in will be stratocumulus (layers or round clouds with flat bottoms) and nimbostratus clouds (a thick, dark gray ceiling). You might get a bit of precipitation from the stratocumulus. Nimbostratus are rain bags, ready to soak you.

If the progression from the high, wispy clouds to the thick ceiling comes quickly, the rain will pass over you quickly. If it is a slow progression, the rain will edge over you with slow deliberation.

Short notice, soon to pass
Long notice, long will last.

There are many other jingles that aid in predicting the weather. One of our best known refers to the color of the sun.

Red sky at morning, sailors take warning;
Red sky at night, sailor's delight.

If a deep red sun climbs through gray clouds, expect rain before night. A brilliant red sunset, however, indicates good weather the next day.

Rainbows are another good indication of weather future. If you see a rainbow to windward, brace for some foul weather. A rainbow to leeward means the rain has passed you.

Are you cooking breakfast over an open fire? Look at the smoke. If it rises and vanishes, you're enjoying a high-pressure system and good weather. If the smoke hugs the ground and stays with you, the air pressure is lower and a weather change is in the offing.

A clearly defined ring around the sun or the moon often warns of approaching rain. Those high cirrostratus clouds that look like thin layers of gauze are made of ice crystals. Refraction of light from the sun or moon by the crystals creates a definite halo. Like the other high clouds, this is an indicator of high-altitude winds that could be blowing in a weather change, especially if followed by lower clouds.

Ring around the moon or sun
Rain is coming on the run.

Fog is a fact of life for anyone who goes to sea. If a fog raises in the evening or at night, expect it to linger. An early-morning fog, however, is usually caused by the combination of cool air and warm water and as often as not will soon burn away.

Feel your boat when you first get up in the morning. If the dew has made your boat damp, odds are the weather will be good. If your boat is dry, however, don't pack your rain gear too deeply. Dew forms when objects cool below the dew (condensation) point of the surrounding air. Since the greatest cooling by radiation occurs under clear skies, you're more likely to find cooler objects and dew when you can see the stars.

When the dew is on the grass
Rain will never come to pass.

The Spanish might have had kayaking in mind when they said:

When God wills, it rains with any wind.

Build plenty of extra time into your schedule in case of unfriendly weather. A cruising kayak is one of the most seaworthy small vessels ever designed, but its major strength is that it can easily be hauled ashore. If the weather is questionable, enjoy an afternoon on the beach.

CHAPTER TWENTY-FIVE

Sailing

We were camped on a thin pinnacle of rock stuck into the straits on the east side of Canada's Vancouver Island, enjoying the last of the summer light as it bled out of the sky. We had made a long day of it, catching the morning tides to work our way through a maze of islands and overfalls, and it felt good to sit on the beach and sip hot tea liberally laced with honey.

A big tandem kayak came down the far shore, riding easily and forcing the three accompanying singles to push just to stay with it. The bow paddler in the tandem had opened a big beach umbrella, and it scooped a great bite out of the wind—enough to put a "bone" of white foam curling back from the kayak's bow—and the stern paddler rode the rudder pedals to keep the boat on course for the next bay.

Opportunistic? Sure, but that's what kayak sailing is all about for most of us who like to mess about in small boats. Sails allow us to extend our cruising radius while remaining in the comfort and security of our kayaks. We can grab a little power assist from the wind at one end of the spectrum, or we can trick our boats out with a dazzling array of space-age components to push the very envelope of wind-driven performance. All we need is a scoop of fabric to catch the wind and a rudder to control our direction.

We're not necessarily talking about anything new here. John MacGregor in the 1860s cruised through Europe in his yawl-rigged cruising kayak *Rob Roy*. Dr. Hannes Lindemann kayak-sailed the Atlantic twice in the 1950s, once in a dugout and once in an off-the-shelf Klepper folding kayak. Fredrick Voss, in a big decked canoe, sailed around the world. The Polynesians spanned the Pacific in their multihull sailing canoes, and the Makah of the Pacific Northwest sailed out in search of whales. So we have a long history of sailing and a well-earned reputation for quick and comfortable passages.

SAILS

Let's roughly divide kayak sails into two groups: those designed to go downwind and those designed to go across or upwind. That's an arbitrary division and you'll find a lot of crossover, but as a starting point it works.

Downwind sails are set across the wind, and the force of the wind pushes you in the direction the wind is blowing, within an arc of about 45 degrees. That big beach umbrella was a perfect example of how downwind sails work.

If you just want a bit of a push at the end of the day, take a look at the small, deck-mounted sailing rigs. Think of a capital V, with fabric stretched between the booms that form the outside edges. The bottom of the V is attached to tie-downs on your foredeck—the same ones that hold the shock cord strapping your chart case onto the deck—and control sheets lead from the top of the booms back to the cockpit. These are small sails, 10 square feet or so, and are surprisingly effective. Primex of California sells one version of this.

If you're more into sailing as a tool, look at a spinnaker flying from a rigid mast mounted through your foredeck. These are triangular sails, with the peak of the triangle supported at the top of the mast and control sheets from the two clews—the outer corners of the sails—coming back to the cockpit. If there is too much wind, simply fold the sail in half so that the two clews are together, and move one sheet from an original clew to a grommet in the center of the lower edge of the sail. Want to sail more or less across the wind? Pull the sail against the mast, bring the two clews together, and you have an airfoil shape that will allow you to sail efficiently across the breeze. Spinnakers are made by a number of kayak manufacturers.

When sailing becomes as big a part of the sport as paddling, look at the Twins rig offered on a number of kayaks and developed by Balogh Sail Designs. You'll hear more about them; Mark Balogh loves to design sail rigs, and his wife, Sam, loves to sail. The Twins rig is basically a pair of triangular sails joined at the mast, with booms that keep the sails fully extended. Sheets come back from the outside ends of the booms to a short rod that allows one-handed control of the entire rig. The two sails can be folded together for crosswind sailing.

Sailing downwind is great, but the time will come when you'll want to sail across the wind. Now's the time for what they call fore-and-aft sails, because instead of having the sails spread out to each side of the kayak, the sails will be more or less in a line with the keel. They go from the fore, the front, aft to the rear.

You're going to have to add a few more parts to your kayak to use fore-and-aft sails. When you turn sideways to the wind, it will still attempt to push you downwind. You have to counter that sideways slip, and fortunately that's easy enough to do. Let's think about a knife and a cube of soft butter. If you slice through the butter sharp-edge first, the knife moves through the butter easily. If you attempt to push the blade through sideways, it becomes very difficult. If we hang a board off the side of our kayak, parallel to the keel line, it works just like that knife. The board slides easily through the water if you're going ahead, and at the same time helps the kayak resist sliding sideways under the force of the wind. Sailors have been using these for thousands of years, and call them leeboards—because they are boards on the lee, or downwind, side of the sailing craft. In most cases the kayak will carry two boards, one on each side. You put the one on the lee side in the water, where it is held at the top and supported by the hull pressing against it. The other board is raised out of the water.

The simplest fore-and-aft rigs are jib-shaped sails that are supported at the top of the mast and at the bow of your kayak, with the control sheet extending back from the clew to the cockpit. They can be as simple as a triangle of cloth, shaped into an airfoil by the wind and pushing you ahead. Featherlight allows you to halve the sail area easily, by putting a cringle (nautical talk for a grommet or reinforced eye) in the center of the lower edge of the sail. Unhook the tack (that's the place where your sail hooks to the bow of your kayak) and rehook the tack to the center cringle. Fold the sail in half, and attach the sheet to both grommets at what is now the clew. The folded edge of the sail is now the leading edge, and your effective sail area is halved.

Easy Rider developed a jib that can be unrolled or rolled up, much like a window shade. Reducing or expanding the amount of sail takes only seconds and allows a sailor to instantly adjust the sail area to match wind conditions.

Sailing kayaks, for generations, have been powered with gaff sails. The gaff mainsail is a four-sided sail supported on a relatively short mast, stretched out along the bottom edge along a boom, and extended higher than the mast from a near vertical gaff boom supported at one end by the mast and held in its vertical position by halyards from the top of the mast to the midpoint or so of the gaff. They're highly efficient sails, trading off some of the power of a contemporary three-sided mainsail for the stability and greater strength of the shorter mast. Most gaff-rigged kayaks also have a jib sail. On occasion you'll see a kayak with two masts, with a smaller gaff sail on the rear mast.

Then came Mark Balogh, who is passionate about sailing efficiency. He developed a very high-efficiency sail, supported at the leading edge on a mast and extended out along a boom on the lower edge. Thin battens are inserted into the sail, forcing it into an airfoil shape that collects the most potential power from the wind. He calls his sail a Batwing, and when backlit against the sky, it really does look like one wing of a big bat.

Sailing across the wind, or beating upwind, is feasible with the fore-and-aft sails, but you'll soon learn an important truth. The wind blowing against the sails above your head and the leeboard keeping the hull from slipping sideways exert a twisting force on your boat. The kayak will start to lean—or if you want to talk nautical, to heel.

A few seconds of reflection will convince you that your sail will work better when the mast is vertical. You won't be spilling air out of the sail, and a sail held vertical presents a more effective area to the wind than one held at an angle. On the other hand, you'll also soon realize that at some point the heeling motion will overcome your balance. Or, splash-and-glub time.

With small sails and beamy double kayaks, you can counter some of the heel by shifting your weight to the upwind, or weather, side of your kayak. With narrower boats, more sail, or bigger winds . . . you're challenged.

A couple of thousand years ago, the Polynesians were faced with this same problem and developed a super answer: outriggers. They extended *akas,* or crossbeams, straight out from the sides of their boats and at the ends of the *ukus* mounted *amas,* or outriggers. With outriggers, any heeling motion imparted to the boat is counteracted by the buoyancy of the *ama.* If that outrigger extends out 5 or 6 feet from the side of your kayak, the support is tremendous. Kayaks can be rigged with an outrigger to one side or with outriggers on both sides.

Easy Rider has developed a sailing system with outriggers, crossbeams, and sail areas designed to work together, and builds the attachment points into its engineered hulls. Its biggest double is rigged with three masts balanced on a narrow hull between two outriggers. Balogh fabricates an outrigger system that can be fitted to just about any folding kayak with a supported cockpit rim and can be retrofitted to most hardshell kayaks. Easy Rider's outriggers are rigid (with some in take-apart sections), while Balogh's are inflatable.

SAILING

Enough of hardware. Let's go sailing. We'll start in shallow water, where I can hold you as you get ready. First of all, make sure your leeboard and rudder are down in the water. Raise your sail, letting the sheet fly free, and secure your halyard. If you haven't noticed, on this first sail you have a fore-and-aft rig with a single mainsail. Get comfortable, get your feet on the rudder, and pull the sheet in until the boom makes an angle of about 45 degrees with your keel line. I'm holding you (and it's getting more difficult with the pressure from the sail) so that the wind is coming straight in from the side. As I release you, you'll start sailing at right angles to the wind. Hey, it works.

As you start to pick up speed, you'll see that you can easily turn your bow

Wind Direction

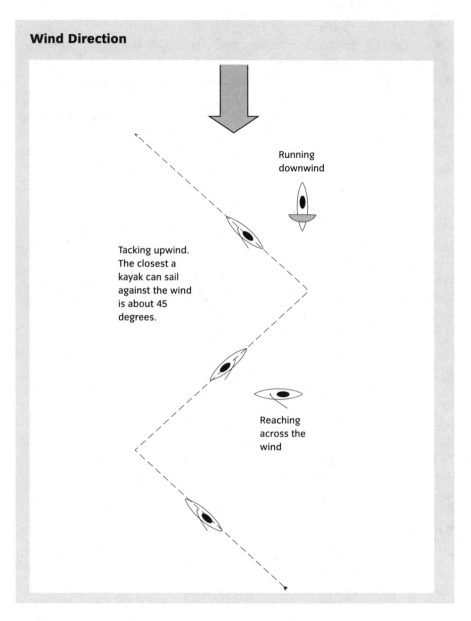

Running downwind

Tacking upwind. The closest a kayak can sail against the wind is about 45 degrees.

Reaching across the wind

toward the wind with your rudder. But as you do so, the back of the sail begins to shake and you lose speed. Try hauling the sheet in a little tighter, until the angle between the boom and your keel is about 30 degrees. You will now be able to turn your bow further into the wind, until you're sailing a course about 45 degrees from dead into the wind. And that's about as close to sailing straight into the wind as you're going to get.

Now you want to come back to the beach. You have two options in turning. You can turn your bow toward the wind, and with enough speed you'll swing your bow right through the direction from which the wind is blowing and will be heading back toward the beach with the wind on your other side. Turning by heading into the wind is called tacking. You could also turn your bow away from the wind, in a curve downwind, and bring the wind across your stern. Your boom will probably swing from one side to the other with a thump (and with more wind this can be awfully powerful) as you complete your turn. This is called gybing or jibing. You will be blown a ways downwind with this kind of turn.

That was fun!

Now you want to go upwind. Pick up a bit of speed and turn until you're headed about 45 degrees into the wind. Sail for a distance—whatever is comfortable, depending on the width of the channel you're in, the force of the wind, the waves, or even your comfort range from shore. Now, with plenty of speed, go ahead and tack—that is, turn into the wind. But don't turn completely around. Instead, stabilize your course until you're sailing at about 45 degrees into the wind, but now with the wind on your other side. You might not be able to sail directly into the wind, but you can zigzag your way upwind like this, and on average you'll be heading right upwind. You're covering more water, but you're working those switchbacks toward your destination.

Going downwind is almost intuitive. Turn your bow downwind. Let out your sheet until your sail is at right angles to the wind. You're on your way. In most cases you can lift both leeboards out of the water to reduce drag. With the wind behind you, you won't slip sideways.

A few warnings about downwind sailing. One, you're going to have a hard time estimating the force of the wind. It won't feel as powerful, because your speed will somewhat disguise the wind velocity. Two, the size of waves is directly affected by the distance the wind blows over the water. The farther you sail downwind, the larger the waves will become. Third, it's a lot easier to be blown downwind than it will be to battle your way back upwind. Fourth, if you absentmindedly turn a little off course, the wind can reach behind the edge of your sail and slam the boom to the other side with great force.

I haven't mentioned kite sailing, because I've never done any and know little about it. It is just what the name implies. Fly a kite from your kayak, and let the wind aloft pull your kayak toward your destination. Sounds like fun, and one day I'll try it. But for now, I'm going to enjoy catching a ride with the technologies that I know.

CHAPTER TWENTY-SIX

Why Go Kayaking?

Why go kayak cruising? We've shared a lot of tips on the "how" of kayaking.

But the "why" of this activity?

I'm not wise enough to link the symbolism of the salinity of the sea to the salinity of your blood, nor the pulse of the tide to the beat of your heart. Nor to reflect on the coincidence that your body and the surface of the earth have about the same percentage of liquids.

I know we live in a stress-filled world, with constant demands eroding our own time and space. And I know that living on beach time with muscles tired from paddling rather than from being tense all day gives me a more positive outlook.

I've seen that folks who paddle along the shoreline under their own power seem not to trash the sea and befoul the shore. Perhaps while making their very good time, they have the breadth of vision to see the folly of not caring wholeheartedly for the land. I can't point with praise at an unblemished personal environmental record. My boats are plastic and 'glass. I wear synthetic clothing. I do the best I can, but I'm not about to crank the clock back to another time. I like the era in which we live, and technology wisely used is such an awesomely great benefit.

But the "why" of this activity?

All my life I've been in small boats and water. A life without the language of water is a foreign tongue, and while I may attempt to translate it, I do not understand the nuances of it. Why go kayaking? How can you *not* go?

How can you not drift along on a sleek gray tide waiting for the sun to come climbing in an explosion of reds and golds, changing the black sky to blue? How can you not watch rain throw itself into the sea? Or laugh at the quizzical expression on an otter's face moments before it leaps from its rock over your bow?

How can you not find that the speed of a cruising kayak matches your own curiosity, and that the ability to explore the byways immeasurably expands your horizons?

How can you not pass on to your children the understanding that the kayaker is responsible for himself or herself—that the freedom to paddle is based forever on the responsibility of paddling?

I launch from my dock and glide over deep purple sand dollars canted up on edge as they feed. How can you not delight in them and work to preserve them?

I met a Native American from the upper Midwest, a birchbark canoe maker by trade and a person who understood that there are meanings underlying our actions.

"You," he said, "are responsible for the next seven generations." He didn't mean some vague, impersonal "you" floating over the population. He meant the person he was talking to, and he would mean the same thing speaking to each of you. Speaking to each of you in the singular, speaking to each of you one at a time.

If a cruising kayak can help any of us to see the magnitude of our task and the pleasures we find in meeting it, how can we not help but paddle?

Appendix: The Beaufort Scale

In 1806 Sir Francis Beaufort devised a scale of wind speeds, vital to a navy that used wind as its fuel source. By using a set of accepted standards, sailors the world over could consistently describe and compare wind speeds.

Wind is the primary cause of waves in the cruising kayak environment. Wave height varies with the length of time the wind has blown and the area of open water over which it has blown (the "fetch"). The heights given in this chart are based on a twenty-four-hour wind and a fetch of no more than 10 miles—for the coastal paddler.

Beaufort Scale

Beaufort Number	Wind Speed (Knots)	Seaman's Term	World Meteorological Organization Term	Effects at Sea	Effects on Land	Wave Height (10-mile fetch)
0	Under 1	Calm	Calm	Sea like mirror	Calm; smoke rises vertically	Flat
1	1–3	Light air	Light air	Ripples with appearance of scales; no foam crests	Smoke drift indicates wind direction; vanes do not move	Less than 1'
2	4–6	Light breeze	Light breeze	Small wavelets; crests of glassy appearance, not breaking	Wind felt on face; leaves rustle; vanes begin to move	Less than 1'
3	7–10	Gentle breeze	Gentle breeze	Large wavelets; crests begin to break; scattered whitecaps	Leaves, small twigs in constant motion; light flags extended	2'
4	11–16	Moderate breeze	Moderate breeze	Small waves, becoming longer; numerous whitecaps	Dust, leaves, and loose paper raised up; small branches move	3'
5	17–21	Fresh breeze	Fresh breeze	Moderate waves, taking longer form; many whitecaps; some spray	Small trees in leaf begin to sway	4'
6	22–27	Strong breeze	Strong breeze	Larger waves forming; whitecaps everywhere; more spray	Larger branches of trees in motion; whistling heard in wires	5'
7	28–33	Moderate gale	Near gale	Sea heaps up; white foam from breaking waves begins to be blown in streaks	Whole trees in motion; resistance felt when walking against wind	6'
8	34–40	Fresh gale	Gale	Moderate high waves of greater length; edges of crests begin to break into spindrift; foam is blown in well-marked streaks	Twigs and small branches broken off trees; progress generally impeded	8'
9	41–47	Strong gale	Strong gale	High waves; sea begins to roll; dense streaks of foam; spray may reduce visibility	Slight structural damage occurs; slate blown from roofs	9'
10	48–55	Whole gale	Storm	Very high waves with overhanging crests; sea takes on white appearance as foam is blown in very dense streaks; rolling is heavy and visibility is reduced	Seldom experienced on land; trees broken or uprooted; considerable structural damage occurs	10' plus
11	56–63	Storm	Violent storm	Exceptionally high waves; sea covered with white foam patches; visibility still more reduced	Very rarely experienced on land; usually accompanied by widespread damage	10' plus
12	64 and more	Hurricane	Hurricane	Air filled with foam; sea completely white with driving spray; visibility greatly reduced		10' plus

Glossary

Abeam: On the side of the kayak, amidships, or at right angles to the keel line. "On the weather beam" means at a right angle to the keel in the windward direction, while "lee beam" means at a right angle to the keel in a leeward direction.

Aft: Toward the stern.

Amidships: In the center of the kayak.

Anchor: A weight that, when dropped to the bottom of a body of water and attached to a kayak by a rope, or line, holds the kayak in one place.

Astern: In the direction of the kayak's stern.

Asymmetrical: Pertaining to a hull shape in which the kayak's widest point, or beam, is either aft or forward of amidships.

Bail: To empty water from a kayak.

Bang plate: A reinforcing plate or "shoe" made of abrasion-resistant material that protects the stems of a kayak from scrapes and impact damage during beaching or launching.

Beacon: A post or buoy placed over a shoal or bank to warn vessels of danger.

Beam: The width of a kayak at the widest point.

Bearing: The direction to an object in relation to the person looking at it.

Bight: A rope bent back upon itself so that it is doubled. Also, a bend in the shore that creates a bay.

Bilge: Area where a kayak hull's bottom turns up into its sides.

Binnacle: The receptacle for a compass.

Bitter end: The end of an anchor line that is attached to a boat at a bitt.

Blade: The wide, flat area of a paddle.

Bow: The front of a kayak.

Brace: Paddling technique used to stabilize a kayak. The "low" brace and "high" brace are two common techniques.

Breaker: Waves broken by shoals or ledges.

Broach: A potentially dangerous situation that occurs when a kayak becomes caught in currents of different speeds. An example is when a kayak accelerates down the face of one wave and collides with a slower-moving wave in front, causing it to veer or yaw abruptly sideways.

Bulkhead: Transverse wall that creates a sealed compartment fore or aft in a kayak. Primarily used for flotation but also used as storage area with access via deck hatches.

Buoy: A floating mark that identifies a location or channel.

Can buoy: A buoy shaped like a cylinder. Most can buoys are black.

Canoe: An open craft with pointed ends that is propelled with one or more single-bladed paddles.

Chine: The intersection between the bottom and the sides of a vee- or flat-bottomed kayak.

Cleat: A device to which ropes or lines may be attached.

Compass: An instrument that points toward magnetic north.

Course: Planned route over which a kayak travels.

Cross bearings: Two or more bearings used to determine the position of a kayak.

Current: Water moving horizontally.

Current rips: Small waves formed on the surface by the meeting of opposing currents.

D-ring: A metal D-shaped ring for fastening ropes and straps.

Daymark: A structure used as an aid to navigation during daylight.

Dead ahead: Directly ahead.

Dead astern: Directly behind.

Dead reckoning: Calculation of distance from time on the water and estimated paddling speed. Derived from the word "deduced."

Deck: Surface that covers the bow and stern of a kayak.

Depth: Vertical measurement from a hull's lowest to highest point, usually from the top of the gunwale amidships to the floor of the kayak.

Directional stability: Tendency of a boat to hold its course under way.

Displacement: The weight of the water displaced by a kayak.

Draft: The depth of water needed to float a craft.

Draw stroke: A stroke that is used to move a kayak sideways. The paddler places the blade in the water parallel to the kayak at arm's reach, then pulls the kayak over to it.

Dry bag: Waterproof storage bag.

Dry suit: Fully enclosed, waterproof garment with latex gaskets at the neck and wrists. Worn by whitewater and sea kayakers for protection from cold water.

Ebb: A receding or falling tide.

Eddy: Area of swirling water down-current of an obstruction.

Eddy line: Transitional area between main current and eddy current.

Eskimo roll: A self-rescue technique used to right an overturned kayak or canoe without exiting the boat.

Fathom: Measurement equivalent to 6 feet.

Feathered: Pertaining to a blade that is canted to present the narrow edge rather than the surface to the wind, thereby minimizing wind resistance. A feathered blade on a kayak paddle is offset at an angle from its opposite blade.

Ferry: To cross a current with little or no downstream travel, using the current's force to move boat laterally.

Fiberglass: Glass-fiber cloth impregnated with resin that can be easily formed into hull shapes.

Flare: A hull cross-section that grows increasingly wider as it rises from the waterline toward the gunwales. Also, a pyrotechnic device used to get the attention of someone beyond shouting distance.

Flat water: Lake or ocean water or slow-moving river current.

Flood: A rising tide.

Flotation: Buoyancy elements built into a craft to ensure that it does not sink when swamped.

Fore: The part of a kayak forward of the cockpit.

Freeboard: The portion of a kayak above the waterline.

Grab loop: Short rope or grab-handle threaded through bow or stern stem of a kayak or canoe. Most often used as carrying handle, but also useful as handhold for swimmers.

Grip: The part of a kayak paddle held in the hand.

Gunwale: The line where hull and deck intersect.

Hatch: Access opening on front or rear deck.

Hull: The underbody of a kayak, which comes in contact with the water.

Hull configuration: Shape of a hull.

Inflatable kayak: An inflatable, open-top craft designed for one or two paddlers.

Initial stability: A boat's resistance to leaning; tippiness.

International Canoe Federation: The international governing body for competitive canoeing and kayaking.

K-1: One-person kayak.

Kayak: A watercraft that a sitting paddler propels with a double-bladed paddle.

Keel: A strip or extrusion along the bottom of a kayak to prevent slipping sideways under the pressure of wind.

Keel line: The shape of a kayak's bottom from a sideways perspective.

Kevlar: A DuPont aramid fiber used in kayak construction.

Knot: Rate of speed based on the time it takes to cover 1 nautical mile (6,076 feet).

Layup: Manner in which layers of fabric such as fiberglass or Kevlar are placed to form a kayak hull.

Lee: The downwind side. "Under the lee" of an object means having it between you and the wind.

Leeboard: A board fixed to the lee side of a kayak under sail to prevent the kayak from being blown sideways.

Lee shore: The shore upon which the wind is blowing.

Leeward: To the lee side.

Leeway: The distance a kayak drifts to leeward, or downwind.

Life jacket: Personal buoyancy device required by law for every person aboard a vessel of any size.

Nautical mile: 6,076 feet.

Navigation: Determining and following one's route.

Neap tide: The period in the moon's first or third quarter when the low and high tides have the least amount of change.

Nun buoy: A buoy with a conical top. Most nun buoys are red.

Offing: Distance from shore.

Overfalls: Short, usually breaking waves that occur when a current passes over a shoal (or other underwater obstruction) or meets a contrary current.

Paddle: Primary tool for propelling kayaks.

Painter: A rope attached to bow or stern for tying a kayak to shore.

Peel-out: The act of leaving an eddy and entering the main current.

PFD: Personal flotation device.

Piloting: Navigation using geographical points.

Polyethylene: Thermoplastic material used in construction of kayaks.

Port: The left side of a kayak from the perspective of the paddler. Also, an opening or hatch.

Pump: A device for removing water from inside a kayak. Also called "bilge pump."

Put-in: The starting place of a paddling trip, where you put your boat in the water.

Ribs: Pieces of wood spaced along the inside of a hull to form its frame.

Rocker: Upward curvature of the keel line from the center toward the ends of a canoe or kayak. A great amount of rocker enables quick, easy turns.

Rudder: A foot-controlled steering device on touring or sea kayaks.

Sea: Waves caused by wind blowing at the time and place of observation, as opposed to "swell," waves caused by a distant wind.

Secondary stability: A hull's tendency to stabilize as it leans to one side.

Shaft: The rod or tube holding the blades, which the paddler holds.

Skeg: Rudder that is fixed laterally but may be raised or lowered and that improves a kayak's ability to move in a straight line.

Sound: To measure the depth of the water.

Spring tide: Tides that occur near the times of full or new moons when the range tends to be greater.

Starboard: The right side of a kayak from the perspective of the paddler.

Stem: The end piece of a hull at bow or stern.

Stern: The rear part of a kayak.

Surf: Large breaking waves along a coastline or tidal area. Also, to ride large waves on a river or the ocean in a kayak or canoe.

Surf ski: A long, narrow kayak used for cruising and racing across open water. The paddler sits in divots on the hard-shelled deck, not in an enclosed cockpit.

Sweep stroke: Stroke used to turn a kayak toward the off-side (non-paddle side) by reaching out and ahead, then "sweeping" the blade in a wide arc fore to aft.

Swell: Waves caused by far-off winds.

Symmetrical: Pertaining to a hull shape in which the kayak's widest point, or beam, is directly amidships.

Take-out: The end point of a paddling trip.

Tandem: Two-person kayak.

Tide: The vertical movement of water caused by the gravitational force of the moon.

Tie-downs: Ropes or lines used to secure a kayak to the top of a car.

Tracking: The ability of a boat to hold a straight course due to its hull design.

Trim: Balanced and level both side-to-side and end-to-end. A trim boat is achieved by shifting the load or the position of the paddlers.

Tumblehome: A hull cross-section that curves inward from the waterline toward the gunwales.

Vee: A hull shape.

Volume: Overall capacity of a given hull shape.

Wake: The path or track of a kayak in the water.

Waterline: The line formed at the edge of the water along the hull of a kayak. The shape of the waterline and the handling characteristics of the boat change as the load changes.

Wave: An undulation on the surface of the water, usually caused by wind. The water does not move, while the wave does.

Weather: In the direction from which the wind is blowing.

Wetsuit: Gear worn by kayakers for cold-water protection. Typically made of neoprene, which creates a thermal shield.

Windward: The direction from which the wind is blowing; opposite of leeward.

Index

About the Author

Dennis Stuhaug is a lifelong paddler who has voyaged extensively along the Pacific Coast from California to Alaska as well as in the interiors of Canada and Alaska. A noted water and boating safety expert and former paddling instructor, he has written for a variety of outdoor publications. His paddling partner is his wife, Suzanne. They reside in Longbranch, Washington.